"Hot Pizza, Cold Shoulder"

Hot Pizza, Cold Shoulder

An Antarctic Comedy

Ricky Ginsburg

©2024 by Ricky Ginsburg

All rights reserved. No part of this book may be reproduced, stored in a retrieval system or transmitted in any form or by any means without the prior written permission of the publishers, except by a reviewer who may quote brief passages in a review to be printed in a newspaper, magazine or journal.

The author grants the final approval for this literary material.

First printing

This is a work of fiction. Names, characters, businesses, places, events, and incidents are either the products of the author's imagination or used in a fictitious manner. Any resemblance to actual persons, living or dead, or actual events is purely coincidental.

Nothing in this story was written by or with the aid of artificial intelligence.

ISBN: 9798338864487

Printed in the United States of America

Also by Ricky Ginsburg

K47
Head Fake
Boulong's Cheese
Putting a Ghost to Rest
When Life Gives You Beef, Make Burgers
Sushi, Burgers, and Rocky Mountain Oysters
A Tasty Murder

The "Bird" Series featuring Detective Valarie Garibaldi:
The Blue Macaw
Shooting Limpkins
Clouds Full Of Ravens

With Many Thanks To...

Carol Miller, proofreader extraordinaire, grammarian, and girlfriend, is without question my most valuable writing asset. All the tiny words my brain misses, she finds. Every plot-hole that needs to be filled is found by her careful assessment of the action as it unfolds. And when I wake at two-forty-five in the morning and need someone to discuss a scene, Carol rolls over and together, we solve the mystery. Every writer should have someone with her talents. No, sorry, I'm not sharing.

Polar Latitudes, the most wonderful expedition company that took us to Antarctica and sparked the plot for this book. Special thanks to John McKeon, the CEO of Polar Latitudes, who was along for this expedition, and added his own magic to a place that was already the pinnacle of enchantment. Even more special thanks to Hannah Lawson, our expedition leader, and the inspiration for Gwendolyn McMartin's character. One of the most talented people I've ever met. Her lighthouse performance was unbelievably funny. If you ever plan a trip to Antarctica, make sure Hannah's in charge.

Stacy Clair, a wonderful beta reader, currently lives in Tucson, AZ with her husband and their rescue dogs. Stacy is best known for her dark poetry. You can find her writings online as well as in several local Virginia journals.

"Hot Pizza, Cold Shoulder" *Ricky Ginsburg*

"Unless you are a pizza, the answer is yes, I can live without you." - Bill Murray

Part One

Chapter One

Kim-Jack kicked the nearest locker, doing minimal damage to the thin metal door but aggravating his sore toe again. It was five minutes to eleven according to his phone, just about dinnertime six hours away in Honolulu where his fiancée should have called from nearly three hours ago. He knew that Madeline had a problem with the time difference when she traveled, but her parents were there, his father and stepmother were there, as was a bevy of helpful hotel employees who already knew his voice over the phone and had promised to have her call as soon as she was spotted.

He tapped the redial button, but canceled the call before it could connect. Staring at the device as though it was to blame, he sighed. "Waste of time and Tito's alone with the pizzas."

Leaving his partner in the middle of an experiment had resulted in disastrous results before and he wasn't going to let *that* happen again. Stowing his cellphone in his back pocket, Kim-Jack hurried back into the science lab and over to the white marble-topped lab bench, currently covered in pizza boxes.

Anxiously, he refreshed the display on his laptop several times in less than a minute, smiling so wide at what he saw that he nearly drooled on his notes. Leaning over to pencil in the time and temperature reading on a yellow legal pad, he nudged Tito awake.

"Two hours and eight minutes with no change in temperature." He shoved his groggy research assistant again. "Yo, Tito, did you hear me? It's working!"

Rolling out a yawn that ended with a loud belch, Tito Czerwinski, co-chair of the science department at Barack Obama High School, lifted the pad a few inches from his eyes rather than dig around in the pockets of his lab coat for his glasses. He was too nearsighted to drive and too farsighted to read. The glasses added to his baldness, making him look twice as old and a hundred times frumpier.

Kim-Jack thought his fellow teacher was fifty when they first met and had been ribbing him about it for the past three school years. Even though they were both twenty-eight, Tito was born six months after Kim-Jack and was a foot shorter, which he thought made his partner look older. However, when speaking to other teachers, Tito always referred to his co-chair as the old man.

"Can we eat the goddamn pizza now?" Tito dropped the pad on the counter and gingerly slid off his stool. "It's so far past dinner that my stomach is wondering if my throat's been cut. Honestly, I'm hungry enough to eat one of your disgusting protein bars, or maybe I'll just gnaw on my fingernails." He nodded at Kim-Jack. "Maybe I'll try *your* fingernails?"

"You want to eat pizza at eleven o'clock at night?" Kim-Jack aligned the pad with the edge of the counter and placed the pencil on the top line. "No wonder you weigh three hundred pounds."

"And you are the skinniest Chinaman–"

"I'm half black and one hundred percent American. Don't start that shit again. Do I even look Chinese?" Kim-Jack bent over so that Tito could see his hair. "How many Chinese do you know with cornrows?"

"Hey, you're the one who got into it with that kid, Marcus about black heritage and black pride and all that angry young man shit...again."

"Goddamn freshman punk, what the hell does he think he knows about black heritage beyond what he's learned on the street?" Blowing out a hard breath, Kim-Jack yanked the probe from the side of their experimental pizza box and wiped it clean with a tissue. "My dad grew up in the sixties. I should bring him into class one day and let him explain what it means to be beat down and shoved out."

Gingerly examining the exterior of the box, Kim-Jack checked for leaks with the precision of an astronaut about to step out of a spaceship. He smiled. "Nothing. Tight as your belt."

Tito raised an eyebrow.

"Okay. No more fat jokes tonight."

"Thank you." Tito took a step back and sneezed. "Sixty-two degrees outside and they finally turn on the air conditioning. Gotta love the way the city spends our taxes."

Kim-Jack nodded toward the street. "They didn't unlock the windows until the first week in October. I had seven students pass out at their desks on the last day of September."

"For real pass out or for I-know-you'll-send-me-to-the-nurse pass out?" Smiling, Tito bent over the box and sniffed. "I can smell pizza."

"As you should. The box may not be one-hundred-percent airtight, but it's definitely thermally sealed."

Tito's stomach rumbled and he reached for the lid. Kim-Jack slapped his hand.

"Give me a minute to double-check the data. We're coming up on two hours, ten minutes."

"I'll give you one more minute and I'm watching the clock." Setting his phone on the lab bench, Tito started the countdown timer. "If this works, we could literally make a bazillion dollars."

"Bazillion or Brazilian?"

"Is there a difference?"

Kim-Jack shrugged. "I don't know. If it's that much money, you could probably buy a country."

"And be king?"

"Of course."

Tito clapped his hands. "I would buy Bolivia and make myself King."

Kim-Jack shook his head. "I'd go with Burundi."

He stopped clapping. "Why Burundi?"

"It sounds better." Kim-Jack held out his left palm. "I'm King of Bolivia." He switched to his right. "I'm King of Burundi. See, Burundi sounds more masculine."

Tito pondered the two names for a second. "Burundi it is. But where does that leave you?"

Kim-Jack waved his arms slowly around the classroom. "Right here, doing what I do best." Smiling, he put the legal pad and pencil on an empty desk, with a quick adjustment to get it square. "I think we're ready."

Tito, whose stomach was now in control of both mind and body, was at his breaking point. Well beyond the point of thinking, he leaned around the six plus feet of the senior partner of their team and opened the box with a flourish.

"The goddamn cheese is stuck to the top of the box where it sagged."

Kim-Jack tapped on his cellphone camera. "Let me get a couple of shots before you screw it up."

"Quickly, please."

Capturing the cheesy stalactites as digital images, Kim-Jack laid his phone on the lab bench. "Go ahead."

Tito ripped off several full sheets of paper towel and laid a slice of pie on them to absorb the grease. While he refused to participate in a diet regimen, keeping his cholesterol below two-hundred meant the monthly checks from his wealthy and extremely health conscious stepfather would continue to flow into his checking account. A teacher's salary was not the fast lane to prosperity.

Shoving him out of the way, Kim-Jack grabbed his first slice out of the box along with a dollop of gooey cheese on the tips of his fingers. "I can't eat like this when Madeline's around."

"Did she call?"

"Of course not." Kim-Jack shook his head. "She probably thinks I'm sleeping."

Tito pointed a slice of pie at him. "Well, there's your sign. Dig in. She's not here, so shut up and enjoy the moment."

Along with his fiancée's disapproval of his diet, the sagging lid was only one of the many problems facing the two experimenters. Their original pizza box was too heavy and the pizza cooled to room temperature in half an hour. They had been using various foils to insulate the box, but the price of the foil that worked the best meant the box would cost over twenty dollars to construct. A Google search revealed that no one else was designing the perfect pizza box, so the task was left up to a pair of high school science teachers.

Digging into the task, the two scientists left the real world several times a week and entered the cardboard box universe. Kim-Jack handled the research, Tito ordered pizza and covered their expenses. They shared the dream of unlimited wealth, perhaps even the Nobel Prize for food preservation, if such an award existed. Their golden goose was an eighty-cent cardboard box that could maintain a pizza at tongue-scorching temperature for at least three hours. They had been working on the box since spring break of Kim-Jack's first year, fortunately with more positive results than negative.

Hot pizza was their goal. Burning their mouths was the danger to avoid on the way, although both men had blistered their tongues dozens of times in the three years they'd been attempting to construct the perfect pizza box. As a reward for teaching in a less than desirable high school, their principal had green-flagged the experiment and personally marched it through the budget approval process. The school's science lab, shared by the two teachers–co-chairs of their two-man department–was theirs to use after hours for as long as necessary.

The search for a modern pizza box that could keep a pie hot and fresh for hours was mostly the result of boredom on the part of Kim-Jack. His only hobby was collecting expensive red wine, and then drinking it. He jogged when struck with the mood, and swam in the lake all summer. The school's gym was loaded with exercise equipment and the basketball coach was more than happy to have a former college star workout with his team. Fitness wasn't an issue.

So, with too much spare time on his hands, and constantly getting cold delivery pizza when Madeline wasn't around, he set about to solve two problems with one solution.

In the back of his mind, he saw riches, but the front door led to the classroom. One evening, not long after they'd been at the project for two school years, Kim-Jack admitted to his partner that no amount of money they made on this whimsical dream would ever make him walk away from teaching. Tito had laughed for a few seconds and then, seeing the serious look on Kim-Jack's face, clapped him on the shoulder and said he understood.

Kim-Jack doubted he was telling the truth.

Pizza boxes aside, teaching had always been his dream. Starting in kindergarten, Kim-Jack fell in love with his teachers. No other female meant as much or had as profound an impact on his life. His teacher was the only person he gave a Valentine to each year, with the exception of his father. While his peers were conquering the sexual torrents of adolescence, Kim-Jack couldn't shake his love for the women who stood in front of the classroom. Rarely dating in high school, he remained a virgin until his second year in college.

He was book smart with a photographic memory. As far back as he could remember, the minute details of life, the never-fading trivia, every story he'd ever read, found its way into his deep gray matter. The dream then, was to release that knowledge to his students. To let it flow from his mind to theirs. Teaching science was the pinnacle of that dream. Teaching science in a city where children were more interested in surviving than learning the botanical names for the local flora led to his daily questioning of whether or not he'd made the right career choice. The answer was always the same.

Most of his students would never live long enough nor spend sufficient time in school to actually graduate. Those few that reached their senior year rarely got jobs, hardly ever continued on to college, and only wanted the degree so that they could join the military and legally carry a weapon. Kim-Jack had followed the school district's curriculum for the first year and then trashed it completely in September of his second year as a science teacher. Most of his lectures revolved around the human body and how to keep it functioning with a six-inch knife in the chest or multiple non-fatal bullet wounds.

He spent a full week on human reproduction. A waste of time with a classroom that had at least four pregnant female students each semester. The district office sent a woman to meet with Kim-Jack in his office, after hours, to explain to the new teacher that they already had a curriculum in place to handle Sex Education and that he was overstepping his bounds. Kim-Jack had a copy of the district's Sex Ed manual, complete with his red circles around every phrase that was misleading, unclear, or written for a first-grader who'd only recently learned the difference between male and female sex organs by walking into the wrong bathroom.

The woman left in a huff and no one ever complained about his daily teaching plan again.

Kim-Jack had been fighting an ongoing battle of the generations with one of his students, Marcus Tigue, age fifteen, since the first day of school this year. The lanky boy who always sat in the front row, with waist-length dreadlocks and a terrible home life, would have been a warrior for the cause at some distant point in the past. Now, he was just a street thug who had somehow made his way into the first year of high school in a city where most kids his age would be working, thieving, or slowly dying. Kim-Jack did his best to avoid physical contact, but he dreamt of beating the kid senseless to save him the trouble of surviving the real world once school ended.

It seemed that every new school year brought with it at least one student who challenged everything Kim-Jack said. Marcus was the current thorn, but he wasn't sharp enough to cause his teacher permanent pain. Knowing that summer would eventually slide in and chase the students away was enough to temper even the worst days for an inner city high school teacher.

Somehow, their feeding frenzy had left the two hungry researchers with a single slice of pizza in the box out of eight possible. It wasn't the first time this had happened, and as before, Tito accused Kim-Jack of eating one more slice than him, insisting that the odd piece was his. Knowing full well that Tito ate twice as fast and that he probably ate two slices at the same time without realizing, Kim-Jack pushed the box over to him and got off his stool. His appetite had faded with the long hours.

"Eat it. I had a big lunch." He turned toward the door. "I'm going downstairs to the teacher's lounge to get a soda. You want something?"

Tito shook his head. "I've got a two-liter bottle of cola in the specimen fridge."

"Are you kidding?"

"What?"

Kim-Jack made a puking motion with his fingers half into his mouth. "There are dozens of Petri dishes in that fridge with all sorts of nasty bugs my students have been collecting from around the school."

"So?"

"So, you are exposing your beverage to all sorts of virulent creatures that will, if nothing else, solve your weight problem if they don't kill you first." Kim-Jack pinched the bridge of his nose. "Good lord, Tito, this is a science lab, filled with scientific experiments in case you haven't noticed. My students and a couple of yours have been swabbing the toilets in all the lavatories. Wiping the drains in the boys' locker room. Inspecting the cafeteria trash. I wouldn't touch anything that comes out of that refrigerator with anything less than four-foot tongs and a hazmat suit."

Tito looked over at the refrigerator covered in bumper stickers that went back twenty-plus years and shrugged. "I've been keeping my lunch in there for years. I could never understand why it wasn't stolen."

***

Due to the high crime rate of the nearby neighborhood, the school had four armed security officers on duty from six in the morning until six in the evening. Overnight, there were just two, and both could always be found hanging out in the most elegant teachers' lounge outside of Beverly Hills. To a first-time visitor, it would appear that they'd walked into a living room designed from the pages of *Architectural Digest*. The four ultra-plush brown leather sectional couches that had plenty of room for six large adults and the marble-topped coffee tables that seemed to be everywhere and in a multitude of sizes were the perfect venue to watch the seventy-inch television that occupied one full wall.

The first floor lounge was equipped with an adequate kitchen: no oven, but there was a cooktop and three microwaves– no waiting. The Home Economics teachers came here to test their recipes before foisting them on their students. The lounge had its own restrooms, vending machines, a refrigerator with an icemaker, and wall-to-wall carpeting. It was a wonder any of the teachers ever went home. Other than the bars on the windows and the bulletproof glass, the room was certainly nicer than any part of a teacher's domicile.

Teachers coming to the school for the first time were amazed at the opulence showered on them. However, the lounge was just one of the many perks the Board of Education had agreed to supply in order to get teachers to accept an assignment far more hazardous than any battlefield. All of the glass, inside and out, was bulletproof. Metal detectors were used at every entrance. A razor wire fence protected their cars. Upon request, a security guard would accompany a teacher to the safe parking area and stay there until the teacher had left the school grounds. Baseball tickets, skyboxes at the football stadium, and prime theater seats were always available to convince a prospective teacher to sign a contract.

Yet even with the benefits, most teachers at Barack Obama High School lasted only a few semesters. Some went on to more fashionable school districts. Some simply retired. All who left swore they'd never return, even for more money and gold-plated toilets.

Kim-Jack scanned his ID card at the door and nudged it open with his elbow. He knew what was growing on the doorknobs, handrails, lockers, and walls outside this sanctuary.

Even though students were never allowed inside, they still made physical contact with the surfaces on the exterior. What they left behind was as dangerous as the contents of the refrigerator in the science lab.

Looking away from the late night, West Coast, baseball game he'd been watching, Fred Washburn, who everyone called "Physical Fred" or just Fizz for short, smiled at Kim-Jack and waved him over.

"Pizza man. How's it going?"

"We broke the two-hour mark again." Kim-Jack pumped his fist in the air. "I'm betting we can reach three hours by the end of the semester."

Fizz winked at him. "Take your time. We love all the free pizza."

"Where's your partner?"

"On the roof, getting some fresh air." Another wink.

Kim-Jack glanced upward. "It's good to know there's a stoned security guard wandering around the building with a gun."

"Protect and serve."

The protectee blew out a short breath. "Live long and prosper."

Fizz had been an actual police officer many years in the past. His reasons for leaving the force were a matter of speculation, and he wasn't talking. Even though he was receiving a pension from the department and healthy social security stipend, Fizz was the first to complain about the lack of pay raises from the Board of Education. Of course, that was his old attitude, before the Board reassigned him to Barack Obama High School with its luxury lounge.

A long fly ball caught the security guard's attention. It went deep into right field before a gust of wind took it foul. Kim-Jack took advantage of the distraction and walked over to the refrigerator.

"Mind if I steal a beer?"

"Just for you?" Nodding, Fizz muted the television. "Professor Tito owes me a six-pack. You keep his fat ass out of my shit, okay?"

"I told him beer will raise his cholesterol." Kim-Jack grinned. "You've got nothing to worry about anymore."

The door lock clicked and both men turned to watch Vincent Giaccomo slide into the room, combing his slick black hair off his forehead. Less than half as old as Fizz, Vincent's background was the military police and the current holder of the number of times anyone had failed the city's police exam.

"Yo, Vinnie, you talk to the birds?" Fizz laughed and got up from the couch. He changed the channel to the streaming service his partner had been watching before his circuit and trip to the roof. "I gotta do the one-o'clock circuit. See you in forty-five."

Vincent jammed his comb into his back pocket and gave his partner the thumbs up. "Don't get lost." Turning to Kim-Jack, he held out his hand. "Hey, glad to meet you. I'm Vincent Giaccomo. I'm Fred's new partner."

Kim-Jack held back his laughter and shook the young man's hand. "We met six hours ago, Vinnie."

"We did?" Vincent pursed his lips. "Yeah. You're right. I remember. You're the pizza professor with the funny name."

"Kim-Jack."

"Yeah." Pausing in thought for a few seconds, Vincent cocked his head to the side. "How'd you get stuck with a name like that anyhow?"

Even though he'd told the story hundreds of times since learning to speak, Kim-Jack sighed and readied himself to tell it again. He took a drink of beer and placed the bottle on the counter.

"My mom was Chinese. My dad comes from Georgia. His family is black. So, I'm half Chinese and half black. They met at a banking conference in Singapore and, according to my dad, they instantly fell in love. The conference was three days. They spent a month in Singapore and got married upon returning to the States. Mom was pregnant."

Vincent clasped his hands and smiled. "That's so cool."

Groaning softly, Kim-Jack continued. "My mom insisted that I was going to be a girl and that I should be named Kimberly. My dad said, okay, then if it's a boy, I want to name him Jackson after my father who died in Vietnam."

"You're a boy." Vincent stammered. "I mean a man. How come you're not just called Jack?"

"My mom died a few hours after I was born. She threw a blood clot and stroked out. My dad told me that she spent the first few hours of my life holding me, and that her death was instantaneous when the clot hit her brain. She didn't suffer." Kim-Jack let loose a long, deep breath and took another pull off the beer.

"You okay, man?" Vincent walked over and put his hand on Kim-Jack's shoulder. "That's some heavy shit."

"Yeah." Switching his beer to the hand attached to his shoulder where Vincent was at this very moment transferring bacteria, Kim-Jack was able slip out of the security guard's embrace to complete his story.

"So, my dad decided to honor my mom by using half of the name she wanted with half of what he would have used. Thus, I became Kim for Kimberly and Jack for Jackson. Rather than make up a middle name, he used a hyphen, so my birth certificate reads Kim-Jack Donaldson."

"No middle name? I thought everyone had a middle name."

Kim-Jack shook his head. "Nope."

A tear slid down Vincent's left cheek. "Wow. That's a beautiful story, man."

Kim-Jack finished the beer and tossed the bottle into the recycle bin. "Yeah. Same one I told you six hours ago."

Stepping onto the third floor, Kim-Jack's phone buzzed several times. Having already watched a teacher get shoved backwards down the stairs, out of habit he walked across the hallway to a row of lockers before reaching for the phone. The caller ID displayed Madeline, his fiancée.

Finally.

"I've been calling you for hours, but my calls went straight to voicemail. Where are you? Is everything okay?"

Really? Kim-Jack checked the time and slapped his forehead. "I guess I must have been busy. I didn't realize it was this late. I hope I'm not keeping you from dinner. I'm just finishing up in the lab and then I'm headed to the townhouse." He paused for a moment. Most of his comments usually flew past her. "We had great results." *And do you care?*

"I'm onboard the flight home from Honolulu with my parents. We decided to leave earlier and skip the dinner. Your dad said to say hello and your stepmom got totally wasted before we left the hotel, so she's passed out in her seat."

As I thought. "So, it's almost six where you are."

"And it must be almost one o'clock in the morning at home. I hope I didn't wake you up."

Mornings. He frowned. She was a terrible morning person. Not a coffee drinker, Madeline's sole morning beverage was orange juice and god help anyone that poured it out of a can, cardboard container, or a bottle. Madeline's orange juice had to be fresh squeezed, a task that Kim-Jack relished, as she always drank it in bed–a precursor to morning sex.

"You're off by a couple of hours." *Big surprise.*

"You would have loved Hawaii. The surfing was awesome. I rode the pipeline!"

Kim-Jack muted the phone and muttered out loud no one in particular. "And survived. Thank god." He switched back to live. "That's great, baby. I hope your dad got some cool photos to add to our travel wall. Did you get a chance to sing?"

Madeline Kloppleman loved to sing, and she had the voice to prove it. If they walked into a bar with a karaoke machine, it would be hours before they ordered something to eat. She loved show tunes and the crooners from a century before she was born: Sinatra, Mathis, Nat King Cole. Any excuse for her to break into song. And if someone was celebrating a birthday and the server parade was led by a cake and candles? Madeline would rush over to their targeted table and sing the Birthday Song so loud that everyone in the restaurant felt safe to join her.

His stepmother's birthday was the same day they arrived in Hawaii, and Madeline had arranged a special dinner. Kim-Jack warned her in advance that Trisha got embarrassed faster than a schoolchild with a porno magazine caught by a parent. He was going to ask about the special dinner since it had been a secret plan that only Madeline knew in detail, but she was already on a roll.

"OMG, you missed the most amazing luau on the beach for Trisha's birthday party! Fifteen Hawaiian dancers with flaming batons. The music was so intense that I nearly climaxed. And then the dancers surrounded your stepmother and sang Happy Birthday in Hawaiian. I got up and we sang again in American."

American. Kim-Jack stifled the correction, but sighed loud enough for the sound to echo through the empty third-floor corridor. "She must have turned as red as your lipstick."

"Your stepmother might have blushed, but she slid under the table before I finished."

Kim-Jack laughed. "I'm sorry I missed it, but the Board of Ed is quite strict when it comes to their teachers having a good time."

"There was a lot of pot smoking."

"I'm sure you enjoyed it."

"Once or twice, but it screws up my throat. Your stepmother got hammered. What a hoot!"

He'd seen his stepmother stoned plenty of times. She started out with the strength of a church candle, but eventually melted into a puddle of spent wax. "It takes a few tokes to get her to unwind, but Trisha's a lot of fun when she gets blasted."

Feeling the urge in his pants, he was going to say how much he missed her and wait for her to argue that he was just horny, but he could hear the announcement about airplane mode in the background. He was glad he didn't get the chance.

"I've gotta go. We're departing. I love you and can't wait to have those big, powerful hands running up and down my naked

body. I want to scream the last three bars of 'My Way' when you make me cum. You can't imagine how horny I am right now."

"Jesus, Madeline. Are you sitting with your parents?" A bolt of fear ran up his spine. "With *my* parents?"

"Oh, hell no." She laughed. *"They're all up front in First Class, planning a really cool vacation wedding for you and me. Oh, my god, you're gonna love it! Your dad is cray, cray when it comes to cool ideas."*

Kim-Jack took a step away from the lockers, glancing up and down the hallway for some non-existent threat. Her parents had planned four different destination weddings in the year and four months they'd been engaged. He'd been able to talk her out of all of them so far. She had almost been convinced to having a simple wedding on her parents' estate. He'd even acquiesced to a rabbi instead of a priest despite his father and stepmother's vehement objections.

"Another vacation wedding?" He took a deep breath. "To where this time?"

She replied with only one word before disconnecting, but he could sense her joy nonetheless.

"Antarctica!"

The word echoed around his brain before locking onto an appropriate image of ice and snow and wind so strong that his cornrows unraveled. His throat constricted. His breathing stopped. But Madeline ended the call before he had the chance to shout, "No goddamn way!" slamming his fist into the nearest locker.

Chapter Two

A block and a half away from Tito's apartment, Kim-Jack pulled over to the curb and parked. They were in a residential neighborhood on a well-lit street, but he rolled up the windows and kept the engine running. The first twenty minutes of their drive had been in silence. Not even the radio was turned on, their nightly battle of the stations paused while the two teachers and recently declared best friends considered the bizarre wedding destination Madeline had dumped on Kim-Jack from half a dozen time zones away.

Tito, his hunger abated after eating most of the pizza, broke the silence as he had already moved on from food to his partner's unique wedding plans.

"My cousins went to Antarctica."

"And?"

Tito shrugged. "They said it was cold."

"No shit?"

"No, cold...really cold. Like frozen testicles on a penguin cold. Colder than you get when your feet get wet in the winter. So cold that no one serves ice cubes at a bar. All the drinks freeze as soon as they're made." Tito shivered to punctuate his comments.

Kim-Jack frowned. "Your cousins live in Key West. Anything north of Miami is cold to them."

"But that's not the worst of it."

"Do tell."

"Giselle, who never gets seasick, said that the Drake crossing was the worst experience in her life. Everyone on the ship was puking their guts out. The crew was passing out Dramine pills like M&Ms. Swells so high and deep that the ship was on a forty-five degree angle most of the time. And remember, she spent five years in the Navy." Shaking his head, Tito continued. "Her husband tied himself into the bed with a bunch of spare blankets and swore he'd never go on another ship if they survived. Not even a canoe."

"Don't worry, man. I can talk Madeline out of this one just like the others. No way are we going to Antarctica." Kim-Jack chuckled. "I do love that girl, but she's got the attention span of a Mayfly unless she's singing or shopping. Great ideas become distant memories faster than a hot pizza cools."

"Look, KJ, that's not the point." Lowering the window just an inch for some fresh air, Tito reached into his pocket and pulled out a pre-rolled joint from a small, green tube.

"You're not going to light that up in my car, are you?"

"Well, normally I'd wait until I'm upstairs in my apartment, but you've parked here and there's apparently something on your mind." From the same pocket, Tito retrieved a gold Zippo and lit the joint.

Sighing, Kim-Jack lowered the other three windows of his Chevy an inch to match Tito's window. He pushed the fan to high and sat as close to his door as possible.

"I'm losing control, buddy."

Tito blew out a cloud of smoke. "I told you that control with a woman like Madeline was a fantasy. Remember me saying those words over a year ago when you got engaged? No way are you ready for marriage, especially after your performance in the bar last Saturday night."

"Because I wowed a bunch of coeds from the University?"

"Because you tried." Tito took another hit. "You went after that redhead like she owed you money."

With a wicked grin spreading across his face, Kim-Jack blushed. "She was hot, yes?"

Kim-Jack loved women the way a bird loves to fly or a fat man loves to eat. Engaged to be married or not, he worked a dance floor with precision, dancing to any beat that flowed from the speakers, joining a group of females as though they were his best friends. Even if he danced alone, just grooving to the beat, women would flock to him faster than a magnet could attract a pile of paperclips.

Turn on the karaoke machine and Kim-Jack was the first to grab the microphone, and no one ever booed *him* off the stage. Unless Madeline was there and then only in jest. In fact, he usually drew a chorus line of female singers to the stage to accompany him. Of course, that would bring Madeline rushing to the stage to join in and eventually shove him off to the side.

So, as often as Madeline traveled with her family, Kim-Jack took advantage of the temporary freedom to mingle, mash, and move. Around town, where he was well known, drinks were complimentary, cover charges were never mentioned, and if he was hungry, snacks from the kitchen arrived without asking. The most troublesome part of his life when she was away was convincing the women he met that marriage was in his future. You can look, but don't touch.

None of this was kept secret from his fiancée. In fact, she encouraged him to dance and sing, knowing that his talent would make their wedding reception a success. The problem was that pinning down a date, place, and venue for their nuptials became more complex with each long distance excursion Madeline took with her parents. To the woman who'd never worked a day and was being groomed as a homemaker and a world-class vocalist, her sole focus in life was the wedding, with procuring a record contract a close second. Her problem was keeping that focus locked on either target for very long.

Kim-Jack had suggested blinders.

Their original wedding plans were for a beachfront service at sunset in Negril, Jamaica with Madeline's father renting the entire Rick's Café for the reception afterward. Everyone was going to stay at the same five-star resort to guarantee they wouldn't be late for the ceremony. He'd even chartered a flight from Miami to keep the flock together.

Kim-Jack's father and stepmother had been going to an adults only resort in Negril where clothing was banned and all-over tans were the orders of the day for nearly a decade. They were thrilled with having the wedding at their "home away from home," but a bit dismayed that they would have to dress for the ceremony. They'd been to dozens of au natural weddings at their resort and made a half-hearted attempt to convince the Kloppleman clan to consider a change of venue.

Sadly, this plan went out with the tide when it came time to assemble the guest list. From his and her parents, the ensemble grew exponentially as cousins, their spouses, best friends and their significant others, and children were considered. By the time everyone who either Madeline, Kim-Jack, or their parents wanted at the wedding, the resort came back and told them they had exceeded the number of available rooms, even if the guests slept four to a bed.

From Jamaica, the wedding arrangements moved to a very large private yacht owned by a friend of Madeline's father. The yacht could sleep twenty. The guest list could only be pared down to forty-seven. Next up was a resort in upstate New York on a magnificent lake that was stocked with trout, her father's favorite. The location was perfect. Unfortunately, the timing was off. The resort was available to the two families only one weekend in the early autumn or a midweek stay just before Christmas. However, the winter dates depended on snow removal to allow everyone safe passage from the city to the mountainous area where the resort was located, but the resort refused to guarantee clear roads.

April in Paris was the closest Kim-Jack had come to agreeing on a destination. Her father knew the French ambassador, who could arrange for a private ceremony on the Eiffel Tower's observation deck. Madeline's allergies squashed the plan before her stepmother could start contacting hotels. On both of her previous trips to France, his fiancée spent the time in the hotel room with the windows shut, the air conditioning on high, and a bottle of antihistamines close at hand.

Nearly two months went by with no further planning until Kim-Jack's father suggested Hawaii. Never having traveled there, he saw it as an opportunity to wipe two items off his bucket list: visiting the last of the fifty states and seeing his son finally put a ring on a woman's finger. There was even a resort with a separate beach for clothing optional guests.

Kim-Jack was thrilled with the plan. He never imagined that the Kloppleman family would see Hawaii and then consider anywhere else for their wedding. Much less somewhere as cold and distant as Antarctica. It just didn't make sense. But then again, *his* dream was the perfect pizza box.

Tito crushed the end of the joint with his thumb and forefinger, sliding the oversized roach into its plastic tube.

"You're going to end up getting married on the moon if she has her way about it."

"I'm certain that conversation has bounced around their dinner table." Kim-Jack put the Chevy in gear and pulled out from the curb. "I'm thirsty and everything's closed between here and the townhouse. You got any beer?"

"Nothing but wine coolers." Coughing, Tito reached for the open bottle of water that was jammed into the center console.

Kim-Jack bit his lip. No one drank those fizzy wine coolers anymore. He knew at least one place that would be open, but it was out of his way and he really didn't feel like opening a bottle of wine. He shrugged. "I'll come upstairs and grab a couple for when I get home."

Noisily, Tito gulped the water then nodded, followed by a belch. "Home to the townhouse that's in her name because she refused to live in the combat zone. Home to a refrigerator filled with sport drinks and some green shit in a bottle that I think you can also use to wax your car. Home to where the woman of your dreams still doesn't understand your penchant for neatness. Home to a woman who'd rather listen to a bunch of thousand-year-old drunks who all died from lung cancer instead of Taylor Swift."

Taking a deep breath, Tito was about to continue, but Kim-Jack held up his hand.

"You are working your way off the guest list."

Tito groaned. "Again?"

***

Kim-Jack parked at home and twisted the top off a wine cooler. Sitting in the car, with the windows down, the night air blew across his face and gave him a chill. Autumn had replaced summer with a vengeance. Hot nights had tempered and then turned cold without warning. The humidity was gone, only to be replaced by the occasional icy drizzle and gray skies. He lived for this weather. Clouds, rain, and wind gave him a strange sense of comfort. Autumn and spring were far easier to deal with than the frigid winter with its snow and ice or the blazing hot summer that brought mosquitoes, sunburn, and traffic. For Kim-Jack, the simpler the weather the better.

Chugging the icy beverage and staring at the stars, he sighed, getting home this late meant missing his favorite part of the day. Because school ended more than an hour before his working neighbors punched out for the day, Kim-Jack would usually sit on his balcony with a cold beer and oversee the parking lot. He loved to watch his neighbors come home from work, park their cars, and stumble into their townhouses as though they'd been whipped all day long.

School was tough, but the hours were short and no one was going to whip him. His father worked the building trades for too many years. The jobs left him bent and scarred, but he'd managed to accrue enough savings that he was able to retire in his fifties. Kim-Jack listened to his moans and groans every time they got together and swore he'd never have a job that required that much bodily sacrifice.

Teaching was his passion and his dream. He'd grown up at the fringe of the bad neighborhood and watched kids his age succumb to its poison. His closest friends went on to either college or trade school. Casual acquaintances signed on with the military. Too many children he knew only from their photos in the newspaper or their weeping parents on the nightly news. From the moment he could read and understand the words, Kim-Jack knew that teaching was the only logical solution.

Kim-Jack saw his students as blank canvases, notebooks still fresh from the stationery store. He did his best to pass on the knowledge he'd collected in school, to educate the kids that everyone else thought were incapable of learning. Avoiding the rich neighborhoods and the private schools, Kim-Jack found his podium deep within the inner city. He knew that many, perhaps most of his students had neither the capacity for learning nor the desire, but even if he could light the educational spark in one student each period, he was accomplishing his goal.

Locking the car and tapping the alarm on his keyfob four times just to be sure, Kim-Jack crossed the parking lot and climbed the stairs to their third-floor townhome.

The mail consisted of mostly junk, but there were three postcards from Madeline, all sent on the same day from the hotel in Honolulu. She missed him, wanted his body, and was having another argument with her stepmother. Kim-Jack shook his head. Same three postcards every time she went away. A handful of bills went into the upper shelf of his desktop organizer unopened. He had a hard and fast rule that bills were only paid on Sunday morning while he watched cartoons on television. The annoyance of the bills was tempered by the animated humor. He told her it was the perfect display of yin and yang.

At first, Madeline had called it childish. On their fifth Sunday morning together, Kim-Jack opened a bottle of her favorite wine and poured two glasses. By the time the second show began, she was hooked and quite drunk. Their Sunday morning ritual culminated in sex most of the time, but occasionally, she would pass out with her head in his lap and sleep in that position for several hours. Either way, the bills were paid.

Gulping the rest of the now warm wine cooler, he glanced at the clock on the microwave.

I've got a class in five hours. Thank god, it's Friday. No Marcus today. Kim-Jack slapped the countertop and dropped the empty bottle in his other hand into the trash. Sniffing his armpit, he blew out a sharp breath. *I need a shower and I've got to go food shopping before she gets home.*

The siren of a passing police car caught his attention and Kim-Jack looked out the window to follow its progress down the avenue and out of sight. Spinning around, he focused on the calendar hung next to a framed photo of him and Madeline getting out of a helicopter somewhere in the Florida Keys. She was smiling. He looked as though a dentist had just yanked out his four wisdom teeth at the same time without any Novocain.

Shit. She's due to land at seven-fifteen. Even with getting their luggage and the hour and a half drive from the airport, she'll be home before my third class ends at eleven. Well, there goes food shopping during last period.

Logging onto his computer, Kim-Jack went to the supermarket's website and placed an order for delivery at noon. He'd be home by eleven-thirty with no classes scheduled until Monday morning. The school district had enacted half-day Friday before he was hired. The kids loved it. The teachers were thrilled until they learned that their pay would reflect the change. Legal action by the Union produced no results, but they kept trying anyhow.

Tofu. She's gotta have her tofu. Christ, that stuff looks like snot. We'll go for sushi, so nothing for dinner, but we're out of oranges. Good lord. We must have oranges. Madeline needs her orange juice. Kim-Jack needs Madeline. Therefore, we shall order two bags of oranges instead of just one.

He filled the rest of the order form with the usual staples: two-percent milk, rye bread, no seeds of course, the soft butter he liked that had enough chemicals to make a decent explosive, and Fig Newtons, his reward for handling the grocery order.

Man, I hope we're not going to end up with his and hers refrigerators once we move in together for good. Thank god, she's not kosher.

Kim-Jack walked over to the fridge and opened the door. A quick scan of the shelves told him everything he needed for continued survival was present with the exception of beer.

Madeline frowned on his drinking what she called "a poor man's beverage." White wine was her choice. Red, only if the bottle was very old and very expensive. Of course, she came from wealth. Kim-Jack was still climbing that ladder. Tito said he was being a "gold-digger," and apologized moments later while Kim-Jack was searching Google for the definition.

    Several spices were running low, and he added them to the delivery list. The wine refrigerator that she'd donated to his appliance collection was filled with her requisite beverage, but his tiny corner of the unit was missing his six-pack of imported beer. Madeline had acquiesced to his needs but insisted that he drink only the highest quality brew. Her theory was that the more expensive the bottle of beer, the less he would drink thus avoiding the inevitable beer belly. To keep her happy, he drank the high-end beer at home and whatever was on tap when they went out.

    Satisfied that the provisions list was complete, he clicked send, entered his credit card information, and shutdown the laptop.

    If I missed something, she'll just have to go shopping for it.
He shook his head.

Bad idea. We'll end up with a family-size bag of kale, a year's supply of flavored tofu, and some weird fruit that's only eaten by a tribe of indigenous people from the headwaters of the Amazon.

    Taking another glance into the fridge, Kim-Jack found nothing missing from the list and then double-checked the pantry as well. He reopened the online order and added another box of Fig Newtons and a spare bottle of hot sauce. Madeline's eating habits aside, the woman loved her food hot and spicy. Her condiment choice was always the same: Scared to Death hot sauce with a picture of a screaming skull on the label. He'd tasted it once and had to drink three ice-cold beers to quench the fire on his tongue. She claimed it was great for her vocal chords.

    Oddly enough, their freezer was empty with the exception of a few medical cold packs and an old-fashioned ice cube tray. The sound of the icemaker dumping fresh cubes in the middle of the night was annoying to his fiancée, so he'd shut it off and bought a plastic tray at the supermarket. The ice in the tray was at least two months old, since Madeline complained that too much ice hurt her teeth and was bad for her voice.

For his part, Kim-Jack rarely drank anything that required an ice cube, and agreed that the rattle of the machine-made cubes was an impediment to a good night's sleep.

Saving the changes, Kim-Jack shut down the laptop again and plugged in the charger. Initially, he was surprised that Madeline didn't own a laptop. Her sole connection to the outside world was a smartphone that she constantly forgot to charge. He'd offered to buy her a tablet so that she could communicate without the need for glasses. The larger size text would reduce her eyestrain and be easier to use with her long, manicured nails.

Madeline refused, saying that it was too big and bulky and why was he so concerned about her eyesight anyhow? She ended the discussion with a statement about "girl power" before he could retort. It wouldn't be the last time their conversations would park in that cul-de-sac. Kim-Jack saw it as a valuable lesson. With just two words, she taught him to think twice about further efforts on his part to change anything about his future wife.

Kim-Jack stripped off the clothes he'd been wearing since seven o'clock the previous morning and got into the shower. Those nights that Madeline spent at their townhouse meant he would be taking a cold shower in the morning after she went first. The water heater in the unit was fine if you wanted to wash the dishes, but a shower used up the hot water and it took nearly an hour for the aging device to replenish the supply.

Early on, he'd solved the problem by taking his shower after she'd fallen asleep at night or waiting until morning while she was still in bed. Even when their evening ended with a rollicking bed rodeo, she rarely showered at night. Madeline said that she loved his animal smell and didn't want to wash it off. So, on those rare occasions when she was away, he had nearly fifteen minutes of luxurious hot water to scrub away the dirt and grime of the inner city.

As with most of his personal items, Madeline had a problem with the shampoo that Kim-Jack used several times a week. According to her, the potion had too many chemicals and she was all about organic. He argued that after almost a dozen years of employing the same product to keep his oily, black hair clean nothing else worked as well. He'd grown an afro in his last year of high school, as a statement of black unity, but keeping it dirt free and somewhat less oily was impossible. A woman he'd dated the year before meeting Madeline braided his hair into cornrows, which was the style he'd maintained ever since and his hair sucked up oil faster than a French fry to keep them tight.

His shampoo had a pungent fragrance that she compared to mixing bug spray with witch hazel and a touch of wet dog. Rather than upset his bride-to-be, Kim-Jack kept his shampoo in his nightstand, only taking out the bottle to shower and only after she'd finished in the bathroom first. Fortunately, she had no problem sharing the soap and found his choice of toilet paper acceptable for her sensitive fanny.

Stepping out of the shower, just as the water went from hot to lukewarm, Kim-Jack dried himself off and walked back into the living room naked with the towel over his shoulder. He stood in front of the windows, staring at the street for a few seconds before turning his gaze toward the full moon.

It'll all get better once we're married. She'll compromise. I'll insist on certain things and we'll find common ground. He shook his head. *Who am I kidding? I'll compromise. She's worth it.* He smiled. *Plus, we can always get a bigger place with two bathrooms.*

Chapter Three

The school day exploded before first bell. A boy who was stabbed in the arm broke his assailant's nose before Kim-Jack could stop the fight. He'd pinned the wounded student in the back corner of the classroom and was holding him there when the security guards stormed into the room. Ever conscious of blood-borne disease, he'd showered and changed clothes in the teachers' lounge before returning to the empty classroom. Less than four months into the new school year and the students were already ramping up the body count.

Tito came in while he was lifting the overturned desks and lining up the rows. Chelbe Udulu, an English teacher who'd graduated from the school when it was still named after the wealthy black philanthropist who paid for the land, was right behind him. Years ago, a student fight brought out a crowd. These days, the lack of toilet paper in the boys' room drew more attention. Teachers looked out for each other, though, and a stabbing was cause for alarm or a possible opening for advancement.

"Did you get cut?" Chelbe had twenty years of scars and could recite each one's history in English, Spanish, and Swahili. She didn't carry a knife or a gun because that would be illegal. However, three nights a week, she fought mixed martial arts and enough students had seen her fight to maintain a legend.

Kim-Jack shook his head. "That kid with the orange hair literally flew over the desk. I couldn't have stopped him even if I had a hand on his shoulder."

"Ulysses?" Chelbe smiled. "You can see his hair from the opposite end of the corridor. He was blue for most of last year."

"Xavier's the kid who got stabbed?" Picking up the outer wrappings of a bandage, Tito walked over and tossed it in the trash.

"Xavier San Phillipo." Kim-Jack smiled. "Took out Ulysses with a right hook that would have made Mike Tyson crumple to his knees."

Chelbe cocked her head. "Who?"

"I thought you followed boxing." Rubbing his shoulder where he'd hit the wall, Kim-Jack grinned. "You were throwing around some serious cash last week in the lounge while the fight was on television."

"And I won." She winked. "Just a lucky guess."

"He's the boxer with the weird tattoos on his face. Looks like a Maori warrior." Stretching, Kim-Jack kicked a couple of spent vape tubes into a small pile. Kids smoked cigarettes when he was in high school. He sniffed one of the tubes and wrinkled his nose.

Tito found another bandage wrapper and carried it to the trash. "You should get a janitor to scrub the floor."

"Is it that time of year already?" Kim-Jack laughed. "I thought the third floor wasn't due to be cleaned until December. No sense asking, I'll just dump some disinfectant from the lab where the EMTs worked on Xavier. It'll dry eventually." He pointed at the coagulated puddle of blood. "Sure was a deep cut."

"He'll be fine. If they leave the building alive, they usually make it back before the end of the week." Sitting on the window ledge, Chelbe glanced at the two city police cars still blocking traffic in the parking lot. "The police were asking if it was gang related."

With a quick shake of his head, Kim-Jack held out his hands. "No, not this time. I believe it was a disagreement over who would be valedictorian at this year's graduation ceremony. The cops really pressed me on that issue. They have gangs on the brain."

Tito laughed. "Ten dollars says that neither one will survive the rigors of high school until that fateful day."

Chelbe opened her cellphone. "My cash app says I've got twenty."

"I'm in for twenty, as well." Straightening the last desk, Kim-Jack looked up at the clock. "Third period is in seventeen minutes."

Waving his arms slowly around the room, Tito was satisfied. "Looks ready for class, professor."

"The room is ready, but I can't swear that the teacher is in the groove." Kim-Jack walked over to the window ledge and joined Chelbe. "I don't know if I can teach today."

"You're a teacher. You can teach anytime you have to. Any day that your words of wisdom are needed." She put a hand on his shoulder. "No one died today, Kim-Jack. Look at it like that."

He stood and crossed his arms over his chest. His voice was coated with sarcasm. "Gosh, that makes it all better."

Kim-Jack walked over to the large flat screen monitor and powered it on. Whatever lesson plan he'd set for today's class was trashed. It was Friday and he'd be on the street in four hours and seven minutes. Madeline would be waiting and they would either be discussing her fling in Hawaii at high tide, the pending lunacy of a wedding at the South Pole, or a valid reason for him to continue teaching in the combat zone.

Connecting to the Board of Education's massive database, he loaded a Japanese movie from the 1980s titled *Antarctica*. Dubbed in English with all Japanese actors, it was the tragic story of an expedition and its dogs. Kim-Jack found it on a Google search just before leaving the townhouse that morning and planned to watch it with Madeline tonight. The stabbing changed those plans. He just wasn't in the mood to teach.

***

Madeline was waiting for him in the foyer, wearing nothing but a fake grass skirt, an all-over tan, and a smile that said, "Take me now or lose me forever." She'd tied her blond hair into a bun that she let drop down her back with a single tug. Kim-Jack was out of his khakis and polo shirt before the door locked behind him.

They had sex on the sectional couch in the living room. Then again, on the thick padded carpet in front of the couch. And, as he'd been holding back with every ounce of determination he could muster, they finished on the freshly made bed. Lying naked alongside each other, Madeline wrapped one leg over and the other through his, dragging herself as close to Kim-Jack as she could. He was still catching his breath, but managed to get an arm around her back. Everything else that happened that day was already a distant memory and one that he'd never reveal to her.

Moving his fingers slowly up her side, he smiled. "Nice tan."

"Amazing beach." She leaned closer and whispered, "I went to the nude beach with your dad and stepmom."

All the wrong muscles in Kim-Jack's body tensed. "And your parents?"

"Don't know." She nibbled at his earlobe. "And relax, nobody's gonna tell them. Okay?"

He took a deep breath and then paused. "You got that tan in one day at the nude beach?" Kim-Jack raised his eyebrows. "How is that even possible?"

She laughed. "Not one day, silly. I went there almost every day during the week we were in Honolulu. My parents were entertaining business clients and hardly spent any time with us. The beach bar had an awesome karaoke machine. Lots of country music. I sang *Stand by Your Man*."

His tension doubled. "Must have been an awesome experience. You, my stepmother, and my dad on some tropical beach with dozens of naked strangers watching you belt out Tammy Wynette tunes in the nude. Wonderful."

"It truly was." Loosening her grip, Madeline rolled away and sat up with her pillow behind her back. "The last time I was naked in public, I was five-years-old. I got away from my mother at the mall and climbed into the fountain where everyone tosses their change. By the time she caught up to me, I had stripped off all my clothes and was collecting coins in my socks."

Closing his eyes and taking a deep breath, Kim-Jack tried not to see the image he'd already verbalized. He'd seen his stepmother naked, by accident, when he'd arrived early at his father's house for a barbecue and she was having an afternoon swim...in the nude. However, his father's body below the waist was a mystery and not one that he had any desire to solve.

Madeline's fingers worked their way down his side and across to his crotch. "One more time?"

"Not right now." He shook his head. "Not after you've laid that image on me. I need to absorb this recent development and give my equipment time to recharge."

"What's there to absorb?"

"You, naked with my parents and a crowd of people who've already shared their photos on the web." Kim-Jack grabbed her wrist. "Try to imagine me naked with your stepmom and your father."

Madeline scrunched her face. "Ewww. That's disgusting."

"Why then is it okay for you to be naked with my parents?"

"Because they're naked with everyone." She grinned. "You know how they hate clothes and love to show off their bodies."

He nodded. "Fair point, but I'd rather that 'everyone' not include my future wife."

"Well, when we go to Antarctica no one's gonna be nude. So, you won't have to worry about that problem." Madeline got up from the bed and started for the bathroom. "I'm going to shower. Want to join me?"

Kim-Jack opened a bottle of red wine while his fiancée showered. He'd finished half the bottle before Madeline came into the living room wearing the largest bath towel he owned around her midsection and a smaller one as a turban. Sitting down next to him, she looked at the bottle and frowned.

"You could have opened a bottle of white."

"I don't like white wine."

She shrugged. "But I do."

"What's wrong with red once in a while?" Kim-Jack refilled his glass. "I hear it goes well with tofu."

"Speaking of which, you bought the wrong brand."

"It's the same one I bought last time."

Tugging the towel off her head, Madeline took the wineglass from his hand and gulped the last of his wine, placing the glass upside down on the coffee table when she was done. "It was the wrong tofu last time and I asked you not to buy that brand again."

"Can you really tell the difference?"

"Taste it yourself." She smiled at his grimace. "I thought so."

Kim-Jack lifted the glass and wiped the damp ring it had created on the marble top with her turban towel. Walking over to the wine refrigerator, he retrieved an open bottle of white and filled his now empty glass for her.

"You're not going to wash it first?"

He shook his head. "I paid the water bill last Sunday and couldn't believe how much water we use. Maybe if you didn't take long showers, we could afford to wash out the glassware more often. A bit of red isn't going to ruin the flavor. In fact, it will probably enhance it."

"Do you want your girlfriend to stink?"

"Of course not."

"Then don't complain about hot water." Madeline grabbed the turban towel from him and retreated to the bathroom, slamming the door so hard that a picture on the wall next to it fell and shattered. She came out several minutes later, fully dressed, and headed for the door.

"I'm going shopping."

"For tofu?"

"That and some white wine to drink with it." She walked over and kissed him on the lips. "One of these days, you're going to come home from that hideous school with a smile on your face and your last paycheck in your hand."

"And one of these days you're going to get your recording contract and I'll be your manager and I won't have to work like all those other husband managers of famous singers. And we'll hire someone to buy tofu."

Madeline sang a few bars of Buddy Holly's *That'll Be the Day* and left, blowing him a kiss just before the door closed.

Kim-Jack walked over to the window to watch her get in the car and leave. He dumped the white wine down the kitchen sink, washed out the glass, and refilled it with the last of the red wine.

She's been eating that same goddamn tofu since we met.

Taking a long drink of the wine, he set the glass down on the windowsill and opened the window for some fresh air. Even though Madeline refused to admit it, every time she returned from a vacation without Kim-Jack, she brought home tension from being with her stepmother. He'd done his best to temper those feelings, hoping that a massive amount of sex would be the perfect release. After all, he got along just fine with his stepmother and couldn't understand why the other two women failed to connect. However, sex only served to fan those flames and he was beginning to wonder if there was another path he could take her down that wouldn't be so stressful.

There's no argument that my situation is different. Thank god, there's no divorce. Of course, never knowing my mother, it's a lot easier for me to accept Trisha even though Dad refuses to let me call her mom.

A late fall breeze, too warm for November, blew through the window and Kim-Jack shoved it closed and turned on the air conditioner. He'd never been a fan of warm weather and yet, despised the snow, ice, and cold winter winds. When they'd met, he told Madeline that their perfect place to live would be in Nebraska where it never got too hot in the summer nor too cold in the winter, according to his limited research.

Madeline wanted to live in the south, but not Florida. She identified with Southern culture, loved barbecue, and would occasionally drop phrases like y'all and sho-nuff into her conversation. Having moved north shortly after the death of his mother, Kim-Jack had no interest in the South, its politics, or its food. When she acted less than the white, Jewish princess she'd been raised to be, he would call her out and chide her for pretending to be what she was not. Once, she'd even affected a Southern accent while they were on vacation seeing some of her father's political friends in Atlanta. The woman, who'd known Madeline since she was a baby, told her that the accent would be seen as offensive to most Southerners. It was the last time the two women ever talked.

So, with all this jabber about warm weather and naked beaches, why the hell is she talking about a wedding in Antarctica? What else happened in Hawaii that changed her mind?

Swishing the wine around the glass several times, Kim-Jack inhaled its fragrance and swallowed the rest of the glassful in one gulp. He was about to open another bottle when his phone rang. Tito was calling, and there was no doubt from his coughing that he'd been hitting his bong with gusto.

"KJ, was it as good as you thought it would be after eleven days?"

"Tito, why do you ask such stupid questions?"

Kim-Jack could hear him suck on the pipe, followed by some more intense coughing before Tito could respond.

"I don't know. It's been several centuries since I got laid."

"Women don't want to have sex with an orca."

Tito took another hit, coughed several times, and then sighed. *"Blame my out-of-control metabolism."*

"Is that a fancy way of saying you eat too much?"

"Yeah, and that it's not my fault." Tito paused, but then asked before taking another toke, *"So, what did she say about Antarctica?"*

Kim-Jack pulled a fresh bottle of red wine, a Chianti, from the mini-fridge and uncorked it while he spoke. "It didn't come up in conversation. In fact, what little talking she did, was more about me and my inability to buy the correct groceries, as usual. Oh, and we had an in-depth discussion about the nude beach in Honolulu where she spent most of her time."

"Your fiancée went on a nude beach? Jesus!"

"It gets worse."

"She had sex with someone there?"

"You are such an asshole." Kim-Jack laid the phone on the floor while he filled his glass. He could hear some of what Tito was saying, but after his partner's last comment, he had nothing else to talk about. Tito's comments always got out of control when he was stoned and became abrasive.

Tito, not hearing a response to some question he'd posed, shouted, *"Did you hear me?"*

Picking up the phone, Kim-Jack answered him with, "More than I care to hear from you right now. I'll call you in the morning." And with that, he ended the call.

No sex in decades. If you weren't such an asshole and lost a hundred pounds or so, you might have a chance. He took a gulp of wine. *I'm facing a trip to the coldest place on Earth and my best friend is too stoned to hold a normal conversation. Jesus, why does this madness only stop when I sleep?*

He'd learned early on that Madeline found shopping to be a Zen experience and that she could do it for hours. He'd gone with her plenty of times and always marveled how he slipped into the background when she entered a store. Until she returned to the planet, he'd plant himself in the recliner, drink fine wine, and watch cartoons. Anything else was a waste of time as far as the universe was concerned.

True to form, Madeline rolled in just before nine in the evening laden with packages. One look told Kim-Jack that she'd been to Valhalla and back. The gods were pleased. He clicked off the television and followed her into the bedroom, but stopped in the doorway.

"So, what did you buy?"

Dropping the boxes on the bed, she sat down next to them and gazed at Kim-Jack as though he'd grown horns.

"Do you really care?"

"No." He shrugged. "But I thought it would be a good conversation starter."

Madeline kicked off her shoes and fell backwards onto the bed. "How about a good sex starter?"

He frowned. "Is that all I am to you, a hard-on with a brain?"

"Are you complaining?"

Kim-Jack saw the jaws of the trap spring open and took a step back to safety. "How could I ever complain with a woman as wonderful as you? I've waited my whole life for someone who could put up with my weirdness."

"Weirdness? Excuse me, but is there a bullshit shovel nearby?"

"Why do you do that?"

"What?"

"Diminish my feelings for you with a nasty comment." Walking into the room, Kim-Jack placed his wineglass on top of his dresser. "I love you more than any woman I've ever met. Why do you think I chased away all the other women so soon after we got together?"

Madeline smiled. "Because you were tired of one-night-stands and you wanted to get into my pants without putting a ring on my finger." She chuckled. "I still have the napkin you signed, swearing that you would love me forever. Remember, I started singing *Paradise by the Dashboard Light?*"

"I tried to sing along, but you shushed me."

"You didn't know the words."

He smiled. "Okay, but I tried."

"And then we managed to squeeze into the backseat of your Chevy for the most awkward sex I've ever had." Madeline blew out a short breath. "Thank god, you knew what you were doing."

"You as well, as I seem to recall."

"But I said there was no more intercourse until you put a ring on my finger." Madeline waved the hand wearing the two-carat diamond engagement ring in the air. "You knew that from day one."

Kim-Jack laughed. "But that plan went to hell the first night in your parent's lake house."

"You got me drunk."

He grinned. "You grabbed the bottle out of my hands and chugged it. Two hundred dollars worth of fancy white wine and you drank it faster than a street wino with a camel's thirst."

"And then you took advantage of me." Madeline put on a pouty face. "I was helpless."

"For about fifteen seconds and then you put some kind of wrestling move on me and the next thing I knew, you were on top, holding me down."

"Girl power rules the day."

The two sets of parents met for the first time last summer at Madeline's family home in the country. It was the weekend after Memorial Day and the invitation mentioned barbecue. Kim-Jack and Madeline had been dating for almost a year. Her father suggested sending a limo to pick them up, but Kim-Jack insisted on making the drive in his Chevy. Because she had dressed as though on her way to meet the Queen, Trisha, his stepmom, demanded the front seat. That left his six-foot tall father to squeeze his bulky frame into the backseat for the two-hour drive.

Expecting a standard barbecue–hamburgers, hot dogs, and maybe some pulled pork–his father had dressed in jeans. Kim-Jack made him change out the Rolling Stones t-shirt for a Polo shirt still in the original polybag from last Christmas. Unwinding himself from the car upon their arrival, his father sniffed the air and asked why he didn't smell smoke.

The answer was nothing they were served that afternoon required cooking. Kim-Jack was stunned to see the sushi spread alongside the Klopplemans' Olympic size swimming pool. The vegetable platters at either end of nearly fifteen feet of freshly prepared sushi pieces and rolls had more options than most restaurants. Four sushi chefs, complete with whites and toques, stood behind the tables, sharpening their knives, and waiting for special requests.

The other surprise was the guests. No one had told Kim-Jack that there would be other people at this "little afternoon barbecue by the pool." As they were escorted through the nine-bedroom mansion and out to the pool deck, he lifted his sunglasses and nudged his father.

"Is that the Governor?"

His father blew out a sharp breath. "Holy crap. What's that scumbag doing here?"

"Dad, keep it down." Kim-Jack grabbed his father's arm. "We're guests here, honored guests in fact. Make nice with everyone and you can curse them all you want on the drive home. I'll even let you sit up front."

Larry Kloppleman, Madeline's father, was the number three real estate developer in the state. More than a quarter of a million people lived in a house, townhouse, or condominium that he'd built. Larry told a reporter on live television that his company had cleared more land than six international airports combined. It was no surprise that he'd rubbed knees with the political elite over the years. His public donations were always to Israel, but his private ones were delivered personally, in cash, and only when he and the recipient were behind closed doors. Everyone in the real estate development business knew that Larry was tilting the scales in his favor by throwing around more cash than any of them ever hoped to accrue. While he may have skirted the law on several occasions, no prosecutor in his right mind would ever bring charges.

Gliding over to greet them, Cassidy Kloppleman, Larry's second wife and not Madeline's actual mother, froze several steps away. Kim-Jack noticed, but his father was still glaring at the Governor. Trisha was the first one to speak.

"Cassidy?" She took a step closer. "Cassidy, from Cincinnati? Wow, I haven't seen you in what, four years? Do you still go to Jamaica? Did you ever get the tattoo finished?"

Cassidy seemed to recover in the few seconds it took Trisha to embarrass her. Glancing at the Governor, as though checking to see if his attention had shifted, she nodded quickly. Then, much more composed, the short-haired blonde walked over and hugged Kim-Jack's stepmother, whispering something in her ear. Moments later, the two women simply turned, Cassidy guiding Trisha by the elbow, and walked back through the house without another word. Neither was seen for over an hour, before they came joyfully skipping out of the house with champagne flutes in their hands.

To this day, no one in either family has mentioned the incident again.

Their engagement happened so quickly that Kim-Jack still wasn't sure he was the one who proposed. Her stepmother bought the ring, saving him the embarrassment of giving his future spouse something less than she expected. The chasm between his middle class salary and her sky's the limit spending habits would always be too wide for him to cross. He remembered walking through the mall with her and mentioning a jewelry store they were approaching. She stopped and grabbed his arm.

"You're joking, right? You don't really expect me to be seen wearing some trinket you can buy in the mall, do you?"

Once again, he spotted the trap and jumped over it. "No. I was just kidding. Let's get something to eat."

The summer passed and the two families developed a friendly, but often distant relationship. Kim-Jack and Madeline, who were engaged a week after the barbecue, toiled through the arduous and often frustrating process of intermingling their lives during that time. His food, her food. Which side of the bed she favored. Which side of the bed he felt was best for sex. Nightly, daily, whenever she was in the mood, sex was the fuel that seemed to keep them going. Everything else was background noise.

Not having to work, Madeline spent the time planning their wedding, shopping with her stepmother when they got along, and occasionally lunching with her father and some politician that

"Hot Pizza, Cold Shoulder"   Ricky Ginsburg

needed to see a pretty face. Breaking ground for a shopping center with the Governor, Madeline wore a company hard hat and stood in-between the Governor and her dad. The Mayor was running for re-election? There was Madeline on the stage with dad and the rest of the local political manpower.

The future groom was not so lucky. His third year of teaching high school started at the end of that summer. Kim-Jack's focus was on his students, staying alive during his five daily trips to the educational oasis of the combat zone, as he'd come to call the school, and inventing a pizza box that could keep a pie hot for hours at a time. If there were politics happening around him, Kim-Jack wore blinders to keep them at bay.

    Madeline closed her eyes for a few seconds and opened them, pointing at Kim-Jack's crotch.

    "How about we forego sex for a while? Maybe that will clear your brain."

    "So, you think it's *my* brain that's in need of a dust-off?" Kim-Jack crossed his arms over his chest. "You can't go without grabbing my crotch for more than a day."

    "I'll bet I can hold off longer than you can." She winked. "I've got more of that mysterious girl power that you refuse to accept."

    "Let's make this interesting." He lifted the wineglass off the dresser and took a drink. "If you win, we'll go to Antarctica and get married on an iceberg with an audience of penguins."

    She smiled. "And if you win?"

    "We get married in St. Anthony's on Brighton Avenue." He paused. "With both Father Kennedy and your rabbi performing a dual service."

    Madeline got up from the bed, walked over, and kissed him. "You better go shopping for some kickass winter clothes, buddy. Our wedding day is six weeks away. We'll be crossing the Antarctic Circle right after Christmas." She held up a hand. "Wait. Cancel that."

    "What?"

"Shopping for clothes."

"I can't go shopping for clothes? Gee, I thought I was old enough to handle that task."

Madeline shook her head. "You can buy any clothing you want as long as it's not for our expedition to Antarctica."

"Oh, so now it's an expedition?"

She smiled. "Yes, KJ, that's what it's called. An expedition to Antarctica."

"And not just a wedding?"

"You are such a putz."

He held up a finger. "I know what that means."

"And to think you graduated college."

"Somewhere on my sheepskin it mentions clothing."

Madeline sighed. "I'm sure it does, but not in the context of being stylish around your future wife. I'll go shopping with you. Better yet, I'll take you shopping. Your entire wardrobe for this expedition will be my treat."

"As you wish, dear." Kim-Jack nodded toward the bed. "So, is our wager already in effect?"

Reaching down, she unzipped his fly. "It starts in ten minutes. Hurry up and make me sing. Then I'm going home, so you won't be tempted to sink the bet."

Chapter Four

She was gone when Kim-Jack got up to pee before dawn. No note. No kiss goodbye that he could remember. The ten-minute sexual romp had morphed into a full hour and he had passed out while she was in the bathroom. He walked into the living room and checked for her car from their third-floor window. Her parking space was vacant.

More out of curiosity than apprehension, he'd taken a glance into her closet. Nothing appeared to be missing. Her jewelry box, what she deemed to be her less than valuable spares, was still loaded with sparkling gems. Pretty much everything in the box he deemed to be gaudy, but then again, his only jewelry was his high school ring. They already had several spats in their time together where she'd fled to the safety of her bedroom at home and her father's shoulder. Only once did she take the box, returning with it hours later, when her temper had cooled enough to accept his apology.

However, there was more to her going home this time beyond the trip to Antarctica. Something had happened in Hawaii, something he couldn't yet explain. For her to make a bet like that was totally out of character, especially after she insisted they continue well beyond her ten-minute barrier. No, this was Madeline with a plan in mind, and he had little chance of discovering its details.

We were apart for eleven days. No sex for either of us for eleven days. That's a new record. And now we have a no-sex competition. What a stupid idea. Why did I agree to that?

He shook his head and shut off the light in her closet.

What's going on in that head of yours, Madeline? You really want to stifle such a large part of our relationship for some crazy idea about Antarctica? What the hell are you thinking? He kicked the bed. *What the hell was I thinking?*

Sleep was out of the question, despite his total lack of energy. Shuffling into the kitchen, he grabbed a couple of her oranges from the fridge and made himself a cup of fresh squeezed. He turned off the kitchen light and, guided by the glow of the streetlights, made his way out to their one-chair balcony, wearing only a towel around his waist. It had been weeks, even months, but the doubt had returned.

What am I doing? Is Tito right or just stoned?

Slowly sipping the juice to savor every drop that he'd denied himself in favor of his future wife, Kim-Jack looked up at the stars and asked the question again. The response was silence.

Tito asked me if I love her. He paused for a few seconds. *Of course I do. It's not just about the sex...or is it?* Another longer pause. *Nah. I can get laid without trying very hard. That redheaded girl at the bar last Saturday night was proof of that.* He shook his head. *No, there's obviously more to my feelings about Madeline than just sex.*

Finishing the juice with a gulp, Kim-Jack set the glass down on the floor of the balcony and his bare feet up on the railing. The autumn night air was warm and dry, but the breeze was constant. Without a care for the moment, he was enjoying the peace and calm until sirens in the distance grew louder. Two fire engines made the turn from Brooksville onto Madison and roared past his townhouse. They were followed moments later by a city police car and an ambulance.

Staring off into the distance, he could see the dull glow of a fire at least half a mile away. More sirens were approaching and he was tempted to throw on some clothes and drive down the avenue to see the action firsthand. However, the orange juice had tempted him and he wanted more. Back into the kitchen he strolled. This time using four oranges and a much bigger glass.

Why have I deprived myself of this simple treat? Before we met, I was fine with frozen juice from a can or the occasional bottle of Tropicana from the supermarket. But this? This is liquid gold.

He tilted the glass to his mouth and gulped half of it without taking a breath. The temptation to use every piece of fruit in the refrigerator was strong, but then he'd have to go the market to replenish the supply in the event Madeline returned before the following morning.

I really don't want to go shopping today. I thought we'd spend the day together. Maybe go to the lake and people watch.

Kim-Jack checked the time and decided it was still too early to call her, even if it was a useless effort.

I don't know what I'd say right now. Maybe it's best that I wait until she calls me. He sighed. *As usual.*

In the sixteen months they'd been together, that's how these disagreements were ended. Madeline would call. He'd be apologetic, even if it wasn't his fault, and then she'd come over and jump on him as though nothing had ever happened. The apology meant nothing to her. His act of contrition was worthless, but it gave her more of that girl power that she relished, so each time, he followed the same script.

An explosion from the fire scene lit up the early morning sky. The blast was powerful enough to rattle the windows and the streetlights flickered for a moment. When he was a little boy, Kim-Jack wanted to be a firefighter. His father took him to all the firehouses in the city. Occasionally, they would follow a fire engine to watch the firefighters battle a local blaze. It took a fireman falling four stories from a burning building, screaming in pain, to convince him that a safer career choice made more sense. Of course, teaching in the combat zone was only slightly safer than fighting fires.

Then again, look at the risk I'm willing to take to get married. And what if she wants kids?

The children discussion was still waiting in the wings. Both of them were the only child their parents had created. As far as Kim-Jack was concerned, having a child after several years of teaching them was forever out of the question. Madeline hadn't voiced an opinion yet, but her father made it clear that he wanted grandchildren and as soon as possible.

So, it will be my father-in-law who will make the decision? I don't think so.

Madeline was aware of the circumstances surrounding his birth and the sudden death of his mother due to his arrival in this world. She had denounced his fear of a repeat, but never declared that she was willing to take the risk.

I'd make a shitty father. He nodded. *Especially after dealing with my students.*

A parade of emergency vehicles interrupted his musings and the temptation to drive down the avenue to witness the carnage in person returned. Kim-Jack went into the bedroom and put on a pair of shorts and socks. He was about to tie the laces of his sneakers when his phone rang.

It was Madeline and she was sobbing.

"We're at the hospital. I think daddy's had a heart attack."

"Jesus! Which hospital?" Kim-Jack finished tying his laces and grabbed a hoodie from the chair by the bed.

"Mercy Memorial. Hurry, KJ, please."

"I'll be there in forty minutes." He took a deep breath. "I love you, Madeline. Hang in there."

He made the drive in just over thirty minutes, running the red lights and pushing the Chevy into the danger zone once he got onto the freeway. Pulling into the hospital's parking lot just as the sun was cresting over the distant tree line, he rushed into the emergency entrance and asked where Larry Kloppleman was being treated.

A receptionist told him room four, but that the patient was probably on his way to surgery.

"Did he have a heart attack?"

She shrugged. "You'll have to ask the doctor. Are you family?"

"Not yet." He smiled. "But soon. Larry's daughter is my fiancée."

The receptionist gave him a look that expressed condolences and then grabbed a ringing phone. She pointed to the hallway on the right before answering the call. Kim-Jack jogged down the hallway, spotting Madeline as she came out of the last room on the left.

"Is he okay?"

She hugged him so tightly that Kim-Jack found it hard to breathe and pushed her away by the shoulders.

"Tell me what's going on."

Getting her sobs under control, Madeline held his hands. "The cardiologist says it's a heart attack, but they're unsure of how much damage it's caused. Daddy's on the way to the operating room where they'll evaluate his condition and do whatever's necessary to save him."

"Where's your stepmom?"

Madeline nodded toward the room she'd just walked out from. "In there, lying down. They gave her a shot of valium to calm her down."

"And you?"

"I'm okay now that you're here."

So, all is forgiven from earlier. He grinned. "So, we're still going to Antarctica?"

She managed a limp smile and punched his shoulder. "Only if I win."

Kim-Jack was going to suggest getting something to eat while they waited. He'd been with Tito when his partner's father had his heart attack and knew that they could be hanging around for hours before getting an update. But Madeline told him that other than fresh squeezed orange juice, there was nothing else she wanted to eat.

Just then, a doctor wearing scrubs with a stethoscope hanging from his neck came through the large doors with the NO ADMITTANCE signs and walked over to them. He took Madeline's hand.

"Your dad is stable, but he's going to need several stents to clear his blocked arteries."

Madeline grabbed the doctor's wrist. "How many? Is he going to be okay afterwards?"

"At least three that I can see right now. There's a lot of damage. Your father is lucky he got here when he did." He pulled his hand free and turned to Kim-Jack. "You and your family should go home. This is going to take at least four hours, probably six, and then two hours in recovery. I can have the cardiac unit call you when your father is out of danger and can have visitors."

"Her father and my future father-in-law." Kim-Jack smiled. "But I already feel like family."

The doctor shook his hand. "Well then, congratulations are in order and don't worry, we'll get him fixed up and he'll be able to dance with the bride on the big day." A loud page summoned the doctor and he again took Madeline's hands in his own. "I promise, okay?"

She sobbed, but managed a weak nod.

Turning toward the off-limits doors, the doctor stopped and looked at the couple. "Where are you getting married?"

Kim-Jack shoved his tongue into his cheek. "Downtown at St. Anthony's on Brighton."

Madeline kicked his shin and looked at the doctor with a sly smile on her face. "Antarctica."

With some help from the nursing staff and wheelchair, they were able to get Cassidy Kloppleman into the front seat of his Chevy. Madeline rode in the back with her hand on her stepmother's shoulder for the entire drive out to their country estate. Several of the staff were waiting and carried the limp woman into the parlor.

The head chef had been called back from his weekend off and was busy preparing breakfast. Kim-Jack found his way into the main kitchen and convinced the chef to let him make fresh orange juice for his fiancée and her stepmother. Within fifteen minutes, the kitchen team presented mom, Madeline, and Kim-Jack with enough food to feed a classroom of starving children.

Scooping scrambled eggs onto a homemade waffle, Kim-Jack doused them with pancake syrup and put a second waffle on top to create a sandwich. Cassidy's injection of valium had worn off during the drive home, and she watched in awe as he bit through the massive sandwich.

"Your future husband has some appetite." She took Madeline's hand. "You're going to have to spend some time in our kitchen and learn how to cook."

"Or, I could just hire a chef." Madeline smiled and stared into her stepmother's eyes. Her voice was laced with sarcasm. "So, just how much do you cook, Cassidy?"

Kim-Jack noticed the change in her tone and intervened in what sounded like a rising storm between Madeline and her stepmother.

"Madeline isn't going to need to cook, Mrs. Kloppleman."

"Cassidy, if you please." Madeline sighed. "The real Mrs. Kloppleman lives in San Francisco and doesn't give a shit about her daughter. Everyone around here that matters calls her Cassidy."

"Well, either way...Cassidy, my dad taught me to cook, so I'll handle that task with pleasure." Kim-Jack turned to his future spouse. "I already deal with the fresh squeezed orange juice each morning and buying the tofu."

"And you really know your way around pizza." Madeline grinned. "You should see the magic box he's building so that astronauts on the space station can get it delivered hot every time."

Kim-Jack raised his eyebrows and shook his head. Now it was his turn for sarcasm. "I'm so glad you support my efforts to make this dream come true."

"Ah, the sarcastic tone so early in the day." Raising her eyebrows to match his expression, Madeline pursed her lips. "I'll do everything I can to make your dreams come true, KJ. You know that, right?"

"Sometimes I wonder if you know the difference between nightmares and dreams."

Madeline was thrown off guard. "What's that supposed to mean?"

Walking over to her, Kim-Jack whispered in her ear, "Let's talk about this later. I don't want to argue in front of your stepmother."

"Sorry, Cassidy." Getting up from her seat, Madeline took him by the hand. "Let's go somewhere private so you can argue without worry."

They strolled out to the pool deck and took seats facing each other at one of the glass tables. One of the housekeepers saw them leave and followed to ask if they needed anything. Madeline thanked the woman and told her they didn't want to be disturbed unless it was a call from the hospital. Sitting back in the chair, she pulled her knees up to her chest and rested her head on them for a minute or two.

Finally looking up at him, she asked, "Do we have a problem?"

"Other than your crazy plan to get married in Antarctica, your middle of the night disappearance, and the bug that's crawled up your ass over the last eleven days that you were gallivanting around naked on a beach in Hawaii with my parents? Nope. Nothing that I can think of, other than those few minor details."

"What's wrong with getting married in Antarctica?"

"What was wrong with getting married in Jamaica, or at the lake house, or even the observation deck of the Eiffel Tower?" He shook his head. "What was wrong with Hawaii?"

"Nothing was wrong with any of those places. I just found something more unique."

He nodded. "Ah, so that's the determining factor. It has to be unique. How about someplace that's not only unique, but warm?"

"Everyone I know got married in the Caribbean or on a cruise ship or a beach in Hawaii. I don't know anyone who's declared their vows on the seventh continent. That's what I call unique." Reaching across the table, Madeline took his hands. "We're never going to do this again. It's a one-shot. Why not do something really memorable?"

Kim-Jack pondered her logic for a few moments. "Okay, I see your point, but I'm not convinced. There have to be other places equally unique, but without exposing ourselves to weather that would freeze a polar bear's penis."

"You know that polar bears are only in the Arctic, right professor?"

"Fine. A penguin's penis. Okay? Is that cold enough?" He squeezed her hands. "Do you know anyone who's been married on the International Space Station?"

She yanked her hands back. "I'm being serious and you're making jokes."

"Hey, it's just as dangerous as getting to the South Pole."

Reaching into her pocket, Madeline pulled out her cellphone and asked it if anyone had ever been married in outer space. The reply was instantaneous and left her giggling her way into tears.

"Astronauts Lucinda Breckinridge and Phillipe Cortez were married on the International Space Station on..." She clicked off the phone and laid it on the table. "Your next question?"

"Look, there's gotta be an alternative." Kim-Jack got up from his chair and walked over to the pool. "Your father's not going to be well enough to travel to Antarctica. Have your researched the Drake Passage?"

"Somebody mentioned it."

"Did they mention how dangerous it is, especially for those not in the best of health?" Kim-Jack returned to the table and bent over with his knuckles resting on the glass top. "Is it really worth risking your father's life for this stunt?"

Madeline pushed her chair back from the table. "Stunt? That's what you think this is?"

"Okay, bad choice of words."

"We're talking about making this trip six weeks from now. Daddy will go through rehab. He'll lose the weight and be as healthy as you or me long before it's time to make the Drake thing and survive." She slammed her palms on the table. "Look, KJ, this was his idea, his dream, and we're going to make it happen."

Now it was his turn to be surprised. "His idea? This wasn't something you concocted?"

She shook her head. "It was half your father's idea as well."

Kim-Jack slapped his forehead. "Well, that explains everything."

Twenty-four hours after the surgery that rebuilt the plumbing in his chest, Larry Kloppleman was transferred by helicopter to the airport and then on to a rehab facility in Seattle. Madeline flew out with him. Cassidy stayed behind. Even though he had classes to teach, Kim-Jack made plans to make the trip later in the day, but his fiancée insisted his students needed him more than she or her father did. Kim-Jack told her it was nice to know just how unnecessary he was to her family and ripped up his ticket, smiling the entire time.

Madeline made it as far as the airport in Seattle before they turned her around and sent her home. Apparently, the staff from the rehab facility made it clear that *she* was unneeded there as well. Cassidy required her support and as much as Madeline detested her stepmother, she knew her father would never forgive her if she refused.

Chapter Five

Monday mornings on most jobs started slowly and built to a crescendo as lunchtime approached. The pace at Barack Obama High School peaked several seconds after the doors were opened at seven and never slowed until they were locked again at six in the evening. Keeping order in the hallways was of paramount importance and the teachers took turns maintaining control. Kim-Jack had been using pizzas to bribe his fellow teachers to handle his hall monitor duties for several weeks. No one was left to bargain with this morning.

    The students came to school loaded up on energy drinks and roasted coffee beans that they chewed instead of gum. Between the time the doors opened and the late bell rang–thirty-five minutes by the clock–the hall monitors broke up seventeen fights that were reported to the office and another twenty that were not. One stabbing required a trip to the emergency room accompanied by a security officer. That same incident brought city police to the school an hour later when the process of revenge rolled down the hallway.

    As the hallways emptied and the din became a soft murmur, Kim-Jack let himself relax a bit. The janitor was still cleaning up the dried blood from the last stabbing incident, but the slamming of lockers and anxious running to avoid being late for first period had ended. Peace was restored, at least until the classrooms emptied out in fifty minutes.

    Kim-Jack walked into his classroom at seven-forty to find Marcus standing behind the lectern and clapping his hands to the music coming from his headphones. The boy thrust a folded sheet of paper at him without missing a beat and stood there with an expectant look on his face.

    "What's this?" Kim-Jack lifted a cup from the boy's nearest ear and repeated the question, louder.

Marcus slid the headphones off his head and smiled. "My written permission to skip class this week."

"From who?"

"My moms."

Kim-Jack took the paper and unfolded it. Scanning the page, he laid it on the lectern and shook his head. "You told me that your mother was in jail."

"I took this to her and she signed it."

"You traveled six hours across the state to have your mother sign a piece of paper?"

He nodded. "Yeah. Your sillybus says this is Sex Ed week. I don't need no Sex Ed. I know how to satisfy a woman already. What do you think you're gonna teach me that I don't know?"

Kim-Jack read the note again and stared at the signature. Rubbing his finger over the written words, he came away with fresh ink.

"When did she sign this, Marcus?"

The boy shrugged. "It was over the weekend. I took the bus."

"I see." Folding the paper, he handed it back. The temptation to play along with this obvious scam was strong. Not having to deal with the rebellious teen for a week was tempting, but Kim-Jack knew the Board of Education would hang him for letting the kid slide.

Marcus was confused. "What?"

"Something you don't know about me Marcus is that I have a photographic memory. I know exactly what your mother's signature looks like. She's a lefty, or at least she was on the last note you gave me from her. This is the signature of a right-handed person." Kim-Jack shook his head. "Nice try, though."

"She hurt her signing hand and had to switch." Marcus offered the paper again. "Come on, brother. You know I wouldn't try to scam my favorite teacher."

"Marcus, you'd do or say anything to get back on the streets."

The boy crumpled the paper and dropped it on the floor. "Screw you, man. Wasting my time like you paid for it. Sex Ed." He blew out a sharp breath. "I got more Sex Ed than you'll ever experience, brother. Everyone knows teachers can't party." The boy grabbed his crotch. "Teach this, man."

By now, the classroom had filled with students. In the back of the room, four students were tossing dice and cash. Someone had unlocked the window and a group of smokers had gathered to blow their fetid exhaust out with the breeze. Music blared from a variety of sources, barely drowning out the arguments, boasting, and foreplay.

"Take your seat, Marcus."

Kim-Jack turned away from him and started for his desk. Someone else threw the tennis ball that hit his back, but Marcus picked it up from the floor and began tossing it from one hand to the other.

Imagine that ball being shoved down your throat, you little prick.

Walking back to Marcus, Kim-Jack held out his hand. "You want to skip today's class?"

"Now, you're talking." Marcus dropped the ball into his hand and started for the door. He paused and turned around. "What about tomorrow?"

Kim-Jack pointed toward the door. "Get the hell out of here before I change my mind."

The first day of Sex Ed week was taught by a video that Kim-Jack had procured from the middle school down the block. It was the only piece of the district's curriculum that he used, as it gave him a free period and guaranteed that most of his students would attend class. They loved videos. Bees pollinating plants, volcanoes erupting, farm animals copulating. Every natural image that had a sexual connotation was featured in the thirty-minute movie.

Toward the end, when the action contained people and bars and dim lighting, the hoots and clapping from the class punctuated the action. If they were learning anything, Kim-Jack would call it a miracle. But the attendance numbers looked good on his weekly report to the district, and that meant his job was secure for another year.

It would be a peaceful day for Kim-Jack once he got through first period. None of his other students this semester had shown the aggressiveness that Marcus foisted on him. Last year, there were two such problem children. One made it to Thanksgiving before he was knifed in the boys' locker room. The other never returned after Christmas break, and no one seemed to have any information about her whereabouts.

His last class of the day featured one pregnant student and another who already had a two-year-old at home. The two girls sat side-by-side and cracked jokes through the entire video. Kim-Jack decided to find a different video for next year.

Tito was waiting for him in the science lab they shared between their two classrooms. The jack-and-jill space was wide enough for laboratory benches down one wall and ample storage capacity on the other. Kim-Jack, in a moment of generosity, decided to purchase the dozen pizzas they would need for the evening's experiment. Tito had been moaning about his empty wallet all day.

Two of the pies went to Fizz and Vincent. One pie was Tito's dinner that he offered to pay for next week. The balance went into the various boxes the two scientists had constructed, which were then connected to a series of computer monitors and temperature probes. It was as though Dr. Frankenstein had opened a pizzeria.

Having delivered the two pies to the security guards already on station in the teachers' lounge, Kim-Jack handed his partner the pepperoni and mushroom pie he'd requested. He slid the remaining pizzas into nine identical boxes and started the timer.

"Here's to three hours."

Tito sighed. "Here's to you remembering to get hot seeds tomorrow night."

Kim-Jack reached over and grabbed a slice out of his open box. "Every time I get you hot seeds, you complain about your stomach. Give it a break already. I don't need to sit here for three hours and listen to you belch and fart."

"What's going on with your future father-in-law?"

"Getting better, I hope. Madeline's still at home, taking care of Cassidy. I haven't seen her yet, but I think she's coming down here for the weekend."

"Still going to Antarctica?"

Kim-Jack bowed his head and blew out a breath. "Yeah. It looks that way. Madeline's taking me shopping for winter clothes before she moves back into the townhouse."

Tito swallowed the lump of pizza he'd been chewing and grabbed Kim-Jack's wrist. "Don't do it."

"Why?"

Tightening his grip as Kim-Jack tried to pull his arm away, Tito shook his head. "Whatever you buy will be the wrong thing. It won't be stylish enough for Madeline. She'll claim that you embarrass her by wearing it. From what I know of your future wife, and the control freak that she has become, you better wait for her to select what she thinks is appropriate for you to wear."

"She's not like that."

"Really?"

Kim-Jack relented. "Okay. I let her select my sneakers because she thought the ones I picked out were too gaudy."

"And the incident with the sport jacket?" Smiling, Tito took a massive bite out of the slice in his hand. "You still refuse to wear the one she liked and made you buy."

"So, I like to please her. Keeping your wife happy is a virtuous goal."

"Being pussy-whipped is not."

Tito's abrasive comments were never filtered and Kim-Jack had done his best to ignore them, but his patience had been worn thin by recent events and he struck back verbally.

"What the hell do you know about women, anyhow? Jesus, Tito, your entire life revolves around food and making fun of my attempt at a normal relationship. Let's face it, if this experiment was all about keeping salad fresh, you'd probably lose some weight. And, if you lost some weight, you might stand a chance at getting laid once in a while, even without hair on your head or being able to find your way around the bedroom in the dark."

Tito paused with a slice of pizza halfway to his mouth. Slowly, he laid the slice down on his paper towel stack and slid back from the lab bench.

"I don't need this shit."

"I think you need to hear it though, and I think you need to start taking control of your life before it's too late." Getting up from his stool, Kim-Jack headed toward the door. "I need to get some fresh air. There's too much bullshit floating around this room."

Kim-Jack was one of the few teachers that knew the combination to the locked door that led to the roof. However, the door was ajar and Vincent was already out there getting high. For a moment, Kim-Jack considered sharing his joint, but he hadn't had a toke since middle school and didn't relish the thought of coughing his lungs out.

"Yo, professor pizza, what brings you up to the observation deck tonight?" He offered the joint to Kim-Jack. "Want a hit?"

"No thanks, Vincent. The Board of Ed is still doing random testing."

"Not for security guards."

Kim-Jack pinched the bridge of his nose. "Go figure."

Vincent took a long toke and stubbed out the joint. "I've been thinking about going back to school and getting a degree."

"College?"

He shrugged. "Well, I need to get my GED first."

"You never finished high school and you're walking around with a gun?" Kim-Jack couldn't believe that the city would hire an armed guard with less than a high school diploma. "Did the Board of Ed know that when you were hired?"

"Yeah, but they needed guards for this school and said that I could get my GED while I was working."

Kim-Jack pursed his lips. "And are you working on it now?"

Vincent held out his hands. "I wish I could, but the job keeps me too busy at night and I sleep during the day."

"Too busy?"

"Forty-five minute circuits every two hours. Me and Fizz take turns." He smiled. "It's an undemanding job, but time consuming. Three floors, all those doors, all those keypads to verify that I've checked. Who has time to study?"

"What about the hour that Fizz is making the circuit?"

Vincent scratched the top of his head. "That's when I watch Netflix." He sighed. "I don't get it at home, so I have to watch in the teachers' lounge. I'm four seasons into this weird heist movie. It's in Spanish with English subtitles, but I'm also trying to learn Spanish at the same time. There's an opening at Cortez Middle School for the day shift, but you gotta be bilingual to apply."

Gunshots from nearby interrupted their discussion with both of them ducking below the perimeter wall for cover. Vincent looked up first, but not before instructing Kim-Jack to stay low until he was sure it was safe.

"The city is a crazy place at night."

Kim-Jack snorted. "You should spend some time in my classroom in order to really get a feel for crazy."

The radio clipped to Vincent's belt beeped twice and he keyed once in response.

"That's Fizz." He checked the time. "Shit, I didn't realize I'd been up here so long."

"Go ahead down. I'll lock the door."

Vincent offered him the roach. "Last chance."

"Nah. You'll want it later."

Reaching into the pouch that should have held an extra magazine for his weapon, Vincent pulled out three plastic tubes with pre-rolled joints. "Don't worry about me, professor. I've got plenty to spare."

Kim-Jack spent a few minutes alone on the roof after Vincent left. The night air was cool and moist with the occasional mosquito attacking his ears. Sirens in the distance faded. He wondered who fired the gunshots. Was it one of his students? That wouldn't be a surprise.

He pulled the door shut and tried it twice to ensure it was securely locked. Walking into the lab, Tito was gone, but he'd left a note saying that he was tired, pissed off, and not really in the mood for any more pizza tonight. Kim-Jack checked the probes and found them all to be registering correctly.

Well, at least he hasn't had another temper tantrum and pulled them all out.

Tonight's pizza box test was already running for ninety minutes. He didn't need Tito to finish the experiment. A few photos with his cellphone would be sufficient to record and verify the results. With Madeline still on her way home from Seattle, he felt no burning desire to return to an empty townhouse. His lesson plan was already set for tomorrow. Day two of Sex Ed week meant he'd be using his own video with his own lecture about reproduction. It was the same material he'd already used during the two school years he'd taught so far. Even without his notes, Kim-Jack felt confident that he could recite the lecture from memory.

Marcus would be there tomorrow, probably with another forged letter from his mother. But Kim-Jack needed to reel him in, maintain a level of control in the teacher-student chain of command, and if the kid tried the same stunt tomorrow, he'd simply rip up the letter and embarrass the shit out of the little punk.

Kim-Jack nodded twice and rubbed his hands together. That's what he remembered from college: keep control at all times. Never let the students have the upper and hand.

And do your best not to murder them.

He went downstairs to the teachers' lounge to bum a cold beer. Fizz was in his usual position, eyes glued to the television, watching Australian Rules football. When Kim-Jack asked for a brew, he simply waved his hand without looking away from the screen. Kim-Jack drank a cold one while watching what appeared to be football without the pads, helmets, or common sense rules that accompanied the NFL.

"Those guys are insane."

Fizz nodded. "Yeah. Totally insane, but I'd take any one of them as backup when the shit hits the fan."

"No padding? How come they don't get hurt?"

"Oh, they get hurt." He pointed at the screen. "Number twenty-three has a broken nose from earlier in the period and the goalie on the other team has a broken arm, but they splinted it and he's still in there."

"Jesus!" Kim-Jack twisted the cap off a second beer. "They should teach here."

Fizz laughed. "You got my vote on that one."

Two players collided midfield, and the remaining players jumped into the fray. Whistles sounded and the officials did their best to separate the combatants. The television switched to a series of commercials, and Fizz muted the sound.

"I heard you put some kid into the wall."

Kim-Jack nodded. "Ulysses Wilson. Right after he stabbed another student."

"I know the kid he stabbed, Xavier San Phillipo. Can't believe he's still in school. Must be five years now." Fizz blew out a sharp breath. "Blacks and Puerto Ricans, you'd think after all these years they'd have settled their differences."

"Hate is a tough emotion to bury."

"Well, I'd watch your back for a week or two. Ulysses belongs to a gang of radically bad kids. They're not gonna take your actions lightly. You dis one of them and it's like you're calling out the entire gang. Cops are only gonna hold him for forty-eight hours at the most before they cut him loose." Fizz brought the volume up slightly as one player smashed another in the throat. "He'd be good at this kind of football."

"If he lives long enough."

"Well, that's the standard problem around here, professor." The game was back to full speed and the security guard pushed the volume up to maximum level.

Kim-Jack watched for a few moments and left the lounge with his beer. He paused outside the door and took a long gulp of the icy brew, before heading back to the third floor to check his pizzas when his cellphone jingled. It was Madeline, and he held his breath as he connected the call.

"Is everything okay?"

"I'm going to slit her throat while she sleeps."

"I'll take that as a no."

"I'm on the highway. I'll be at the townhouse in an hour and a half."

"With or without a knife and an all-points police bulletin looking for you?"

"I'm not in the mood for your corny humor, KJ."

Kim-Jack held the phone at arm's length for a few seconds. "Are you staying?"

"For now." She honked the horn several times and screamed, *"Asshole!"*

"Are you okay to drive?"

"Does it matter? I'm already on the way. I don't care where you are or what you're doing, just be at the townhouse when I get there, okay?"

Shaking his head slowly, Kim-Jack sighed once, loud enough for her to hear. "I'll be there. You can count on it."

She ended the call without another word.

Chapter Six

Beating her to the townhouse, Kim-Jack stripped off his clothes and put on the grass skirt Madeline had worn the other night. It was too small to snap closed, so he twisted it around to the back and used one of his belts to keep the skirt from falling. The effect became even less seductive as his junk kept peeking through the green nylon strands. He gave a moment's thought to grabbing a towel from the shower instead, but seconds later, Madeline came through the door.

"I'm not here to play peek-a-boo with your penis, KJ."

"Even though it wants you?"

She shook her head. "It *always* wants me. God, you have such a one-track mind."

"Okay, we'll deal with that later. What's the big emergency?"

Madeline pulled her cellphone out of her back pocket and started a call. He heard a voice answer, and then she handed him the phone.

"It's my father."

Kim-Jack took a deep breath. "Hello, Mr. Kloppleman." He caught himself too late. "Sorry. Hello, Larry. How are you feeling?"

"I'm feeling concerned, Kim-Jack. Madeline tells me you're against having the wedding in Antarctica."

Tapping the mute button, Kim-Jack turned to his fiancée. "Double-teaming me? Wow, I never expected that." He unmuted the phone. "I was really hoping that you'd like Hawaii instead. I've never been there."

"How many times have you been to Antarctica?"

Blindsided. Shit. "None yet, but some day I'd like to go."

"Then why not for your wedding?"

Kim-Jack's eyes launched tiny daggers at Madeline. "It just doesn't sound very romantic."

"How so?"

I am so totally screwed. "I'm trying to imagine that first night, after the ceremony and the celebration when we're back in our tiny cabin, in the frigid cold, trying to consummate our union."

"You never had sex in the winter?"

"Sure, in a heated cabin on a king-size bed." Kim-Jack grinned. "It was at your lake house as I recall."

Madeline fired the daggers back at him, mouthing the words, "Shut up, you idiot."

"I remember. You two were louder than the coyotes and made more noise than an avalanche. Cassidy thought a bear had gotten into your cabin."

Kim-Jack shook his head. *We weren't that loud.* "I didn't realize your hearing was that acute."

"Son, I can hear a bee fart at thirty paces. I know when a bear is grinding its teeth while sleeping in its cave. My eyesight may not be the best, but I know when two people are having sex. Especially when one of them is my daughter."

"Okay, but the cabin was still warmer than a ship in the Antarctic Ocean and I'm sure the bed was much larger than what they offer onboard."

"Well, don't worry about the bed. I'm booking you two into the owner's cabin."

"And the cold?"

"Wear socks."

A spate of coughing came over the line and Kim-Jack could hear voices in the background urging Larry Kloppleman to hang up. He must have covered the phone for a few moments, but the anxious voices came through nonetheless.

"Listen, son. They want me off the phone, so I'll make this short, sweet, and to the point. My little girl wants to get married in Antarctica, so that's what we're gonna do. If you're there to slip a ring on her finger, I'll see to it that you'll never have to work in that stupid high school again. For that matter, I will make sure you never have to work anywhere ever again. How's that sound, sport?"

"I don't know. What would I do all day long?"

"How about working for me?"

Yikes. Kim-Jack closed his eyes and listened to the sound of his breathing for a few seconds. "It's a very tempting offer, Larry."

"Tempting, my ass. I'm the genie in the bottle, son. Don't waste your wishes."

"What about my pizza box?"

"You're still fooling around with that idea?"

Madeline's eyes opened wide and she shook her head several times.

"Yes, and we're having significant results. This box could make us millions." Throwing her a silent kiss, Kim-Jack winked. "Tito has a lead on some very inexpensive foil that could bring the cost per box down to under two-dollars."

"Tito? He's that fat communist science teacher at your school?"

Pinching the bridge of his nose, Kim-Jack sighed. "He's not a communist, Larry. His parents come from Canada, and I think they're Polish descent."

"A Canadian?" Larry coughed and then spit. *"That's a thousand times worse."*

Kim-Jack muted the phone and looked at Madeline, who was doing her best not to throw something at him.

"What's he got against Canadians?"

"The bartender who convinced my mother to leave him was from Montreal."

"Oh." Kim-Jack unmuted the phone. "So, we'll leave the pizza box as an open item for now."

"Son, you can do whatever the hell you want with your pizza. If you like, I'll buy you a pizzeria and you can make pies all day long."

Oddly enough, Kim-Jack had a momentary vision of tossing a spinning pie over his head and smiled. But then the flimsy dough collapsed over his head. It was a message from the beyond, and Kim-Jack accepted it with a sigh.

"That's a very tempting offer, Larry. Can I have some time to consider it?"

"I'll count backwards from ten."

Once again, Kim-Jack muted the phone while his future father-in-law and possible boss, counted down. However, there was no need for Larry to count. Politics, excessive wealth, and a father-in-law's eyeballs boring into his skull all day long were never part of his dream. The collapsed pie over his head was as stifling as having Larry Kloppleman for his boss. Plus, the pizza box idea aside, he truly wanted to teach, to pass on the knowledge he'd learned. The memory of his father's joy when he told him that a job was available in the city and that he'd be educating the grandchildren of his friends would never fade.

Walking away from her father's offer might mean walking away from Madeline, but it was a risk he'd have to take. Now or in the future. He weighed the element of losing her against believing their bond had already grown strong enough to make her side with him against her father. The odds were strong that she'd be pissed off for a few days, but would eventually see the future through his eyes. Or so he hoped.

He waited until he heard the number zero before replying. "Okay." He turned to Madeline and smiled. "Fine. We'll get married in Antarctica if that's what will make you and Madeline happy. But as far as working for you, I think I'll pass. I not only want to teach, I need to teach. I need to make a difference. Too many children are growing up dumb, even though free education is available to them. I've already seen too many fights and stabbings in a place where they should never happen. Call it corny or the ranting of a dreamer, but I really want to change their lives."

"You really want to continue teaching in that hell hole?" Madeline blew out a sharp breath. "I think you're making a mistake. I think you're risking your life to teach children who can't see the value in an education that doesn't involve guns and knives."

Kim-Jack shrugged. "Maybe, but it's my mistake to make."

"I've seen many men make mistakes, son. You're making one now, but at least you have the balls to admit it. But I'm pleased that you're onboard with our Antarctic expedition. It will make Madeline happy and that makes me happy, and without happiness all we have is pain."

Another roaring cough and more anxious voices in the background that he shushed.

"I'll reach out to Trisha and your father to make the final arrangements. We'll leave the day after Christmas, so plan for a New Year's Eve wedding on the ship."

"Is the ship's captain going to marry us?" Madeline had concern in her voice. "I thought we were going to have a rabbi."

"I'm going to book a cabin for Rabbi Horowitz and his wife."

Kim-Jack held up his hand. "What about a priest?"

"You got a favorite one?"

"Father Kennedy's too old, but there's a young married priest at the Catholic Church across the street. I've never been there, but my dad knows the priest."

"From the nudist colony in Jamaica?" Madeline was aghast.

"Not likely. Before my dad retired from his carpenter job, he did some work rebuilding the rectory. The minister is new, but the elders of the church know him and they'll convince him to take on the task if he's reluctant." Kim-Jack smiled. At least he was getting a tiny bit of input for the most important day of his life.

"How is a Catholic priest married?"

"He got married as an Episcopalian minister and then converted." Kim-Jack shrugged. "I guess they can do that these days."

"Get me his name and number. I'll have my secretary reach out to him and make the arrangements."

Kim-Jack nodded and looked over at Madeline. "Anything else?"

She shook her head and reached for the phone.

"Thanks, daddy."

"Whatever you need, Maddy. You know that."

There was silence once the call ended. Kim-Jack slid off the grass skirt and put on a pair of sweatpants. Madeline took a seat on the couch, kicked off her shoes, and opened the top three buttons of her blouse.

Standing in the doorway to the bedroom, he shook his head and tied the strings of his sweats.

"You've got to be kidding."

She raised an eyebrow. "What?"

"You ambushed me like that and now you want sex?"

"You don't?"

Kim-Jack nodded toward her phone. "Is daddy listening?"

Madeline took the phone from the coffee table and slid it under the couch. "Okay?"

"No. Not okay." His face was hard, sullen, and he held his ground even as she leaned forward and held out her hands. "Are we playing on the same team?"

"Of course."

He shook his head. "It sure didn't seem that way. I got backed into a corner and double-teamed by this weird father-daughter combination. Sort of a mixed martial arts battle that I lost before the first bell. Right now, I'm feeling like I'm still wedged into that corner even though the fight is over and I've lost."

"What did you lose? We're still getting married and you're going to be able to brag that you've been to Antarctica."

Crossing his arms over his chest, Kim-Jack slipped into his teaching voice. "You can't simply force your way into someone's life with money and power. That's your father's modus operandi. When you try to act like him, you make me wonder if you've ever really cut the cord that ties you to his purse strings and beliefs. It's frightening to think that you might side with him over your future husband. There shouldn't be this much stress over our wedding. We should be able to compromise. Both of us should look forward to the day with optimism and joyful expectations. Right now, I'm scared shitless that something monstrously bad is going to happen."

"Wow! You're seriously that pissed off?" Madeline took a step back.

"Not as bad as Custer at Big Horn, but enough that my sex drive engine is cold right now."

She smiled and got up from the couch. "Let me warm you up then."

Kim-Jack tightened the bow on his sweatpants. "I can get past you using your sick father to sell the Antarctica thing. But you could have done this with a bit more finesse."

"Oh? I already told you this was his idea."

"And half my father's." He looked down at the floor. "And my father never said a word about it."

Madeline walked over and pulled one string on the bow. "Poor Kim-Jack, everyone's ganging up on him." She pulled the other and let the sweatpants fall to the floor. "And look. Even your love muscle thinks Antarctica is a good idea."

Every argument he had fell to the floor with his crumpled sweats. Kim-Jack picked up his future wife and carried her, with her legs wrapped around his waist, into the bedroom. Smiling, she sat on the edge of the bed and slipped her blouse over her head, but he stopped her, grabbing her hands.

"You better hope that ship has really warm cabins."

Madeline pulled her hands free and took him by the butt cheeks. "Warm or cold, it'll be hot when I'm done with you, KJ." Looking up at him, she broke into song. "Unforgettable, that's what you are. Unforgettable, though near or far."

He hummed the Nat King Cole standard along with her until the humming became moaning and her singing led to loud thumps from their neighbor on the common wall.

Kim-Jack slipped out of bed just after midnight and tiptoed into the living room. Madeline was snoring, not as loud as she sang, but with enough volume the he wasn't going back to sleep until she rolled to the other side. The thermostat was set cold enough to frost the windows from the inside, and he wrapped himself in a blanket. Walking over to the balcony, he slid the door open but stayed inside. The cool air at his back and the warm night breeze was a pleasing contrast hitting his face.

I must be crazy. He smiled and nodded once. *Yep. That's the answer. All that hot cheese has clogged the arteries into my brain. I've actually become a cheesehead. How is that possible? I've got a Master's degree in Education. I don't know what my IQ is, but I'm sure I'd get into Mensa if I took their tests. Is pizza making me stupid?*

He laughed and dropped the blanket to the floor, letting the breeze filter through his legs.

I must have my dad's gene for nakedness. Kim-Jack slapped his forehead. *I can't imagine being on that beach in Hawaii when Madeline sang naked in front of him. He swears that they never gawk at other naked bathers in Jamaica, but she's got a body that would make a blind man blush.*

Dropping down into the one chair that fit on the postage stamp balcony, he put his feet up on the rail and closed his eyes.

A beach in Hawaii, watching the sunset. Dolphins jumping in the surf. Steel guitars playing in the background. A waiter is coming toward me with a tall glass topped by a paper umbrella.

He sat up straight in the chair.

But he's naked.

Reaching down, Kim-Jack retrieved the blanket and tossed it over his shoulder. He made his way inside, closing and locking the slider before returning to the bedroom. Madeline was quiet. She'd rolled to the opposite side and squelched her snores. Slowly, he slipped back under the covers and pulled them up to his neck.

Her hand came over his belly and danced without stopping until her fingers were wrapped around his tool. She squeezed him softly and whispered in his ear, "I thought you'd never come back to bed."

Carefully, he turned toward her. "I was trying to remember how orcas have sex."

She tightened her grip. "I'll bet they like it cold."

"You know that they're mammals not fish, right?"

"Duh." Madeline ran her fingers up his belly and poked him. "Everyone knows that whales are not fish. But maybe it's different if the water is that cold."

"Well," he sighed with a bit of resignation in his voice, "We're going to find out one way or another."

She rolled over and lay on top of him. "I'll bet I can make you spout like a whale."

Kim-Jack grabbed her hips. "And I bet I can make you sing like a penguin."

"Penguins sing?"

He shrugged. "Something else for us to explore on this expedition to madness."

Chapter Seven

Tuesday arrived several hours too early for Kim-Jack. With their wager no longer an obstacle to sex, they had turned the bedroom into an adult playground. Chairs were turned upside down and built into a massive fort that currently held all the bed linens. They'd shoved the bed over to one side of the room and tilted the mattress up against the windows to guard against intruders that only existed in their minds. Madeline's appetite for sex was insatiable. Kim-Jack considered tying her hands and legs together with pillowcases as dawn broke outside the windows.

Standing in the doorway of their bedroom, he surveyed the destruction and shook his head.

"You going to clean up this mess before you go home?"

Madeline rolled over and pushed the nearest chair out of the way. This caused the roof of their fort to collapse, bringing the extra pillows and shams down on her head. Tossing them off, she pulled the blanket over her chest and smiled at him.

"I could leave the fort like it is and we could continue when you get home."

Kim-Jack shook his head. "You know I can't stand coming home to a mess."

She pulled the blanket down toward her waist. "Then don't leave."

Checking the time, he closed his eyes and took a deep breath. Kim-Jack was out of his shirt and slacks before the echo of her words faded.

He made it to class moments before the first bell. Thankfully, traffic was light and the new basketball coach remembered not to park in his spot. Students were still rushing into the building with the urgency of salmon swimming upstream. Kim-Jack rounded the corner with the sound of lockers slamming and students shouting. Pulling the door shut behind him, he turned around just in time to see Marcus break a chair over Xavier San Phillipo's head.

The assailant was screaming and cursing so loud that several of the female students were covering their ears. Jumping up onto a desk, Marcus pointed at Xavier. "You broke my cousin's nose and got him expelled. You lowlife piece of Puerto Rican shit." Then, faster than an exhaled cloud of vape, he pulled a knife from his back pocket and lunged at the kid. "I should cut your balls off and shove them down your throat."

Xavier managed to steer clear of the knife, but suddenly brandished his own blade, swinging it wildly with his arm holding back the blood from a gash in his forehead. Kim-Jack hit the panic button on the wall and grabbed a four-foot-tall model of a Saturn V booster rocket from the display by the door. Using it as though he was a knight with a lance, Kim-Jack was able to separate the two combatants until the security guards rushed into the classroom.

By the time the dust settled and the two boys were in restraints, the knives had mysteriously disappeared. None of the students remembered seeing a knife. Most of them said it was just a verbal disagreement and that Kim-Jack overreacted. Of course, the security guards heard this line of crap on a regular basis and searched everyone as they left the classroom. The knives were never found.

Police were called, but a bank robbery with a hostage situation and a seven-car-accident on the expressway had all available units tied up. Security escorted Marcus and Xavier off the school property and waited while the two boys jogged off in different directions. Everyone knew they'd be back at it tomorrow, but for the balance of the day, the two warring factions were too far apart to battle.

The remainder of the school day was calm and normal, if such a term could be applied to the madness of the high school corridors. Kim-Jack ran through his Sex Ed lesson plan for day two without a hitch, but the tension in his classroom remained high.

Apparently, each of the rival gangs had spread the word that the other side had started the confrontation and by lunch, extra security guards were brought in to quell any potential conflict.

A few small skirmishes broke out in the cafeteria, but they were quickly handled without anyone getting tossed out of the building. Several girls cornered a female member of an opposing gang and threatened her, but no punches were thrown, although someone wrote an ethnic slur in lipstick on the girl's locker. According to the teachers who met for lunch in their lounge, it was a fairly uneventful morning.

Pleased that attendance had been higher than usual, Kim-Jack was wrapping up the lesson in his last class when English professor and lover of all things Shakespeare, Chelbe Udulu slipped into the classroom and took a position at the back. She waited until he finished and the students filed out before walking up and handing Kim-Jack a folded sheet of paper.

"What's this?"

"One of Marcus' cousins gave it to me right after lunch."

"Another cousin?" Kim-Jack shook his head. "I think he's related to everyone in the school."

She shrugged. "It's a gang thing. Sort of like King Duncan and Macbeth."

"Didn't Macbeth kill the king?"

"Correct. Same thing that's going on here. Cousins killing cousins. You're not the only one who calls this place the combat zone." Chelbe pointed at the paper. "Read it."

Opening the paper, he noticed that the words were written in red paint. But then he looked closer.

"Jesus. It's written in blood."

"An awful lot of blood." Chelbe pointed at the paper. "Those letters are half an inch wide and the dried blood is so thick that you can feel it through the folded sheet."

"Pick a side?" He scratched the back of his neck. "What's that supposed to mean?"

"I think the gangs want you to decide which of them you're going to support."

Kim-Jack laughed. "I'm not joining a gang."

"You might have to join one in order to survive."

He shook his head. "I'm certain the Board of Education has a policy against its teachers participating in gang activities."

"I don't think the Board has any idea what's going on in this school."

"Fair point, but if we all start sporting gang tats and bandanas they'll come running."

Tito strolled into the room from their jack-and-jill laboratory. "You in a better mood today?"

"I'm fine." Kim-Jack raised his eyebrows. "What about you?"

"My stepfather's check hit my bank last night. I'm in a splendid mood." He turned to Chelbe. "What about you, madam professor? Willie the Shake working for you today?"

Chelbe grinned. "You should read Shakespeare, Tito. He loves fat characters."

Tito flipped her the middle finger. "Fat is just a state of mind."

"Largest state in the U.S. I believe." She responded in kind and then nodded at the paper in Kim-Jack's hand. "Show Tito your love letter."

Kim-Jack placed the note on the desk in front of his partner. "Is this an invitation or a threat?"

Lifting the paper, Tito sniffed the writing. "That's blood. Might not be human, but it's definitely blood. Where'd it come from?"

"Chelbe got it from a member of Marcus' extended family." Walking over to the window, Kim-Jack glanced at the trickle of students still dripping out of the building and into the rain. "I don't need a gang war in my first period class."

"So, pick a side." Tito smiled. "But pick the right one."

Chelbe smacked Tito on the back of his head. "You are a fetid pond of poor advice."

"Ow! You wouldn't do that if I was a student." Rubbing his head, Tito stepped out of her reach.

"I'm not picking a side or joining a gang." Kim-Jack picked up the letter and crumpled it. "Somebody remind me what the syllabus was for Gang Membership 101."

Chelbe pulled at her earlobe for a second and then held a finger in the air. "Page one said something about never joining."

"Now there's some sound advice." Kim-Jack fist-bumped the English professor.

Hearing the last bell of the day, Chelbe looked at her watch. "Are you two working late tonight?"

Kim-Jack nodded. "Not too late. Madeline's back."

"Tell her where you're going for your wedding." Tito chuckled and slapped his thigh. "The last place on Earth you'd imagine."

With her head cocked to the side, Chelbe stared at Kim-Jack for a few moments. "The last place on Earth?" She smiled. "And the coldest one?"

Tito was crestfallen. "You told her?"

"Nope." Smiling, Kim-Jack pretended to shiver. "Brrr."

"You're getting married in Alaska?" Chelbe's eyes went wide. "Wow."

"Close, but the wrong pole." He walked over to the globe and spun it around so that the South Pole was on top. "My fiancée and her family have decided that we should marry in Antarctica. They want a 'unique' wedding. You know. Penguins, humpbacks, icebergs, something memorable that we can talk about as the years go by." Kim-Jack closed his eyes. "I'll write a book. How I got frostbite and lost my fingers and toes on our honeymoon."

Chelbe clasped her hands. "You are so lucky. I've always wanted to go to Antarctica."

"Are you gay?" With his tongue jammed into his cheek, Kim-Jack shrugged. "Maybe my future wife would prefer a woman. I'll ask her if you're really interested."

"Switching sides at this point in my life?" The gray-haired woman chuckled. "Tempting, but I'll stick with men, especially if they're younger than me."

Tito leaned in. "Like our new basketball coach?"

She grinned. "News travels fast around here."

"He's a year out of college." Kim-Jack whistled. "You're more than twice his age."

Winking at him, Chelbe growled. "Cougars are fierce, no matter how old we get."

Kim-Jack blinked. "The image is rough around the edges, but I can see you and the kid on the dance floor."

"Screw that. You should see us in bed." Menacingly, Chelbe growled again and turned toward Tito. "Lose some weight white boy and I might even give you a spin." With that said she left, purring and clawing at the air.

Tito wiped his brow. "Thirty-one years in this school is enough to make anyone crazy."

An argument in the hallway drew both teachers' attention, but it ended too soon for them to go out and check. Tito walked over to the door and locked it, drawing the shade for privacy.

"We've always had two goals in the design of our pizza box."

Kim-Jack nodded. "Keep the pizza hot and not screw up the environment."

"Correct." Reaching into the pocket of his lab coat, Tito retrieved a small folded packet and laid it on the nearest desk. "Our current box lasts for over two hours, but it costs a dollar-eighty-one to produce."

"And we need to get the cost under eighty cents in order to compete with plain cardboard."

"Correct again." Tito smiled. "Our stumbling block has been the foil. Everything we've tried so far that works, also lasts for centuries in a landfill."

"Okay."

Tito unfolded the packet and smoothed it out on the desktop. "Behold bone foil."

Kim-Jack picked up the sheet of foil and examined both sides. "It's light, but it's still foil. What's the metal? Aluminum, tin, some composite?"

With a grin cracking across his face, Tito shook his head. "Calcium. They've developed a process to extract pure calcium from bones and turn it into a metallic foil with amazing insulation properties."

"What kind of bones?"

Tito shrugged. "Doesn't matter. Big bones from butchered cows. Small bones extracted from chicken waste. For all I know, they're digging up graves and using human bones. The process removes all the organic matter and just leaves the calcium and some trace elements."

"Please tell me you're joking." Kim-Jack held the foil at arm's length and leaned away.

"Okay, I'm joking about the human bones, but the folks that are producing this foil have contracts with all the major beef and pork slaughterhouses. They get hundreds of tons of bones for mere pennies and convert them into that magic foil you're holding in your hands."

"For real?" Kim-Jack flexed the foil and rubbed it with his fingers. "How do they get it so shiny?"

"Trade secret. But that's not the best part." Snatching the foil from Kim-Jack, he walked over to a laboratory sink and ran the water. "Watch this." Tito balled the sheet and held it in the palm of his hand. Moving it under the water, the foil ball grew smaller and smaller until it was gone.

Kim-Jack whistled. "Holy shit. Foil that dissolves in water. It must cost a fortune, though."

"And that's part two of the magic. The process to make foil out of bones is surprisingly economical. I did some rough calculations and we can produce a full-size pizza box with this foil for eighty-four cents. No pizzeria owner is going to fuss over four cents, especially when they can get a box that will keep their pies from getting cold."

There was silence in the lab for a few seconds as the two scientists stared at the sink. Kim-Jack recovered first. "Oh, my god. We've done it." he held out his hand. "We're gonna be rich, Tito."

However, instead of shaking hands, Tito shoved his hands in the pockets of his lab coat. "There's only one problem."

"Don't tell me. The foil is carcinogenic."

"Nope."

"Radioactive?"

"Nope." Tito's mouth screwed into a frown. "The rights to its manufacture and use are held in perpetuity by Kloppleman Pharmaceuticals."

Kim-Jack's jaw dropped. "My future father-in-law owns our foil?"

Tito nodded. "Yep. One-hundred-percent. They use it to line their push-through pill packages and seal their bottles. My guess is that every one of their employee cafeterias uses the foil to wrap hamburgers."

Closing his eyes, Kim-Jack replayed Larry Kloppleman's offer. The man's laugh echoed in his head and made him grimace in pain.

Tito witnessed his partner's reaction and put an arm around Kim-Jack's shoulder.

"If there was ever a doubt in your mind about marrying Madeline Kloppleman, I hope you can bury it and never look back."

Kim-Jack ducked away from the embrace and walked back to the window.

"Somebody else has to have figured out how to make foil out of bones." He threw his hands in the air. "The last thing in the world I want to do is to work for Larry Kloppleman, and you've just told me that I have no choice. The way it looks, if we want this pizza box to succeed, it's only going to happen with his help. God dammit, Tito, I thought my only problem with marrying Madeline was buying the right tofu."

While they ate one of the pizzas, Kim-Jack told Tito about the phone call with her father. Realizing that his path to wealth and fame was tied to his partner's successful marriage, Tito's opinion of Madeline reversed course.

"She'll make a wonderful wife, KJ." Sprinkling his third slice with hot seeds, Tito folded it in half the long way. "You can teach her to cook and she'll teach you how to get along with her father."

"I already know how to deal with her father."

Tito nodded. "Yeah, that phone call you had with the old man certainly puts the relationship in the proper prospective."

"Hey, I had the situation under control until you dropped the bomb about the foil on me."

"You caved on the Antarctica trip pretty quickly."

Kim-Jack shrugged. "I had no choice. Larry opened the trap and I walked in smiling."

"Thanksgiving is two weeks away. Maybe she'll change her mind if you cook an amazing dinner for everyone." Tito added more hot seeds. "Speaking of which..."

"Forget it." Kim-Jack jumped off his stool and shook his head several times. "You ate so much turkey when we invited you last year that I had to cook hamburgers in the microwave while everyone was mumbling about the lack of food."

"It was a small turkey."

Slapping his forehead, Kim-Jack was too stunned to speak for a moment. His voice went up an octave. "Twenty-six pounds of meat for seven people! That's too small? Jesus H. Christ. That's not enough food?"

"If I'm coming to dinner? No."

"I'll invite you over the next time I cook a whole cow." Shoving his slice of pie away, Kim-Jack rested his elbows on the lab bench and cradled his head. "She's not going to change her mind. Not at Thanksgiving dinner, not at Christmas dinner, and certainly not when her father's limo picks us up at the townhouse."

Tito pointed the peppershaker at him. "Then you better buy some seriously warm clothing, my friend."

Sliding his six-foot, two-inch frame into a chair designed for a student, Kim-Jack laced his fingers behind his head and stared at the ceiling.

"We're going shopping on Saturday. Madeline is buying me everything I'll need to survive this expedition." He stopped and sat up as straight as possible in the small chair. "She wants me to be stylish. It's critical that I don't embarrass her."

Tito laughed. "Professor button-down shirt and khaki pants? Stylish?"

"I'm thinking a winter parka in purple with yellow amoebas and green worms."

"Orange snakeskin boots so they can see you when you get stranded on an iceberg." Tito slapped his thigh. "With blinking lights in case you get lost at night in a blizzard."

Kim-Jack held his hands up. "I want bear claw gloves. Real gnarly ones with three-inch claws."

"A hat." Tito reached into his back pocket and pulled out his wallet. "Look at this photo of my father in the hat with the furry ears."

"Oh, my god. That's perfect. And see how the earflaps have snaps to attach them to the top of the hat? Damn thing is convertible." Kim-Jack handed the photo back. "I'll order it on Amazon with my account and hide it in my suitcase."

"KJ, you're either going to be dressed for the South Pole or an insane asylum."

Kim-Jack laughed. "I already wear the right clothes for an insane asylum."

"A white lab coat?"

"And a panic button."

Tito shook his head. "Yeah, but are you ready for a real one?"

Unwinding himself from the chair, Kim-Jack thought about the question for a few seconds.

"Tito, my friend and partner in pizza, I ask myself that question every time I walk into this building." He smiled. "If not for my love of teaching, of imparting knowledge into the vast empty wasteland of a student's brain, I would probably open a pizzeria."

Chapter Eight

The week plodded along with Kim-Jack dreading the shopping trip Madeline had scheduled for Saturday. Finished with Sex Ed a day early, he scheduled a field trip for the science classes. News of the city zoo reopening after major renovations came through in the middle of the week. Prodding the Board of Education on Thursday, he was able to procure fifty passes and the promise of a bus to transport the students to and from the zoo.

However, when the bus pulled up in front of the school, it had bars across the windows. The rear emergency door was welded shut, there was a wire fence between the driver's seat and the rest of the seats on the bus, and the words Department of Corrections could be faintly discerned on both sides. Two of the male students and a female refused to get on the bus, claiming they'd already taken the ride on that bus and didn't believe it was really going to the zoo.

Because it was Friday, Kim-Jack didn't have to worry about Marcus and Xavier getting into a brawl. Marcus worked somewhere on Friday, and Xavier was still nursing his wounds. There was a strong possibility that the author of the "Pick a Side" note was on the bus, but a security guard had checked each student for weapons as they boarded.

Tito went along, presumably to keep his flock in order, but in reality, he didn't want to miss a day in the fresh air and a chance for some free hot dogs. The remainder of both teachers' classes were combined, with a substitute teacher being called in for the day. The school had a list of approved substitute teachers with the number of times they'd taught at each school in the district. Very few of them ever got called to Barack Obama High School and even fewer returned for a second appearance, regardless of the triple bump in pay.

Their first stop at the zoo was the penguin enclosure. Kim-Jack gave a brief lecture about the flightless birds and several students asked if the material was going to be on a test.

"Perhaps." He smiled as they scribbled furiously on their tablets. "Everything you learn in life is a test. The questions don't end just because you're not in a classroom."

Tito leaned close and whispered in Kim-Jack's ear, "You'll be eating penguin at your wedding reception. Maybe you should have the students Google a few recipes for extra credit."

Kim-Jack elbowed him in the side.

"Almost all the penguins on Earth live in the Southern Hemisphere with the bulk of them in South America and Antarctica." Having spent a few hours researching the birds, Kim-Jack fancied himself knowledgeable when it came to the wildlife they'd see in the zoo. One of the key lessons he remembered from college was always know more than your students. At Obama High, this was rarely a problem unless hand-to-hand combat was the subject.

"Three of the largest species of penguins live in Antarctica." Kim-Jack turned to the students. "Can anyone name them?"

From the middle of the group, someone shouted, "Moe, Larry, and Curly!" Another voice responded with, "Manny, Moe, and Jack." This led to dozens of students yelling out three-name combinations until Kim-Jack was able to restore order by blowing a whistle he'd borrowed from the new basketball coach.

Moving from the penguin enclosure into the three-story aviary, one of the female students received an aerial welcome in the form of bird poop on her head. This brought waves of laughter and pointing from her fellow students until they were attacked by several large toucans who found their long hair perfect for nesting material.

Tito was the expert when it came to birds and took over the narration as they made their way through the wire mesh enclosure. Naming the birds in flight, he would follow them with his finger and then start fresh with the first bird that crossed its path. One of his students managed to sneak a slingshot into the zoo and nearly took out a macaw with a six-foot wingspan that he was following before zoo security wrestled the weapon from his hands.

Finished with flying creatures, the group gathered around the first of five large mammal enclosures, and stared in awe as giraffes, elephants, and cape buffalos strolled through a faux African landscape. A river ran through the middle of it, and someone thought they saw an alligator, but it turned out to be a log.

Denise, a senior who had to stand on her tiptoes to see over most of the fences, pointed at a pair of elephants that she could barely see and asked Kim-Jack which one was the female. Before he had a chance to respond, the boy behind her made a comment about the size of the male elephant's penis and the moment devolved into pornographic comments about an elephant's sex life.

Boasting their sexual prowess, several shoving matches broke out, but they were friendly in nature, and Kim-Jack let them run their course. One of the basketball players, a senior more than an inch taller than him, claimed that the elephants had less sex than most of the team. A cheerleader, who wasn't in either of the science classes had come along for the ride and punched him in the side.

Someone shouted to Tito to confirm their statements about large animals having sex, but he ignored the query. One of the boys groped one of the girls, which brought an immediate response from her friends, and in seconds, the boy was on the ground with a girl twice his size sitting on his chest. Kim-Jack ran over and restored order, suggesting they continue on to where the big cats were displayed.

The zoo featured some of the healthiest lions and tigers in the region. The birth of a cub would capture the lead story on local and several national newsfeeds for at least two cycles. As it was getting near to their afternoon feeding, all of the massive felines were prowling close to their perimeter fences.

Of course, this led to a series of challenges among the students. Who was willing to put their fingers through the heavy wire mesh fence? Who had the nerve to stick their tongue through the tiny opening? Several of the boys were about to pee through the fence, but Tito herded them away. Zoo security rushed in and moved the students back, admonishing Kim-Jack for not keeping them safe.

Fifty children who had never been this close to an animal that could eat them for dinner before, reacted with more exuberance than Christmas morning. Several groups began pacing with the beasts, running or charging the fence in unison with the animal on the other side. Growling and making monkey noises, even though they had yet to see their hairy ancestors, the boys would bare their teeth and paw at the wire mesh.

Kim-Jack knew they couldn't possibly reach the teeth or claws of the lion that was more yawning than growling at them. However, the screeching and shoving was having its toll on his patience. It was almost noon and they were well behind on his plan to cover the entire zoo in time to get back for the last bell. Apparently, letting these marginally behaved teens loose in the blistering sun and fresh air released their inner animals. He was regretting the decision until they stumbled into the reptile pavilion.

An odd silence fell over the students as they entered the cool, dark, manmade cave with its glass exhibits. Walking up close to a snake that could kill a person in less than ten seconds, they stared in frightened amazement at a creature that was more deadly than any of them with a blade or a gun.

Tito made his way over to Kim-Jack and pointed at a group of students gawking at a boa constrictor. "Killa know killa." He grinned. "Snoop Dog."

"That's not funny."

"But it's true."

Kim-Jack shook his head. "They're not all killers, Tito."

Nodding, Tito put his hand on Kim-Jack's shoulder. "No, they're not. Some of them will be victims."

As they reached the far end of the reptile cave, the students gathered around a large pool with several sleeping crocodiles. Someone made a comment about luggage. Another claimed to have wrestled an alligator on a trip to Florida. Kim-Jack stood in front of the pool and explained the difference between alligators and crocodiles. When he was done, a member of the zoo staff came over and corrected him. Apparently, he had the details backward. This brought out a round of catcalls and cheers from the students that ended when another staff member brought a bucket of meat chunks and began feeding the hungry animals.

Breaking for lunch, Kim-Jack passed out food vouchers worth twenty-five dollars each. Several students sold them to other students for ten dollars cash and went off to smoke cigarettes or vape. Tito parlayed his voucher into a tray full of hot dogs and found a seat in the shade. Not wishing to risk his digestive tract on zoo food of any genus or species, Kim-Jack sat down next to him with a bottle of water and a granola bar.

"That's your lunch?" Tito bit off a third of a hot dog.

"You must have a death wish."

"Because I eat hot dogs?"

"Because you eat food that's been sitting in the hot sun for hours and growing enough bacteria to turn your digestive system into mud."

"Remind me to never take you to a ballgame." Tito took another bite and added mustard to the remaining piece. "Would you even drink the beer?"

Kim-Jack smiled. "Beer has alcohol. Alcohol kills bacteria."

He gave them an hour for lunch. Fifty-five minutes too long as it turned out. The students dispersed throughout the zoo, and it took an additional hour to round them up. Gathered with his flock in front of the monkey exhibit, Kim-Jack pointed to a group of spider monkeys in a tree at least thirty-feet in height.

"We have more in common with those skinny apes, swinging from the branches like they were born to fly, than any other creature on Earth."

"Professor Czerwinski must be related to that big ass gorilla, leaning against the trunk of the tree." The anonymous jab came from deep in the crowd, and it made Tito blush. It led to several annoyingly long seconds of laughter before Kim-Jack could continue his lecture.

"Keep in mind, that gorilla could crush your skull like a soda can, so being related to him is probably more of a positive attribute than negative." Kim-Jack stared at the general direction the comment had come from, hoping to spot the offender, but no one moved in reaction to his retort.

"Okay then, let's talk about the chimpanzee."

With little more than three Wikipedia articles, Kim-Jack had cobbled together a five-minute lecture on the life and loves of man's favorite ape. He ended the piece with a few sentences about favorite chimps from the movies and outer space. Looking up from his notes, he noticed that many of the students were holding their cellphones in the air, aimed at him.

"Since this afternoon's performance of Professor Donaldson and the chimpanzees is about to go viral, I would like to say for the record that all of the information I just presented comes from various internet sources."

Someone shouted, "Did you use AI?"

Kim-Jack laughed. "You don't need artificial intelligence if you've got the real thing."

A mockup of the Serengeti plains from East Africa was the last stop on their visit to the zoo. Sparse vegetation over sand, a large freshwater pool, and a deeply rutted road composed the canvas for the exhibit. All of the students knew the zebras. The inner city slang for a black person who tried to be white had been around when Kim-Jack was in middle school.

I've heard worse. He shrugged. *Much worse.*

Denise, who was finally in a place where she could see clearly, pointed at a tiny deer-like animal, standing on its hind legs to chew leaves off a tree.

"Is that a baby deer?"

Kim-Jack shook his head. "No. That's a dik-dik–"

He was about to tell them that the animal was actually a miniature antelope, indigenous to East Africa, but the roar of laughter drowned him out.

So mature.

It was useless to continue, so he smiled and gave them a few minutes to prance around and make monkey noises. With control once again in his hands, Kim-Jack checked the time and ordered the group to follow him to the bus. Tito took up the rear and urged stragglers to move faster with the threat of a quiz for the last five students to board the bus. A race ensued as the exit gates came into view and Tito was left sweating and breathing hard in the sun.

By the time the bus pulled into the school parking lot, social media had been flooded with videos and stills from their adventure to the zoo. The district allowed its members to have a presence on most of the common platforms, as long as they shied away from politics, porn, or anything that might make the Board of Education look bad.

Kim-Jack's newsfeed exploded with tags to their posts.

Most of the images were of animals doing what animals normally do, even if people are watching. Of course, those actions when seen through the eyes and processed through the brain of a teenager will always produce humor, even when other humans are involved.

Kim-Jack was the focus of many of the shots, especially when apes and his backside were in the same frame. He untagged himself in all of them, but added a smiley face to the image on the student's page. None of the photos that featured Tito appeared on his page, although a few of his butt crack were circling the ether faster than a comet raced around the sun.

The two science teachers walked out to the parking lot together. Kim-Jack had been expecting to drive his partner home, but Tito pointed to a red Chevy pickup truck that appeared to have spent most of its early life on a farm.

"It's twenty-one-years-old, but it runs like it just came off the dealer's lot."

"Did it spend its early life in a demolition derby?"

"It's got new tires."

Kim-Jack walked over and kicked one. Bending down, he examined the tread.

"It needs new tires."

Tito threw up his hands in surrender. "It was what I could afford. Look, man, I don't have a wealthy girlfriend to buy me a car."

Taking a step back, Kim-Jack jammed his tongue into his cheek. "Madeline has not bought me a car."

"My apologies. It was just a townhouse."

"Jealousy doesn't become you."

Tito took a long breath, finally letting a smile come through. He held out his hand. "I'm tired. It was a long, hot day, and we worked the last three hours for free. Cut me some slack, okay?"

Kim-Jack shook his hand. "You don't have to ask."

"We need the weekend."

Shoving his hands in his back pockets, Kim-Jack shook his head.

"Tomorrow's the big shopping day."

"Oh, shit."

"Pray for me."

"You know I would, but I'm an atheist. Your god might take my prayers the wrong way."

Kim-Jack grinned. "I'll take the chance. Go ahead and pray."

Chapter Nine

Their expedition to the shopping mall began Saturday morning, an hour after sunrise. They weren't going to the outlet stores or the budget mall where he usually shopped for clothes. Instead, the senior Kloppleman had dedicated a limo and two assistants to help with their purchases. The mall they were headed for not only had limo parking, but valet service for those who drove themselves and offsite parking for anyone with a car more than two-years-old.

The drive was a bit over two hours, but Madeline had prepared, or at least instructed the chef to prepare, sandwiches, potato salad, and a pitcher of spiked lemonade for the drive. At the last minute, Cassidy begged to come along, but Madeline had other plans for the long journey to the mall. She told her stepmother that her outfit was an embarrassment and they left while she was changing.

Their driver dropped them off at the north entrance, closest to the men's shop Madeline had selected for the first part of their task. Walking into the mall past the three-star Michelin restaurant and the drone store, she had to drag Kim-Jack away from the distractions, keeping him aimed toward their intended target.

ManPowr, a shop for men with more money than common sense, was in-between Jewels from Heaven and Cloud Cosmetics. Kim-Jack made a joke about shopping with the gods before Madeline shoved him through the door.

The music hit him first, followed by a blast of air so cold that he shivered and immediately regretted wearing shorts. Pulsing dance music played on synthesizers roared through his ears. Kim-Jack had gone to a few raves growing up and always sat as far from the tower of speakers as he could. The music was EDM– electronic dance music–as popular with the teen dance crowd as the drugs they took to enhance the beat.

He shouted his second observation into Madeline's ear. "Where are all the salesmen?"

Madeline pointed at the statuesque brunette that was dancing in-between the racks and making her way toward him. "Saleswomen. No men."

The smile that filled Kim-Jack's face was far too obvious for his fiancée and she kicked him in the shin. "Keep it in your pants, KJ. This is not one of your karaoke bars, and that woman has no interest in what's between your legs."

Stopping in front of them, the saleswoman blinked her soft blue eyes and nodded toward a sign on the door. "I'm sorry, ma'am, but we don't allow women to shop here."

Madeline smiled. "Can you read the fine print below the ManPowr sign?"

She nodded. "I have perfect eyesight."

"Read it, please." Madeline crossed her arms over her chest.

"A Kloppleman Industries venture." The woman shrugged. "So?"

Madeline held out a hand. "I'm Madeline Kloppleman. Pleased to meet you."

"Oh, my god. Someone called from corporate yesterday and said you'd be coming."

"Victoria, my personal secretary."

Recovering faster than a child accidentally dressing for school on Saturday, the woman shook Madeline's hand and introduced herself as Rebeka. "With a K and no Cs."

Kim-Jack offered his hand as well. "I'm Kim-Jack with a K and a C, but you can call me KJ."

Rebeka shook his hand with a grip that made him wince. "Kim-Jack. What an interesting name."

"Don't get him started." Madeline put a hand on his shoulder. "He loves to tell the story. Suffice it to say, the name is a blend of Kimberly and Jackson. His mother's choice and his father's choice."

"My wife says that if the choice had been left up to her, she would have named our little boy Hurricane Tornado." Rebeka smiled. "He just turned three and we've firmly decided not to adopt another one. The cost of patching and painting walls has ripped into our budget and we can't afford to go through this madness again."

Kim-Jack jumped in. "We haven't discussed children yet, but I teach high school and love the kids."

"Even when they're threatening him with a knife." Madeline sighed. "After we're done today, I'm taking him shopping for a Kevlar vest."

"Where does he teach? In a combat zone?"

Kim-Jack smiled. "Exactly. Barack Obama High School in the city."

Rebeka took a step back. "I went to Bohi."

"And you ended up working in a men's shop?" Nodding, Kim-Jack turned to his future spouse. "See? The school does lead to success if you put the effort into your education."

"Success?" Shaking her head in disagreement, Rebeka laughed. "I applied to forty-seven colleges and was rejected by each one. My SAT scores were good enough for the inner city but worthless in the real world. Bohi is where children go before either prison or the army. I got lucky and came here the day the mall opened ten years ago. Every store was hiring. ManPowr wanted sexy-looking women and I fit the bill."

Kim-Jack was unfazed. "How much did you make last year?"

"Why?"

"I'm curious. That's all."

"Just over seventy-five-thousand." Rebeka raised her eyebrows. "And you?"

"Just under forty-two-thousand and I've got a Master's degree in Education." Shaking his head, Kim-Jack pointed at her. "You sell clothes. I teach. Is my job more important than yours?"

Madeline jabbed him in the side. "You're channeling your father, the nudist."

"Well." She grinned. "You can't teach naked."

"But it's easy to sell clothes to a naked man."

Another jab from his fiancée.

Rebeka blew out a short breath. "So, this is how Saturday is going to be this weekend." She turned to Madeline. "What's the special occasion?"

"We're getting married."

Taking a step toward the nearby rack filled with tuxedos, Rebeka reached for Kim-Jack's hand. "Let's go."

Madeline shook her head. "The wedding's going to be in Antarctica."

"Where they have polar bears?"

Kim-Jack chuckled softly. "No. That's the North Pole, we're going south."

"Really?"

He nodded. "Trust me, I teach science."

"But at Bohi." Rebeka whistled. "Too bad you weren't teaching science when I went there." Switching hands, she led him across the store to the outdoor section. Another saleswoman came out from a back room and offered them champagne.

"Let's get liquored up and go shopping." Kim-Jack slapped his thigh. "I love it."

"None for you until we're done, KJ." Walking over, Madeline kissed him on the lips. "I don't want you to say you agreed to any of this because you were drunk."

He put on a sullen but fake expression. "Party pooper."

Rebeka started from the inside and worked out. Thermal underwear that made him itch. Wool socks that made him itch. Thick wool gloves that not only made his hands itch, but also made it impossible to scratch every other place that was now reminding him of his last encounter with poison ivy. The itching quickly overcame his sense of modesty. Ripping off the gloves, Kim-Jack reached into the thermal underwear and scratched his privates as though they were being attacked by mosquitoes.

"KJ!" Madeline tossed a floppy hat at him. "There are people watching you from outside the store."

"Good. Let my agony be a warning to them to stay away from woolen clothes." Glancing at the front of the store, he noticed a pair of well-dressed senior women pointing at him. He waved with his free hand and then turned away.

Replacing the wool with synthetics solved the itching problem, but Kim-Jack's lanky, six-foot-two frame required some searching in the back room for clothing that would fit.

"Do I really need the thermal underwear?" He was doing his best to position his manhood in the tight-fitting garment. "There's no way I'll be able to sit in a chair and eat anything with my nuts crushed into this tiny sack."

"You don't want to let those precious jewels freeze, do you?" Rebeka grinned. "Men and their testicles. God must have laughed herself silly when she came up with that idea."

"You can't make babies without them." Kim-Jack grabbed the largest size off the rack. "If these don't fit, we'll just have to rely on shared body heat to keep the family jewels from freezing."

Fortunately, the larger size gave him enough room to sit, squat, and scratch as needed. Rebeka picked out thermal socks woven with copper threads that were guaranteed to keep his toes from getting frostbite. The entire expedition was scheduled for nine days. Madeline told him to get a pair for each day.

"My feet are going to get that dirty?"

"What if you fall in the water?"

"Nine times?" Kim-Jack shook his head. "You might think about tying my ass to the deck after the second dunking."

Rebeka placed a sealed box with a dozen pairs on the counter.

Waterproof pants weren't a problem. It seemed that tall people favored them in the winter to keep their ankles dry. He asked if they sold bear claw gloves with actual claws on the fingers. Rebeka said no, but to try the children's' store next to the indoor pitch and putt. The place featured an enormous selection of costumes and probably had bear claws left over from Halloween.

Madeline selected a ski mask in neutral colors for him. The expedition company that was running the show supplied each adventurer with a list of items they would need while onboard and on land. The list had three sections: required, suggested, and optional. She intended to get every item from each group and checked them off as they filled the sales counter.

The store sold the hat with the floppy ears in three sizes and two different shades of leather. Kim-Jack found his size in the darker of the two shades, and went into the dressing room with it and a pair of thermal underwear. Coming out, dressed solely in the thermals but wearing the hat, he grabbed a ski pole and goggles.

"I'm ready for anything, baby. Let's go feed some whales."

Madeline turned to Rebeka. "He's normally better behaved."

"He teaches at Bohi, that's what normal looks like."

The last item they required was a lightweight winter parka. The expedition company was supplying each passenger with a bright red external coat with silver stripes front and back. It was good as an outer layer, being both waterproof and warm down to twenty degrees below zero. Kim-Jack had questioned whether they were talking Fahrenheit or Celsius, but then decided that twenty below was too cold regardless of the side of the thermometer being read.

Entering the outerwear department, Kim-Jack was stunned by the selection. Every color combination possible from a collision of rainbows was glowing from the racks. With a hood, without a hood, with a detachable hood that could go both ways, the coats formed a fabric sea.

"Wow." He stood in the entrance to the department with his hands laced behind his head. "Do you have a purple one with yellow amoebas?"

Rebeka cocked her head to the side. "Yellow what?"

"Never mind." Glancing at the various signs, Kim-Jack zeroed in on the extra large section and headed that way.

The first jacket that caught his eye was blue with large yellow stripes. He lifted it off the rack and removed the hanger. Slipping it over his head, rather than messing with the zipper and the collection of tags hanging from the end, the coat bunched up on his back.

"I'm stuck." Kim-Jack waved his arms. "Somebody?"

Rebeka pulled the coat off his head and opened the zipper. "Here. Try it now."

The slick nylon and thick cushioning slid onto his upper torso as though it was greased. Gathering the two sides together, Kim-Jack turned to look at himself in the full-length mirror. Nodding that he was pleased with his selection, he walked over to Madeline.

"I like this one. Splendid colors and you can see me from the distance if I get lost."

Madeline lifted the zipper and read the price. "You have expensive tastes."

"What? How much?"

"Twenty-four hundred."

"Dollars?"

"This isn't Burundi, so it's not francs." Madeline looked at Rebeka. "I'm not thrilled with the colors."

"He wanted amoebas."

Madeline pinched the bridge of her nose. "He's a science teacher." She stage-whispered, "And such a nerd."

"I heard that." Taking off the overpriced jacket, Kim-Jack rehung it and looked around the field of brightly colored winter jackets. "What do you have for under a hundred dollars?"

Rebeka shook her head. "Nothing."

"I'm paying, so what do you care?" Grabbing another coat off the same rack, she held it up to him. "This is your size and a more conservative color combination."

Kim-Jack tried on the coat and was pleased with the fit, but not with the colors. He then went through every coat in his size on four nearby racks, finally returning to the original blue and yellow jacket with the silver stripes.

"I'll take this one."

Madeline groaned.

All told, they spent more in ManPowr than Kim-Jack had laid out for all the clothes he currently owned. Madeline sent a text to their driver, who appeared a few minutes later and carried all their purchases to the limo. It was after three and they had shopped right through lunch, with the exception of two bottles of champagne.

Kim-Jack wanted Italian food, she was in the mood for sushi.

Seated across from him, a few minutes later, Madeline scanned the sushi menu and placed their order using an app and QR code that was pasted to the table. A server who looked too young to drink came over with water and asked if they wanted anything else to drink.

"After spending nearly ten grand on clothes, I need sake."

Madeline sighed. "You need to get used to this lifestyle, KJ." She turned to the teenaged server. "I'll have a ginger ale."

"I need a two-thousand-dollar coat like I need a third eye."

"That's what a good one costs."

"How many times do you think I'll wear that coat after we get home from Antarctica? How many really bad winter storms do we get in a season?"

Madeline shrugged. "I usually go south when it snows."

"I know." He'd been left behind to celebrate snow days on his own several times last winter. She had the luxury of fleeing a winter storm. He watched it from their third-floor window, waiting for that all-important call that the roads were too bad for the buses. No school today.

"What if we go back to Antarctica in ten years to celebrate our anniversary?"

Kim-Jack grabbed the table. "Go back? We haven't survived the first expedition, and you're working on a return trip?"

She smiled. "Who knows? Maybe we'll fall in love with the place."

Silence floated over the table as they waited for their food to be delivered. The restaurant was busy with takeout orders, and it wasn't long before Kim-Jack's patience faded.

"This might not be the right time, but we need to talk about children."

"Children?" Madeline cocked her head. "Like your students?"

"No. Like babies that come from our wild nights together." Kim-Jack smiled. "At some point, you're going to want to stop taking your little pink pill and let my arrows hit their target."

Madeline leaned back in the chair. "You want children?"

He nodded. "Not a whole schoolyard full of them, but at least one of each."

"What about a dog instead?"

"A pet instead of children?" He shook his head. "You get a pet for your children. I think you've got the process backwards."

"What if I don't want to pump a couple of screech owls out of my vagina? What if I want it to be just you and me?"

Kim-Jack said nothing for a few seconds and then he folded his hands on the table and gazed into her deep blue eyes. "Then we should rethink our expedition to Antarctica."

Chapter Ten

They agreed to table the children discussion for a few weeks. He was sure that she'd change her mind. The maternal instinct would kick in and she'd come about one-hundred-and-eighty degrees. Thus, feeling empowered with his plan for the future, Kim-Jack had suggested cooking Thanksgiving dinner for everyone. He wanted to get into family mode as soon as possible.

However, his cooking experience was on an island between microwave and toaster oven. Despite his boasts of superior kitchen experience, he could grill hot dogs and burgers, but a full meal was beyond his talents. Over the years of living alone, he'd cobbled together several meals with the help of YouTube, but this was different. Spending additional hours late at night on the web, he found a website titled how to cook a turkey dot com, and located a friendly grocer who gave him some helpful tips.

Tito had wrangled an invitation saying that Canadians didn't celebrate Thanksgiving the same way Americans did and that he still hadn't found female companionship. However, Tito knew how to cook, and Kim-Jack decided he would be more of an asset than a liability. Of course, hearing that his friend knew nothing about turkey roasting, Tito withdrew his offer of assistance and opted to let him work out the details on his own just to see if Kim-Jack could do it.

Starting early in the day, so that his future father-in-law, who'd recently returned from cardiac rehab could be in bed before seven, Kim-Jack had prepared all the ingredients in advance and was working off a four-page spreadsheet.

Everything was going fine until the cornbread exploded. Kim-Jack shook his head. *How the hell was I supposed to know you couldn't use popcorn in place of niblets?*

And so there he stood at ten o'clock in the morning, Thanksgiving Day, the microwave a splattered mess of cornmeal, popcorn, and shredded jalapeños, a string bean casserole still waiting its turn for a bath in the radiation, and smoke, pouring from the oven.

Kim-Jack grabbed the insulated mitts from their hiding place in the drawer of rarely used utensils and yanked the oven door open, standing off to the side. The black basin flecked in white, which had been spotlessly clean for the six months that he'd been living in the townhouse Madeline bought to get him out of the combat zone was a sea of smoking grease. Apparently, the foil throwaway pan he'd placed the turkey into for its cremation had sprung several leaks from punctures made by the wire rack Kim-Jack improvised out of a pair of heavy wire coat hangers.

Most of the oven was covered in a layer of burnt drippings. Thankfully, the turkey was still as creamy white as when it had been unsheathed from the Butterball condom. Touching carefully, he let out a sigh of relief. The bird was warm to the touch and appeared unaffected by the greasy soot and smoke. Sliding the wire rack out of the oven, he lifted the pan and placed the whole thing in the sink, being as careful as possible to avoid the droplets of grease that splattered to the tile floor. Thinking about it for a second, Kim-Jack wasn't sure if he had a mop.

With the oven off, he grabbed a fresh roll of paper towel and did his best to remove as much of the grease puddle as possible, singeing the hair on the back of both hands, and searing the knuckles on one of them when he hit the still hot heating element. The clock indicated just after noon when he decided the oven was clean enough to restart the cooking process. Madeline was due back from her father's house at four-thirty with her family. His father and stepmom would arrive at four.

Fortunately, the foil pans came bundled in twos, so he lifted the turkey from the leaky one and placed it into a fresh pan, sans the wire hangers. He wasn't sure what the reasoning was behind their use anyhow and figured the fowl could cook just fine sitting in its own greasy bath. After all, the breast, with its little red popup, was on top and he figured that was the only part of the bird most people eat.

According to the instructions on the Butterball wrapper, the turkey was going to need four and a half to five hours to cook at three hundred and twenty-five degrees. It was in the oven only an hour before the leakage occurred. Kim-Jack figured that he could bring the temperature up a few degrees, and still finish the bird in time for dinner. Setting the dial at four hundred, he turned his attention to the cornbread explosion still waiting patiently in the microwave.

The cornbread recipe came from the same website as the turkey, and he had purchased exactly the right amount of ingredients to make enough for seven people with no spares. Even Tito's insatiable appetite would be covered. With the explosive mess caused by his substitution of popcorn for the elusive can of niblets, Kim-Jack decided that it would be best to abandon the dish and pulled a loaf of frozen garlic bread from the freezer instead. Even though he couldn't remember having garlic bread at any previous Thanksgiving dinner, bread was bread and he figured its only purpose in the meal was to sop up the . . .

Gravy! How could I be so lame? I haven't bought a bottle of turkey gravy!

Glancing at the oven, he was pleased to see that the temperature had finally hit four hundred, Kim-Jack opened his laptop to pay another visit to the turkey dot com website. Sure enough, they had several gravy recipes. However, all of them required the use of something called "giblets."

Kim-Jack slapped the countertop. *Giblets, niblets, my life is suddenly dependent upon items too small to be accurately identified much less purchased on a day when the only businesses operating are the National Football League and every Chinese restaurant in the city.*

He Googled "gravy" and found a recipe that used ketchup, soy sauce, and several other common ingredients, all of which he obtained over the years and still had stored in the pantry. Checking the ingredients, he was relieved to see that none were more than a year past their expiration date.

Feeling more in control, now that he'd solved another difficult problem, he squeezed the last dregs of ketchup from the bottle in the refrigerator along with the soy sauce from a dozen packages saved from Chinese takeout meals into a glass bowl, adding most of the spices mentioned on the website. One of the other recipes on the same webpage suggested adding the turkey drippings, so he scraped several spoonfuls of greasy detritus from the original throwaway pan into the bowl. Covering it, Kim-Jack shoved the mixture into the toaster oven to simmer in peace.

Another check of the turkey, which by now had developed a nice brown color to the skin, and he could smell the odor of success wafting from the oven.

With the cleanup complete and the casserole spinning happily in the microwave, Kim-Jack decided it would be a good time to let the food cook on its own and returned to the balcony with a bottle of wine and a clean goblet to watch football. Earlier that day, he'd moved the small television out to the balcony so he could watch the games and pretend he was actually in the stadium. With the door open, he could live the fantasy, at least until Madeline came home.

Of course, once their company arrived, he planned to serve them in a casual style, with everyone sitting on the large sectional around their sixty-inch flat screen indoors.

He opened the wine, a vintage Rothschild he purchased for this evening's dinner, and poured himself a glass. Giving the wine a few moments to breathe, he slipped off the loafers she'd insisted he buy as part of their recent shopping expedition and slid the recliner into its position of maximum comfort. Just as he was about to sample the wine, his cellphone interrupted the moment.

"Madeline. What's going on?"

"Hey lover, how's the turkey looking?"

"Baby, it's gonna be so good they'll be begging me to sign a contract for a weekly show on the Food Channel."

"And give up your lucrative career as a science teacher?"

He sighed. "The next great chef is waiting for their call."

"Yeah, they'll call. Only if they want someone who can make peanut butter and jelly sandwiches or fry some Spam."

"Now, you don't want to insult the man who can make you sing like Sinatra, do you?"

"And you don't want to get on the wrong side of the woman who can make you scream like a–"

"Okay, okay, we don't need to go into details on the phone." Kim-Jack smiled. "You might want to take a nap before you and the gang roll over here."

"Oh?" She snickered. *"You think you'll have any energy after cooking all day?"*

"Hey, you're not talking to some amateur chef, you know. You said that your dad likes good cooking. I'm ready." He poured another glass of wine and marveled at its wonderful bouquet. "Plus, I've got four bottles of a 1988 Laffite-Rothschild that need to be dealt with and a bottle of white wine for you."

Madeline had been nursing her father for the past week. Kim-Jack had been sleeping alone. He pursed his lips. "Are you spending the night?"

"It depends."

"On what?"

"On whether or not my useless stepmother can take care of her husband without me."

"You have a staff of seven watching over him."

"Yeah, but they need eight." She paused. *"Let's see how good a cook you are. Then I'll decide."*

The line went dead before he could reply.

Kim-Jack drank two glasses of the spectacular wine, savoring each drop as though it would be the last to ever hit his tongue, and lay back in the lounger to drift for a while. When he awoke, the Dallas game, second of the day, was just coming out of halftime, tied at fourteen, and an odd smell–somewhere between burnt hair and burnt rubber–permeated the townhouse. Leaping from the recliner, he ran into the kitchen and found the gravy bubbling through the door of the toaster oven, angry streams of it fused onto the side of the pot and the electric heating element. What was left in the pot had no resemblance to any gravy he'd ever seen, although it could easily pass for used motor oil.

    The turkey had gone from suntan to sunburn–third degree in several places–and the only dish still having the characteristics of food was the green bean casserole, waiting lukewarm in the microwave. He punched the off button on the oven and opened the door to let whatever foul gasses had accumulated to dissipate.

    Was the turkey beyond hope? He gazed at the clock over the sink. His guests would be there any minute.

    The gravy was a total loss. Kim-Jack didn't even have ketchup to put on the table, and his limited culinary expertise told him that mustard was out of the question. With the insulated oven gloves, he pulled the pan out of the oven and placed it on the counter top. The turkey website mentioned letting the bird sit covered for thirty minutes before carving. He gave a moments' thought to heating a bunch of Swanson's chicken potpies from the freezer and tossing the overcooked Butterball in the trash, but he knew that wouldn't sit well with the Kloppleman family.

    "Who was the idiot that volunteered for this assignment?" He screamed at the overcooked bird. "Someone should have marched through 'Caterers' in the Yellow Pages before risking such a task." Kim-Jack was breathing faster and the sweat had soaked so far down the back of his shirt that he needed fresh underwear.

    He moved the turkey from the pan to the cutting board, turning it upside down. The undercarriage looked a lot better than the top, so he figured that if Madeline came into the kitchen to inspect, the disaster would be hidden. There was an accumulation of drippings in the pan that he poured into a coffee cup, hoping it might just work as gravy if needed. With their imminent arrival, Kim-Jack set the table for seven. Silverware, gas station goblets, salt and pepper shakers, even a candle in a silver base–one of the few things he kept from his mother's possessions–went on the table laid out as fancy as he could manage.

Shaking a bag of pre-made salad into a chrome mixing bowl, he placed a mixing spoon on either side. No room remained on the table, so he put the salad on the couch.

In a desperate attempt to get the burnt odors out of the townhouse, he opened all the windows and shoved the thermostat up to critical mass. With the cold November wind blowing in and the steam-driven radiators chugging for all their worth, the worst of the stench would be gone before they knocked on the door. Of course, there was little he could do about the dinner other than hope that the Klopplemans had a jester's sense of humor and that he could get everyone drunk within moments of their arrival.

Madeline walked in moments later and tossed her coat on the couch, sitting down alongside it. "Well, sweetheart, you're in luck. Larry and Cassidy went out on his yacht with your parents and decided to spend the night. Tito has been calling you all day, but you must have put your phone on silent. He met a woman who wants to cook him dinner, so he's not coming. It looks like it's just you and me for dinner and dessert."

Kim-Jack kissed the top of her head. "Poor baby. You must be starved."

She looked up him and wrinkled her nose. "I waited all day to eat. I'm ready for a feast."

In the few seconds that he held his breath and stared at her coat, laying there next to her on the couch, Madeline sensed the delay and sat up straight, looking at him with what he described as her "Oh, no" face.

She frowned. "You couldn't do it."

"Why do you say that?" Kim-Jack got up from the couch and motioned with his finger towards the kitchen. "Follow me."

Leading her over to the counter, he nodded and took a step back with his hands on his hips. Madeline stared at the bird resting on the cutting board, waiting to be carved. "It's upside down,"

"I know." He paused and took a deep breath. "You really don't want to see the other side."

"That's fine, I only eat dark meat."

With a sigh of relief, he stabbed the turkey with a barbecue fork and began cutting chunks from the carcass. Madeline pulled a piece of loose meat from a thigh and was about to taste it when she turned and looked around the kitchen. "Where's the cranberry sauce, and stuffing?"

"Stuffing? Cranberry sauce?" Kim-Jack slapped his forehead, dropping the knife to the floor.

His fiancée jumped back to avoid the falling dagger, shaking her head in disbelief. "How could you forget stuff like that?"

Kim-Jack shrugged. "Spent too much time thinking about you."

"Too much?"

"Okay, not enough."

Leaning in closer to him, Madeline whispered, "But I've been having naughty thoughts about you and the cranberry sauce all day."

Kim-Jack's knees trembled and he asked, his voice starting to crack, "Can we use gravy instead?"

Madeline shook her head. "Nope. It's jellied cranberry sauce or nothing."

With a quick nod, he turned and headed towards the door, yanking his new blue and yellow jacket with the silver stripes from the hook next to it. Madeline ran for the couch, grabbed her coat, and stood next to him.

"We both don't have to go." Kim-Jack took her hands and pulled her closer for a kiss. As best as he tried to hide it, there was an element of concern in his voice. "There's a Korean grocery store two blocks away, I'll get every can of cranberry sauce on his shelves, and be back here in fifteen minutes."

"Nah." She glanced back toward the kitchen, smiling. "Let's go eat Chinese. You can try this again for Christmas before we leave for the South Pole." She took Kim-Jack's hand and opened the door. "But since we don't have cranberry, make sure you save all those little duck sauce packets for later."

Chapter Eleven

With four weeks to go until their Antarctic expedition and wedding, Kim-Jack tried on his new clothes to make sure they still fit. He'd been eating an excessive amount of pizza as their experiment got closer to a conclusion. The long weekend after Thanksgiving would have been the perfect time to get some exercise, but it rained.

Monday morning, after their mini vacation, Kim-Jack's students were lethargic, as though they'd had more turkey for breakfast and the tryptophan was kicking in. He remembered how lackluster they were after the previous Thanksgivings and scheduled a video so that those who needed sleep could do so without fear of discovery.

Kim-Jack told Tito that it seemed to him that most of his students sent their brains out for vacation between Thanksgiving and New Years. Tito replied that several of the teachers always reacted that way as well. Together, they came to the conclusion that regardless of the Board of Education's schedule, the winter break started the day before Thanksgiving.

Marcus was especially sluggish, not even responding verbally to Xavier's taunts. Kim-Jack wondered if the boy was on something. Then again, any one of his students could be stoned, and he wouldn't know it. Drunks were loud. Stoners silent. That was the extent of his modern day drug knowledge.

The video was a broad outline of the various weather patterns experienced throughout the country over a twelve-month span that started midsummer and ended the following spring. He could hear snoring from the back of the classroom, but decided it was better than screaming and let the offenders sleep.

All of the winter scenes had been filmed in Antarctica with the focus on the growth and decline of the icebergs. Forced to watch the movie six times, once in each of his classes, Kim-Jack became increasingly uneasy each time the location moved from the beauty of autumn trees in New England to the stark white of the southern continent. Not even the faux smiles of the seals or the waddling gait of the penguins could tamp down his anxiety.

In less than four weeks, he'd be seeing these cold weather creatures up close and personal. All the questions about the mysterious frozen continent that were colliding with his sense of survival would be answered. Kim-Jack hoped he would be able to learn something other than how to prevent his extremities from turning black and falling off while he slept.

Spending the balance of the week on weather and climate change, his fear of the southern end of the Earth grew exponentially. By Friday, he refused to eat ice cream and was spooning the cubes out of glasses of ice water. The school's furnace had been cranked on just before the holiday and Kim-Jack set the temperature in his classroom so high that his students were stripping down to their t-shirts and rolling up their pants.

The pizza box experiments continued, but their results had reached a plateau. No matter how much foil they used or how thick the cardboard, the pizzas cooled to room temperature at three hours. Kim-Jack was certain they had a temperature leak and sent a request for a thermal imagining camera. It came back denied. Apparently, the Board of Education was not ready to invest twenty-thousand dollars on pizza boxes.

Tito felt that the plateau was a sign that they had hit an impenetrable barrier. His cholesterol had spiked and he was in danger of getting cut off from his monthly stipend. For their nightly experiments, he limited himself to a single slice, washing it down with water rather than beer.

The constant battering of Antarctica winds he had yet to experience wore down Kim-Jack's enthusiasm for pie to where he no longer wanted to open a pizzeria and was giving serious consideration to Larry Kloppleman's offer of a job.

I think I've got allergies of the brain. It's so stuffed up with all this crap, that I can't keep my thoughts on track without headphones and blinders.

Madeline's level of excitement ran in the opposite direction. Coming home each night, the first thing he saw was the kitchen calendar they shared for appointments. She waited for him to take off his blue and yellow parka before slashing today's date with a red Sharpie while he watched, sighing. Each crimson X cut into his courage and gave strength to his fear. Only once did she offer the red marker to him. The X he made had wrinkles and was off center.

On a positive note, Madeline had been moving her clothing into the closet in the master bedroom. Their relationship was solidifying and at least a small part of his anxiety was swept out the door. The cheap jewelry in the fancy wooden box was replaced with baubles fit for royalty. The townhouse was equipped with an alarm system that they'd never used. She enlisted a technician from the manufacturer to enhance its capabilities and teach them how to use the system.

However, it wasn't just clothing that Madeline brought to their townhouse. She trashed his useless collection of dime-store pots and pans, bringing in chef-quality equipment. Next, she replaced his glassware with a spare set from home. She was okay with his wineglasses, but the plastic cups he used for everything else went in the trash.

Coming home one afternoon from school, he found her washing glasses in the sink. Water size, juice size, and some odd size in-between, were drying on towels spread over the countertop.

He lifted one of the largest glasses and held it up to the light.

"You've got spots everywhere."

Madeline snatched the glass from his hand and examined it. "That's because you use cheap detergent."

"Oh? You have a suggestion for something that works better?"

"I'll ask the kitchen manager at home what she uses."

Kim-Jack raised his eyebrows. "I thought this was home."

"You know what I mean."

"Do I?" He checked another glass. "Well, as kitchen manager of this establishment, I suggest you put the glassware in the dishwasher instead of wasting all that water washing them by hand."

"So, now you're the kitchen manager?"

"You want the job?"

She shook her head. "Hell, no. I don't even want to learn how to cook."

"I knew I should have read the fine print on the marriage license."

The reality was that neither of them had much talent in the kitchen. Madeline's talent was her voice. Kim-Jack knew that singing to a rib roast wouldn't convince it to cook itself and agreed to learn the necessities once they got back from their honeymoon on ice. His first goal would be to cook a turkey, even if there was no holiday to celebrate.

***

The pace of time reached breakneck speed and before Kim-Jack realized it, there were only four days left until Christmas. Sitting in his car, in the teacher's parking lot, he knew from experience that the absentee rate would double. Thankfully, the students who remained had the best chance for making it all the way to graduation. They were the ones that gave him the reason to teach.

Thus, seeing Marcus at a desk in the front row that morning, left Kim-Jack with more apprehension than joy.

"The test was last Friday. You missed it."

"Man, you know I work on Fridays. Why you dis me like that?"

"Couldn't you get your mother to write your boss a note?"

Marcus flipped him the middle finger.

"Do you want to take a makeup test?"

"How about a make believe test?" The kid smiled. "Just make believe I took the test and give me an A."

Resting his butt against his desk, Kim-Jack looked down at him and smiled. "If life was that easy, I wouldn't get out of bed in the morning."

"Why *do* you get out of bed in the morning, professor? Shit, good-lookin' stud like you and as tall as you are, you should be on television doin' some sports show." Marcus leaned forward. "You too old to play basketball."

"I get out of bed and come here because I believe every person deserves an education."

Marcus nodded. "That's some heavy shit if it's true."

"Why would you doubt me?"

"Brother, I doubt everyone and everything." Sitting back, Marcus shook his head. "You don't doubt on the streets and you could die and not even know it's happened."

A disturbance from the hallway interrupted their discussion and Kim-Jack walked to the door to see what was happening. Two female students were trading punches. A crowd had gathered in a ragged circle around them and they were cheering for the black girl who was pummeling a white girl half her size.

Kim-Jack waded into the middle of the confrontation, holding the two girls apart while a trio security guards raced toward them. The white girl's face was bloodied and one eye was shut from a massive bruise. Shouts from the crowd as to who threw the first punch were meaningless to him. Seeing that no one died was of greater importance.

The security team ziptied both combatants and led them downstairs. Dispersing the remaining students, Kim-Jack returned to the classroom. Marcus had gotten up to watch and was now looking out the window.

"Somebody called the poleese."

"Tough to get busted just four days from Christmas."

"I spent Christmas in jail two years ago." Marcus rubbed his hands together. "Best Christmas dinner I ever ate."

Not being privy to his students' criminal records, Kim-Jack had to ask the question.

"What were you arrested for, Marcus?"

The boy responded with a note of pride in his voice. "Petty theft. I got caught walking out of the burger joint on Colfax without paying." He smiled. "Made it as far as Seventeenth before that fat ass manager caught up to me."

"Why didn't you pay?"

Marcus shook his head. "Duh. I didn't have no coin."

"I thought you were working. Isn't that why you don't come to school on Friday?"

"You honestly think three-days pay is going to last very long, professor?"

You got that right. "You know that you can get financial assistance, right? The state has a program to help with basic needs."

"Yeah, after you go through ten miles of paperwork and get interviewed by everyone except the Governor and the Mayor."

"Fair point, but it's worth the effort in the long run. You'll get money, food, and avoid jail at the same time." Kim-Jack shrugged. "Sounds like a win-win to me."

Marcus grinned. "You ain't never eaten dinner in the county lockup."

"So that's your plan for the future? Work the streets until you get arrested again?" Blowing out a sharp breath, Kim-Jack shook his head. "You'll be lucky to live until your twenties."

"You got a better plan, professor?"

"Finish school and get a job."

"Boring."

"Well, that's what life is all about. Boredom with the occasional spurt of excitement."

"What if I don't wanna play?"

Kim-Jack held out his hands. "Well, there's always the lottery."

"Or I could rob a bank."

"Which would probably land you in jail."

Walking over to the blackboard, Kim-Jack slipped into teacher mode. Grabbing a piece of chalk, he wrote the word JOB up high, JAIL down low, and joined them with a vertical line. In the middle of the line, he put the word SCHOOL.

"This is as simple as I can explain it. You are in school now, at the middle of the line. From school, you can slide up or down. Up means you get a job and live your life as a productive citizen. Down means you go to jail. Up is a future. Down is not."

"I already have a job. Does that mean I'm headed up?"

Kim-Jack shook his head. "Only if you can stay out of jail. It's obvious that your job doesn't pay enough, so get a better one."

"Easy for you to say, professor."

"Easy for you to do, Marcus."

The boy got up from his seat and walked over to the door.

"Where are you going?"

Marcus turned and smiled. "To look for a better job. I ain't gonna get rich sittin' here listening to your bullshit."

Kim-Jack walked over and blocked his way. "What kind of job are you going to look for, Marcus?"

Slipping under his teacher's outstretched arm, Marcus turned around and nodded once. "I always wanted to be a pirate. I'm going down to the docks and see if anyone is hiring."

With their combined students numbering less than half a full class, Tito and Kim-Jack merged their classes together for the final three days of the calendar year. Some detailed research of Antarctica yielded videos of the famous explorers who had been to the seventh continent before his fiancée had discovered the frozen wedding venue. Starting with Scott, the videos worked their way through Shackleton and Amundsen, touching on the French and German explorers as well.

Most of the students slept through the three days of non-stop videos. Tito spent the time in the teachers' lounge. However, for Kim-Jack, the images of wrecked ships, dead animals, and collapsed shelters added to his mounting fear of disaster on the other side of the equator.

Coming home on Wednesday, the day before Christmas Eve, he brought the videos to show Madeline. They were due to leave for the long haul to Ushuaia via Miami and Buenos Aires on Christmas morning, and he hoped that the horror of the films would lead to a last-minute change of plans.

But she refused to watch them, telling her future husband that everything he was obsessed about had happened over a hundred years ago. That ships were built better and for what her father was paying, everyone would survive.

Her words gave him little solace.

***

Not wanting to suffer through another turkey disaster, Madeline had insisted upon Christmas Eve dinner at her father's house. Kim-Jack's father and stepmother were in Jamaica with plans to fly to Miami in the morning and join up with the other members of the wedding party. The couple would spend their last night as boyfriend and girlfriend at her family home, sleeping in separate bedrooms at her stepmother's request.

They packed their bags at the townhouse, using the same list Madeline had brought to the mall. Kim-Jack found the bear claw gloves on Amazon and shoved them into a pair of deck shoes she'd purchased for him after trashing the pair he'd been wearing since high school. Despite his pleadings, she returned the hat with the floppy ears.

Dinner was strange for him. According the calendar and all the network television stations, it was Christmas Eve, but the Klopplemans didn't have a tree or a wreath. There were no presents scattered around the family room and the fireplace had a menorah on top but no stockings hanging underneath. Madeline's father gave them both envelopes filled with cash and a bag of chocolate coins wrapped in gold-colored foil that he called 'gelt.'

The chef had done his best to duplicate a family's Christmas dinner, but he was Jewish as were his clients, and the meal was a hybrid of the two religions. The turkey was kosher and salted way too heavily for Kim-Jack's tastebuds. Instead of mashed potatoes and stuffing, they were served potato pancakes with bowls of sour cream and applesauce.

A gravy boat sat waiting in front of each place setting but the cranberry sauce was absent along with the fresh from the oven rolls Kim-Jack's father always baked. He was hoping for familiar vegetables, but the ones the chef prepared were all the weeds he refused to eat. Not wanting to insult the man, he placed a single asparagus stem, one ball of Brussels sprouts, and the smallest piece of kale he could find in the corner of his plate. And then, just to ensure they were hidden, he doused the pile with gravy.

The lead housekeeper, a French woman with a tight bun in her hair and a bug up her ass, who spoke little to no English, doubled as sommelier and made sure that everyone's glass was filled. Kim-Jack asked her if there was any red wine and the woman scoffed at him, rolling her eyes, and shaking her head. In very broken English, she explained that red wine was inappropriate for a turkey dinner.

Dessert was an array of traditional Hanukah treats including a sticky mass of dough balls and dried fruits. Madeline pronounced the name of the food items three times, but Kim-Jack couldn't get it right.

"Tagalochhh?" He drew out the guttural last syllable in a desperate attempt to duplicate what his future wife was saying.

"Don't spit." Madeline wiped her face. "The sound should come from your throat."

Kim-Jack licked the honey off his fingers and reached for what appeared to be a miniature croissant. "What do you call these?"

"Rugelach." She picked two of the sugar sprinkled cookies off the platter. "Eat it in one bite."

He took one and popped it into his mouth. "Mmmm. Goof."

"You like them?"
"I said good."
"No, you said goof."

"My mouth was full." Kim-Jack reached for another. "Same throat sound at the end?"

Madeline nodded. "It's a Jewish thing."

He was about to try pronouncing the name of the cookie again when his cellphone vibrated in his pocket. Lifting it out, he stared at the number for a moment and then shook his head.

"Must be a wrong number."

The phone continued to ring several times before going to voicemail. Tapping the appropriate icon, he retrieved the message and put it on speaker.

Marcus' voice was shaky, almost a whisper. "Yo, professor Donaldson. I don't have anyone else to call and I need help. I'm at the Baker Street police station. I've been arrested, but it's a mistake. Help me, man. I called everyone I know and no one can help. I'm in some deep shit, bro. You gotta help me out. We be tight, if you do this for me. No need to pick a side."

The call ended and Kim-Jack looked around the table. "He's a student."

"Really?" Madeline shook her head. "Do all your students come to you when they need bail money?" She looked at the time on her cellphone. "At seven o'clock at night, I might add."

Kim-Jack got up from the table. "I've got to help him."

Larry Kloppleman held up his hand. "We're leaving for the airport in eight hours."

"I'll be there." Kim-Jack turned to Madeline. "Promise."

"Dammit KJ, don't screw this up last minute because you don't want to go. You've been trying to talk me out of this expedition since I mentioned it." She slid her chair back from the table. "You know what? Maybe I should come with you."

Her father crashed the idea. "No. With or without Kim-Jack, we're all going to Antarctica. I want you here, so I know you'll be with us."

Bending down, Kim-Jack kissed his bride-to-be. "Whatever this crap is all about, I'm certain I can deal with it quickly and be home in time to get plenty of sleep before we leave."

Chapter Twelve

Kim-Jack had never been in a police station. Getting to Baker Street wasn't a problem, the high school was at the intersection of Baker and Ginger. However, figuring out where to park to avoid a ticket or tow was an obstacle. Luckily, a car was pulling out on the next block and he slid into the spot behind it without the necessity for parallel parking. A skill he'd long forgotten.

Deciding which door to use to enter the block-long station was the next problem he had to solve. Most of the ones he passed had large NO ADMITTANCE signs. The nearest public door opened into a small reception area with thick glass walls on three sides. A receptionist in uniform asked which detective he was there to see.

"Oh, I'm not looking for a detective." Kim-Jack smiled at the young woman. "One of my students has been arrested."

"A student?"

He nodded. "Yes, ma'am. I teach at Obama."

"A student from Bohi was arrested." Her eyebrows followed her gaze toward the ceiling. "How unusual."

Kim-Jack pushed his cheek out with his tongue. "They're not all bad."

"Sugar, I graduated from Lincoln. You know what we called Bohi back then?" She leaned across her desk. "Advanced kindergarten."

"I can assure you, things have changed."

The officer laughed. "Yeah, this is the first time a teacher's come looking for a student. Most of the time, the students don't even know their teacher's name. You the first teacher I've met on the job since graduating the academy."

Kim-Jack held out his hand. "Kim-Jack Donaldson, co-chair of the science department at Barack Obama High School."

"Beverly Timmons, detective bureau receptionist and martial arts instructor."

Her handshake left his hand sore enough that he shook it. "That's a hell of a grip."

"I can bench press three-hundred pounds."

"Why are you driving a desk instead of patrol car?" Kim-Jack rubbed his hand. "You should be on the streets, kicking ass and taking names."

Stepping from behind the desk, Officer Timmons lifted her right pants leg. A bandage went from her calf to her knee. Unsoiled and unbloodied, the wrapping appeared to have been fresh that morning.

"A couple of your students, a block from their daily playground, got into a gunfight. I was first on the scene with my partner. He was driving. I got out my door and took three bullets in my leg before my foot touched the ground." She let the pants drop back in place. "That was four weeks ago. I took two weeks medical leave and opted for desk duty for five more. Don't worry professor, I'll be back on the streets soon enough."

Kim-Jack shook his head. "At least we've stopped them from bringing guns into the school building."

"Yeah, can't have a bunch of armed kindergarten kids." Nodding toward the door, she glanced at the silent phone on her desk. "Come on. It's quiet for a few minutes. I'll show you the public entrance."

She walked him out the door and pointed to the correct entrance at the far end of the building. As he made his way down the stairs to the sidewalk, Officer Timmons called out to him. "What's your student been charged with?"

Kim-Jack shrugged. "Making a mistake."

The public entrance was partially blocked by a drunk who grabbed at Kim-Jack's leg. Stepping over him, a pair of uniformed officers came out the double glass doors.

"Somebody ought to do something about this guy."

The cop closest to Kim-Jack checked the time. "Too early. The shelter doesn't take them in until nine on weeknights."

"So, he just sits here, drunk, and grabs at people when they try to pass?"

"No. Usually, he lays on the sidewalk, drunk, and grabs at people." The second cop pointed at the damp walkway behind Kim-Jack. "It's wet. The stairs are dry." He pointed at the large awning they were standing under that had the words "Public Entrance" in lighted red letters. "Can't fault a guy for wanting to stay dry."

The two cops kept Kim-Jack between them and the drunk as they made their way down the stairs. One of them turned and shouted, "Have a nice day!"

Kim-Jack stepped clear of the drunk and replied, "It's night. Have a nice night." *Jesus. What am I doing?*

The scene inside the police station had nothing in common with what Kim-Jack had seen on television. Vending machines with every option from candy bars to green salads filled one wall. Off to the side, there was a children's play area, which was empty but well lit and filled with colorful toys. Four round tables with attached seats were in the middle of the room and comfortable chairs that could have come from a doctor's waiting room were scattered about.

A couple of tables were occupied, both had what appeared to be anxious parents with a child who had probably been swearing his innocence for hours before relenting to come clean. A well-dressed woman with a lawyer's brown leather bag was seated as far from the entrance and everyone else in the waiting area as possible.

A row of gray metal desks with wooden side chairs made up an impenetrable wall between the public and the police. Six-foot high partitions that went all the way to the wall on either side were at either end of the row of desks. The only way back was the space between the desks, and that space was filled with a heavy chair. A single desk was manned, and Kim-Jack walked up to it.

Stopping several feet away, he looked around for a ticket machine, thinking that he should probably take a number. The officer noticed and waved him over.

"This isn't the deli counter."

"One of my students was arrested." Kim-Jack eyed the chair. "Okay if I sit down?"

"Have a seat." The officer kicked the chair around. "What's the student's name?"

"Tigue, Marcus Tigue."

Dragging a keyboard closer, the cop typed the boy's name and clicked several places on the screen. Selecting one of the lines that appeared, he read it silently, but with his lips moving.

"You're his teacher?"

Kim-Jack nodded. "His science teacher."

"This kid wants to be a scientist?" The cop shook his head and chuckled. "I think he's puttin' you on, professor." He spun the screen around so that Kim-Jack could read it. "He was arrested for shoplifting a woman's purse from the fanciest store in the mall."

"A purse?"

"Not just a purse, but a five-thousand-dollar, one-of-a-kind Bottega Veneta purse." Whistling, the cop scrolled down. "Here's the fun part, professor." He pointed at the screen. "Your student was wearing a pair of Manolo Blahnik black suede stiletto heel boots that cross the finish line at two-grand."

Covering his mouth with his hand, Kim-Jack said "Holy Shit" over and over.

"The good news is, he was wearing men's underwear and a Mike Tyson t-shirt when he was arrested."

"That's the good news?"

"Hey, maybe he's only half gay."

Clicking a button on the display, the officer brought up the criminal record of one Marcus Paul Tigue and read it silently with Kim-Jack, who did his best not to stare at the cop's lips when he read.

Marcus had been arrested eleven times...on the first page. Another fifteen on the second. Mostly petty stuff, other than the two stabbing incidents. Shoplifting was his favorite pastime, followed by several arrests on minor assault charges. Because he was a minor, all the arrests were forwarded to Juvenile Court, the great cesspool of the city's judicial system. Cases in Juvenile took months, sometimes years, to come to trial. Most were dismissed without ever seeing the inside of a courtroom.

However, this arrest put Marcus over the limit. At seven-thousand dollars, he was into felony territory and at fifteen-years-old, Kim-Jack's student could be tried as an adult if the prosecutor got out of the wrong side of the bed that morning.

"Are you a lawyer as well as a teacher, sir?" Spinning the screen around, the cop sat up in his seat. "This kid needs a lawyer."

"Can I talk to him?"

"Family or lawyer." The officer shrugged. "That's the rule. It doesn't specifically exclude science teachers, but I'm gonna go on the assumption that they just forgot to mention it."

Kim-Jack sensed that he'd come up against the blue wall and there was no way over, around, or through it. "Can I at least get a message to him? Let him know that I was here?"

"Family or lawyer. I can say it over and over until your ears bleed, but that's the only answer you're gonna get."

Kim-Jack got up from the chair and took a few steps back. "You know, we're both city employees."

The cop chuckled and shook his head. "Family or lawyer."

Feeling the frustration about to boil over, Kim-Jack headed for the door.

"Have a nice day, professor."

Stopping at the door, but not turning around, Kim-Jack shouted, "Night! Have a nice night, for god's sake."

He sat in his car, in the safety of the lights from the Baker Street police station, and called his fiancée. From the soft grumble of her voice, Kim-Jack knew that he'd awoken her from a deep sleep.

"Madeline, it's me."

"Who?"

"Kim-Jack, your future husband that you're about to drag off to the end of the world."

"KJ, where are you?"

"Outside the police station on Baker Street."

"Better than inside, I guess." Madeline coughed. "What time is it?"

"A little after nine."

Another cough and he could hear her guzzle some water. "We're leaving for the airport at three. Are you on your way home?"

"Listen Madeline, I need a lawyer."

"What? Have you been arrested? Why do you need a lawyer? Is it us?"

"No, none of that. I don't need the lawyer for me, I need one for Marcus." Kim-Jack shook his head. "Marcus is the student's name."

"The one who got arrested."

"Correct. He's in jail, and only a family member or a lawyer can talk to him." Switching the phone to his other ear, Kim-Jack continued. "Your father has dozens of lawyers on retainer. Ask him if he can spare one."

Madeline was silent for a few seconds.

"Hello? Did you fall back to sleep."

"I'm trying to compose the words that I would use to ask my father to have one of his five-hundred-dollar-an-hour attorneys reach out to one of your students who's been arrested."

"Do you want me to ask him?"

"I'm tempted to say yes."

"But?"

She sighed. "It's taken me months to convince him that you're not crazy. Why should I screw up all that good work?"

"Madeline, I'm serious."

"That's what worries me." She slipped into a fit of coughing, finally quenching it with another gulp of water. "I'm going to talk to daddy and plead your case. If I don't call you back, it's because he's smashed my cellphone with a hammer."

She ended the call.

In the fifteen minutes and forty-three seconds, by his cellphone's clock, that he waited for Madeline to call, Kim-Jack searched the web for the purse and thigh-high boots Marcus had pilfered. The police were correct on the valuation, but the question of why the boy was wearing them lingered in his mind.

I've never been able to tell for sure if someone is gay. Could be that I just don't care or it could be that they hide it better. But Marcus? Gay? A tough street punk like him? I mean, I only know him a few months, but then again, what do I know about the gay lifestyle that would make it obvious to someone straight?

And if I go on the assumption that Marcus is not gay, then why would he be wearing those boots and why steal a ladies purse? If they were supposed to be gifts for some mysterious girlfriend, I could understand. But then why try out the boots?

Kim-Jack laughed.

His girlfriend must have some really enormous feet.

Madeline's call interrupted his analysis. She was much more awake now and he could hear her sipping at a beverage, which he assumed to be white wine.

"So?"

"So, there's a lawyer on the way to the police station. He'll be there in fifteen minutes. His name is Frank something."

"Will he get Marcus released?"

"I don't know what he's going to do or not do, but either way, you better get your ass home as soon as he's done."

"Thanks for this, Madeline."

"No problem, sweetheart. When it comes to getting me married and out of the house for good, my father will move heaven and earth to make it happen."

As promised, the lawyer showed up exactly fifteen minutes later. From the man's wrinkled face and fading brown hair, to the liver spots on the back of his hands, Kim-Jack knew this attorney had been on the Kloppleman payroll since the beginning of time.

Brusquely, he introduced himself as Franklin O'Rourke and marched into the police station, with Kim-Jack in tow.

The confrontation with the police officer at the desk was short and ended with the lawyer being led into the depths of the police station while Kim-Jack considered an ice cream sandwich from one of the vending machines. Only one table of anxious parents and a guilty-looking teenage boy remained. The well-dressed female, who Kim-Jack figured for a lawyer was gone as well, but she'd left business cards on the four tables.

Franklin O'Rourke re-appeared about twenty minutes after leaving and motioned Kim-Jack over to one of the four tables, distant from the waiting family.

"The purse was returned to the store and the manager is satisfied that it is undamaged. He's afraid of the publicity and has insisted on dropping the charges."

Kim-Jack was stunned. "All this in twenty minutes?"

"There's more." The lawyer clasped his hands together behind his head. "The boots are fakes, knock-offs, and worth about a hundred dollars."

"So, no felony. This goes to Juvenile?" Kim-Jack had spent most of the time eating ice cream sandwiches and searching the web for the laws related to juveniles and shoplifting.

"Yes and no." Sitting upright, Franklin O'Rourke pursed his lips. "Unless there's an adult guardian, the police have the right to hold Mr. Tigue for up to forty-eight hours and then place him in a group home with a dusk to dawn curfew until his case in Juvenile Court is called."

Shaking his head, Kim-Jack placed his palms on the table. "His mother is in prison at the other end of the state. To the best of my knowledge, he has no other family. A couple of other students who he claims as cousins, but I doubt there's a true familial connection."

The lawyer nodded a few times. "What about you?"

"Me? His legal guardian?" Kim-Jack took a deep breath. "Jesus, Mr. O'Rourke. You know I'm getting married this weekend."

"Yes, in Antarctica. I'll be there."

"Oh? I didn't know that Larry had invited guests."

"Mr. Kloppleman chartered the entire ship. A hundred and eight of his closest friends."

Kim-Jack's heart skipped several beats. "I wonder if he told my dad?"

O'Rourke shifted gears. "Marcus needs a legal guardian right now, or he's headed to the group home on Monday. If you're willing, I can do the paperwork online and have Marcus released before midnight."

"What do I have to do to be his legal guardian?" Kim-Jack steeled himself for bad news.

"See that he has a place to sleep, food to eat, and adult supervision."

"Do I have to be there or can I just give him the keys to my townhouse and tell him, see you in two weeks?" Kim-Jack crossed his fingers.

"Unfortunately, adult supervision means twenty-four hours a day." The lawyer narrowed his gaze. "Or you can just let him go to the group home and pray for the best. But that's on you, Mr. Donaldson."

***

Kim-Jack waited to tell Madeline the news in person rather than over the phone. He was afraid that she'd either smash her cellphone or would be waiting with a loaded gun if he called her. Walking into the house, he was met by his fiancée, her father, and Cassidy in the main foyer. Everyone was in nightclothes.

"I am now the temporary legal guardian of Marcus Paul Tigue. He will be released from jail within the next two hours, and your lawyer will drive him here."

No one said anything for a few very long seconds. Madeline was the first to recover.

"Here? Why?"

Kim-Jack clasped his hands behind his back, squeezing them as hard as possible. "Because he must have round-the-clock adult supervision or he goes back to jail."

Larry Kloppleman jumped into the fray. "Okay. There are lots of adults around here all day and night. He'll be properly supervised."

Shaking his head, Kim-Jack squeezed his hands so tight they hurt. "The law says that as his legal guardian, I'm the one who has to supervise him."

"What are you saying?" Madeline covered her mouth.

"I'm saying that the guest list for our wedding just got an addition."

Cassidy fainted and several staff members appeared from the wings to aid her.

Madeline turned and ran for her bedroom.

With a single nod, Larry seemed to accept the situation. "Does he have a passport?"

Kim-Jack dropped his hands to his side. "I doubt it. I don't think he's ever left the state."

Another nod. "No problem. I'll call my friend at the State Department. They'll have one waiting for him when we land in Miami." Larry headed off to his study.

Alone in the foyer, Kim-Jack knelt and crossed himself. "Well, that went better than I expected."

One of the younger staff members came over to him. "Can I get you anything, Mr. Donaldson?"

Kim-Jack stood slowly and put his hand on the boy's shoulder. "Yeah. A stiff drink and a one-way ticket to Burundi."

Part Two

Chapter Thirteen

Marcus had never been on an airplane before. In fact, he'd never left the state other than a few trips by car down to his cousin's house by the ocean. Getting through airport security was his first hurdle, and he handled it poorly.

"Why I gotta take off my sneakers?"

The TSA agent shook his head. "For the third time, that's the rule. Unless you've got Pre-Check, you have to take off your shoes."

"I ain't got nothing in them, boss. Jus my socks and feet." Marcus pointed at the intricate lacing pattern he employed to be stylish. "You know how long it takes to tie them like that?"

"That's not my problem, sir." Taking a few steps back from the boy, the agent nodded to his partner and sighed. "I was supposed to be off today."

Bending over, Marcus unlaced his sneakers and tossed them into a bin. "What about my socks?"

"Leave them on." The agent took another step back. "But put your cap in the bin."

"Why? You think I got a weapon in my afro?"

The agent nodded. "It's been done."

Marcus spun around and stared hard at the line of people waiting behind him. Pointing a group of men wearing turbans and kaftans, he shook his head. "Shit, man. I see at least three terrorists over there. How come you ain't hassling them?"

"They'll get their turn."

With his pockets empty, his sneakers and hat in the bin, Marcus looked over at the TSA agent. "Now what, boss?"

The agent pointed at the scanner. "Walk in there. Put your hands in the air according to the picture and wait until you're told to step out."

Marcus stepped in and raised his arms. "Am I under arrest?"

Walking away from him, the agent stopped at a group of his fellow TSA staffers and blew out a long breath. "I'm going to grab some of that pot we confiscated this morning and go outside. If I'm not back in an hour, you'll find my uniform hanging from a No Parking sign and a half-smoked joint in the top pocket."

Kim-Jack, who'd gone through the TSA Pre-Check line with his shoes and hat on, grabbed Marcus before the boy had a chance to put on his sneakers.

"They can arrest you for non-compliance."

"Man, I complied." Marcus held up his sneakers. "I ain't walkin' barefoot."

"Look, Marcus, my ass is on the line here. This isn't the hood. This isn't high school. This is what the adults call real life."

"Walkin' barefoot?"

Kim-Jack shook his head. "These guys don't give a damn who you are when it comes to security. They can throw you in a room and lock the door without giving you a phone call or a reason."

"City cops can do that shit too, professor."

Pushing Marcus out of the way of the crowd, Kim-Jack turned and waved at Madeline. He held a finger to indicate one more minute and told the boy to put on his sneakers.

"Can you walk without going through that elaborate lacing process?"

Marcus tucked the laces into the tops of his sneakers and grinned. "Good enough, professor?"

Having endeared himself forever to Madeline, calling her a "sweet lookin' be-atch" on the way to the airport, Marcus walked ahead of the couple with Kim-Jack giving direction.

They stopped for cinnamon buns, eggrolls, and three new hoodies for Marcus: basketball, football, and a nearby college's lacrosse team. He had no idea what the sport entailed, but their mascot was a snarling bull with smoke coming out of its nostrils.

Marcus said that a cousin came up from Mexico last summer and showed him bull-fighting videos on his cellphone.

Once they arrived at the gate, after a bathroom stop for Madeline and a chicken sandwich stop for Kim-Jack, they were ushered into a private lounge. Larry Kloppleman had rented the entire guest lounge for the wedding party and several dozen of their friends who were all flying to Miami with them.

Marcus kept changing seats, constantly moving closer to the windows so he could stare at the jets. Sensing some apprehension on the part of the first-time flyer, Kim-Jack refilled Madeline's white wine and then walked over to him.

"Are you nervous?"

"I ain't never seen an airplane up close." Marcus shook his head in amazement. "They's huge, professor. How do they fly? I mean, I see them flying overhead all the time, but they look so small. This thing's bigger than a bunch of subway cars all linked together. And look at the size of those motors!"

"Engines." Kim-Jack chuckled softly. "On an airplane, they're called engines."

"How they make it fly?" Marcus leaned against the glass. "Do the wings flap like a bird?"

Kim-Jack lost control of the laughter, bending over and slapping his thighs. "Marcus, if those wings start flapping, we won't be flying very far."

Boarding the jet, an hour and half later, the wedding party and their guests occupied all of the First Class and Business Class seats with a few unlucky ones taking up the bulkhead rows in Economy. Madeline, who insisted on an aisle seat, sat next to Kim-Jack with Marcus glued to the window.

She had spoken as little as necessary following the boy's outburst in the limo, jamming her earbuds in place as soon as she was seated. Kim-Jack reached over and took her hand, holding it just long enough for her to turn and give him her standard "I'm annoyed with you" look. He blew her a kiss and smiled, but the gesture went past her without stopping.

As a virgin in the often-confusing world of aviation, Marcus had the usual difficulty with the seatbelt. First, taking the wrong end from the two between him and Kim-Jack. Then dealing with the loose end used to tighten it.

"Why don't they use the automatic shit like in my cousin's car?"

"Because it wouldn't work for the aisle or middle seat." Reaching over, Kim-Jack tightened his belt. "See how that works? If it gets too tight, just release the buckle and loosen the strap."

"What if I gotta pee?"

Kim-Jack pointed at the lavatory door several rows ahead of them. "You go in there."

"An outhouse?"

"Yes. A small, flying outhouse with instructions on the door."

A bald, black female flight attendant with noticeable biceps stopped at their row and asked Marcus to bring his seat forward. Not realizing that of the many buttons he'd been pushing, he'd inadvertently tilted his seat back.

"I didn't break it."

"It's not broken, dear." The woman leaned across Madeline and Kim-Jack. "This button, right here." She pressed the button and his seat popped forward.

"Shit. You coulda warned me, be-atch."

Kim-Jack elbowed the boy in his ribs. "Apologize."

"Hey."

"No hey." Kim-Jack hit him again. "What did I say about that word?"

Marcus slid closer to the window. "I apologize."

The flight attendant nodded. "Your son?"

Kim-Jack turned to Marcus and grinned. "My cousin. It's his first time on an airplane and he's a bit nervous."

She nodded again. "First time out of the city? It's okay. I was his age once. Then I learned about manners." Without waiting for a reply, the woman continued forward.

Marcus looked at Kim-Jack and pursed his lips. "Damn. Ain't that about some shit, homes?"

A few minutes later, the main cabin door was closed and the flight crew began their safety briefing. Marcus had already pulled the laminated instruction card from the seat pocket and was following along with the announcements.

Finished with the instructions, the same flight attendant passed their row, slowing just long enough to smile at Marcus. Not realizing who the smile was intended for, Kim-Jack smiled back and received a glaring look from Madeline.

"Really?" His fiancée yanked out the bud from her right ear.

"What?"

She raised her eyebrows. "She's gay."

"How do you know? Is it on her name badge?" Kim-Jack laughed. "Why do you think every bald woman with muscles is a lesbian?"

"Because most of them are."

"Ah, stereotyping again."

Madeline shook her head. "If you like, I'll ask her."

"Please don't."

"Then agree with me, KJ." Stopping the musical playback on her phone, Madeline turned toward him. "You're a buff, black male. No one would ever accuse you of looking like a member of the Village People. But take away your dick and shave your head and you look like a gay woman." She leaned over and kissed his cheek. "Admit it. You do have a pretty face for a man."

Marcus slapped his knee. "She's right, professor. You'd be a hit at the County lockup. Damn. Pretty boys are in high demand."

"Thank you both, but I'm going to pass on Hollywood, *People* magazine, and a life of crime for now."

The captain came on the public address system and instructed the flight attendants to take their seats in preparation for departure. Madeline put her buds back into her ears and tightened her seatbelt. With the first backward jarring motion of the aircraft, Marcus grabbed the loose end of his belt and pulled it as tight as possible.

Without a bounce or bump, the huge jet was towed back from the gate. Marcus stared at the ground crew waving their orange flashlights. He waved back and kept watching as they disappeared from view. There was a long pause while the ground crew drove the land tug back to the terminal and the taxiway was cleared.

"How did we move backward? Shit, we headin' in the wrong direction."

Kim-Jack grinned as the engines roared with power and the boy gripped the armrests in fear.

"Are we going now, professor?"

"Not yet." Kim-Jack touched Marcus' wrist. "Relax. He's just turning around to taxi to the end of the runway."

"Then what?"

"Then we will zoom down the runway and when we're going fast enough, the plane will lift into the air and you will be flying."

Marcus gripped the armrests tighter. "What if it don't fly?"

"It will." Kim-Jack nodded. "They always do. Airplanes takeoff and land all day long. It's not magic. It's just physics."

The boy leaned over and whispered, "How come your be-atch is so cool about this flying shit?"

Kim-Jack was about chastise him again, but held back. "Because Madeline, like so many other people, flies all the time. This is no more exciting to her than you traveling across the state by bus to see your mother."

"Ain't no excitement seeing my moms."

"Regardless, the point I'm trying to make to you is that flying is safe. Some folks even say it's boring." Kim-Jack pulled out a pair of earbuds. "We have two airplane flights to take before we reach the ship and three coming home. It's going to be this time tomorrow when we land in South America. But there's plenty of free entertainment on the screen in front of you to keep you occupied."

Marcus nodded. "Yeah. I already been poking around that shit. Not much good music."

"Watch a movie or a show. Once we reach cruising altitude there isn't going to be much to see out that window."

"Cruising altitude?"

"Around thirty-five-thousand feet. A bit over six nautical miles."

Grabbing the seat in front of him, Marcus shook his head. "We gonna be six miles in the air? Oh shit, it's almost six miles to my cousin's house. I know what six miles is, professor."

Kim-Jack pulled the boy's arms off the seat. "Relax. You know how you look up and see those tiny airplanes? Well, this is going to be just the opposite. Everything down there that looked so big will become tiny. Has anything changed? You're up in the tiny airplane. Have you shrunk? Are you tiny?"

Marcus shook his head. "No, man. That's some science fiction bullshit. People can't shrink."

"Well, there you have it."

All this time, the jet had been taxiing and was now in position for takeoff. Kim-Jack was going to embellish the concept of perspective when the engines roared to full power. The jet held position for a few seconds before starting to roll. Marcus wrapped his hands around the armrests and stared out the window, shaking in fear with each small bounce.

And then the jet smoothly tilted back and glided into the air. Kim-Jack watched the boy's jaw drop as thrust pressed him into his seat. Marcus turned to say something to him, but the jet banked to the right and he swung his head back toward the window. They leveled off, but continued to climb. As the aircraft pierced the clouds at five-thousand feet, Marcus moved away from the window.

"We're in the clouds, man. Holy shit. We're in the freakin' clouds."

"Keep your voice down, Marcus." Kim-Jack grinned sheepishly at the couple across the aisle who were staring at them. "Sorry. First time in an airplane."

At ten-thousand feet, the captain came back on the PA and talked about the route they were taking, how long they would be in the air, the temperature in Miami that brought about cheers from their nearby passengers, and finally thanking everyone for choosing his airline.

Kim-Jack reclined his seat and loosened his seatbelt. Marcus followed suit with the exception of his seatbelt. At one of their stops in the airport, between security and the gate, Kim-Jack had purchased a fresh set of earbuds for himself. He'd seen Marcus staring at the display with eyes as wide as soup bowls and offered to buy a pair for him. Marcus laughed and pulled out his earbuds, a much higher quality and certainly more expensive pair than anything in the rack.

The boy was gripping the earbud case and watching the clouds rush by when the flight attendant came down the aisle.

"How's the virgin doing?" She smiled. "Nothing like the rush to thirty-five-thousand feet to get your blood flowing in the morning."

"I think he'll survive." Kim-Jack looked over at Marcus. "You're flying, Marcus."

"Hell, yeah." Slowly releasing his grip on the earbud case, he looked up at the flight attendant with an air of importance. "I'm cool."

About an hour into the three-hour flight, the senior Kloppleman came back to their row from his First-Class seat to check on his guests. Madeline's Xanax had started working and she was snoring with one earbud in and the other blasting Frank Sinatra in Kim-Jack's left ear.

"How's the criminal?"

Kim-Jack looked over at Marcus. "Calm. Listening to what he calls music and staring out the window. He ate Madeline's breakfast and his own. Add that to what he ate in the airport, and I don't know if all that clothing you ordered for him is going to fit."

"Have you thought about what you're going to do with him once you get back?" Reaching down, Larry tapped his daughter's cellphone and stopped the music. "I mean, he's not going to have to live with you is he?"

"No. According to Franklin O'Rourke, this whole thing will be dismissed as soon as he can get in front of the judge."

Larry stood up and looked toward the Economy seats. "Nice of your communist friend to give up his seat in Business Class for the criminal."

"Believe me, he didn't do it willingly." Kim-Jack sighed. "He was really looking forward to a comfortable seat. At his size, Economy class seats are a real squeeze."

"He was the best you could find for Best Man?"

Kim-Jack pursed his lips. "He *is* my best friend."

Larry shook his head. "So Madeline tells me."

Opening her eyes, Madeline smiled at her father. "I heard you mention my name."

"I was asking your future husband if he's planning to adopt the criminal."

"He'll be old enough to drive in a few months." Squeezing an earbud into his right ear, Kim-Jack looked up at his future father-in-law. "Might be time for a new chauffeur, especially if you're going to be coming to the city more often to visit. Marcus knows the hood."

The flight was twenty minutes out of Miami when Marcus finally dozed off. Kim-Jack woke him moments later to reposition his seat in preparation for landing. Coming in, over the Everglades, they were low enough for Marcus to spot a group of airboats speeding over the shallow water.

"Everything is flat."

Kim-Jack nodded. "No mountains in South Florida." He pointed out the window. "That's the Everglades. They call it the river of grass."

"Smokeable?"

"No." Laughing, Kim-Jack pointed at the reflection of the sun off the water. "I should do a few lessons about the Everglades this spring."

"Hey, I should get extra credit for seeing this shit for real, professor." Marcus grinned. "Easy A for me."

The airplane banked hard to the left, lining up with a six-lane highway. The captain instructed the flight crew to take their seats for landing and once again thanked the passengers for flying his airline.

"We're going to have some rain in a few seconds. Nothing to worry about. We'll be on the ground in fifteen minutes and the weatherman has promised sunshine for the rest of the day. Welcome to Miami."

Another shorter bank to the left and the plane leveled out. Marcus watched the ground rush up towards them and tightened his seatbelt.

"Where's the airport?" He searched out the window, scanning in every direction.

"You won't see it from this angle." Kim-Jack returned his seat to the upright position. "But the pilot can see it from up front."

Marcus shook his head. "You put a lot of faith into someone you can't see, professor."

"I put a lot of faith into the science that makes this thing fly, Marcus."

They were now low enough to see cars and read billboards. The sound of the landing gear coming down and the flaps to slow them put Marcus on edge.

"What's that sound?"

"Landing gear and the brakes that slow the plane so it can land."

"Is this the easy part?"

Kim-Jack smiled. "For a pilot, the entire trip is usually easy."

"Usually? What happens when it's not?"

The answer wasn't going to be a good one, regardless of how Kim-Jack back peddled. He folded his hands in his lap and looked out the window for a few seconds.

"Maybe, if you graduate from high school, you can find out for yourself."

"Fly airplanes for a living?" Marcus blew out a sharp breath. "You dreamin', professor."

Kim-Jack nodded once. "Life's all about living your dreams, Marcus." He closed his eyes and thought to himself, *even when they want to become nightmares.*

Chapter Fourteen

Their next flight was scheduled to depart at nine o'clock at night, giving the group a nearly six-hour layover. Kim-Jack wanted to take a cab to the beach and go for a swim. Tito, after having been crammed into a seat too small for a toddler, wanted to lie down on a bed and stretch his back. Marcus wanted to eat. Madeline decided they would all go shopping and ordered a rideshare van to take them to the nearest mall with the caveat that Marcus was not allowed into any shoe stores.

The balance of the wedding party and guests were scheduled to arrive throughout the day. Larry Kloppleman had chartered a jet for the eight-and-a-half-hour flight to Buenos Aires and everyone had been instructed which gate to head for at the airport and what time the flight would depart. Gathering friends from around the world had not been easy, but Larry was an expert when it came to organization.

Cassidy was the flaw in his plans.

She'd started drinking while everyone was getting dressed earlier that morning. Kim-Jack had joined her for mimosas in the kitchen just before they piled into the limo for the ride to the airport. Throughout the flight, she'd been maintaining a pace of a fresh drink every twenty minutes, so that when they landed in Miami, Cassidy required a wheelchair.

On the way to baggage claim, she'd sobered enough to demand a ride to the mall, loudly announcing that she would cover everyone's purchases regardless of price. Madeline was dead-set against taking her stepmother along, knowing that the woman was bragging about spending her father's money and that she was more than capable of doing that without Cassidy's help. However, Kim-Jack saw the offer as a perfect opportunity to bond with the woman who was not only her fiancée's family, but apparently a good friend to *his* stepmother as well.

Arriving at the mall, the group split in half. Kim-Jack, Cassidy, and Marcus headed for the massive sporting goods store. Tito, who was getting annoyed at the constant ribbing about his weight from both Marcus and his fellow teacher, took off with Madeline in search of a music store.

The trio found the sporting goods venue next to a liquor store that was large enough to hold a jumbo jet. Cassidy strolled into the adult beverage dispensary without a word to her partners. Kim-Jack noticed she was missing several minutes later and mentioned it to Marcus.

"Let the be-atch go and drink, professor." He grinned. "She's a lot funnier blitzed than she is sober."

Kim-Jack closed his eyes and considered the suggestion. "What if she leaves the liquor store and goes off on her own?" He pointed at the nearby map of the mall. "This place has over two hundred stores and it covers five acres. What if we can't find her in time for the flight this evening?"

Smiling, Marcus pulled Cassidy's wallet from his jacket pocket. "She ain't goin' far, professor. Not without her coin and cards."

"You stole her wallet?"

"I'm gonna give it back."

"Jesus, Marcus. You're making me think I should have hung up the phone when you called last night, and let you rot in jail." Kim-Jack grabbed the wallet from the boy's hand. "Did you take anything out?"

Marcus shook his head. "Hey, man. I'm not a thief. I told you I was gonna give it back."

"Like the boots and the purse?"

"I gave them back, right?"

"That's not the point."

"Oh?" Cocking his head to the side, Marcus folded his arms over his chest. "You starting to sound like a limp dick, brother."

"Don't go there, Marcus."

"Why not? You already pussy-whipped by your be-atch. She barks and you run like a well-trained Doberman."

Kim-Jack held his temper back, but inside, he was sizzling. "Fifteen-years-old and you think you understand all there is to know about women."

"And you ten years older, still making the same mistakes you made when you was fifteen, I'll bet." Marcus shook his head. "What did you learn 'bout women in college, professor?"

"What did you learn about them in middle school?"

Marcus winked. "I busted my cherry in middle school."

"Impressive to your friends, foolhardy to me."

"You callin' me a fool?"

Kim-Jack chuckled. "Only if it's appropriate. Did she get pregnant?"

"Don't know." Marcus shrugged. "She took one of those morning-after pills just to be safe."

While they were talking, a salesman wandered over and asked if he could help.

"We're talking about sex." Grinning, Marcus raised his eyebrows, a trick he'd learned from watching Madeline. "You wanna join in? We could use a white man's opinion."

The salesman smiled and shook his head. "Come and find me if you need help with sporting goods. I've been married and divorced three times. What I know about women isn't enough to fill a toddler's knapsack."

Marcus walked over to a glass-topped counter with an array of pistols and knives. Turning, he called the salesman back over and pointed at a nine-millimeter semi-automatic pistol with ivory grips.

"I'd like to see this one."

The salesman wrinkled his mouth. "I don't think you're old enough to purchase a firearm, junior."

"I'm old enough to have sex." Marcus argued. "What's age got to do with this shit anyhow?"

"The law says you have to be eighteen in this state."

"Shit. You gonna dis me for three years?"

"Not me." The salesman held out his hands. "Talk to the Governor."

Kim-Jack walked over, hearing the conversation unfold. "Uh, the Governor is at the airport with the rest of our group."

"The Governor of Florida?" The salesman's voice expressed serious doubt. "At the Miami airport?"

Kim-Jack pursed his lips. "No. Our Governor, who's a close friend of my future father-in-law."

Marcus leaned in. "And he's black."

"I don't care if he's orange with purple polka dots. The law says you have to be eighteen, even if the Governor is your father." Taking a few steps toward a group of women who were perusing the nearby tennis rackets, the salesman looked at Marcus and smiled. "My store manager is black. I'll be glad to have him come over and explain the law if you like."

"That won't be necessary." Kim-Jack put his hand on Marcus' shoulder. "Junior here thrives on confrontation."

"Hey, kiss junior's ass, professor."

Kim-Jack was about reply when a woman's scream and a loud crashing noise came rolling through the open doorway to the mall.

"Cassidy!"

Marcus ran toward the door. "Here come the mall cops."

Jogging past him, Kim-Jack rushed over to the liquor store entrance where a large crowd had gathered and three overweight mall security officers were pushing their way through. Reaching the front of the throng, he could see a woman in a bright red dress, face down on the floor with hundreds of bottles of beer surrounding her. Several liquor store employees were trying to help the woman to her feet and slipping on the bottles as they brought her up a few feet and then dropped her with no place to gain footing.

Kim-Jack knew it was Cassidy by the dress. The woman had changed clothes on the airplane after spilling a drink on her original attire. However, her shoes were missing and he suddenly regretted keeping Marcus out of a shoe store that morning.

Squeezing through the crowd, he elbowed the mall cops out of the way and got down on his knees by her side.

"Cassidy. CASSIDY!" Kim-Jack shook her until her eyes opened and a crooked smile formed on her lips.

"KJ. Oh, KJ." She tried to stand, but her legs weren't cooperating. "I'm stuck. I can't get up."

Someone in the crowd shouted, "Call an ambulance!"

Someone else chimed in, "She's fallen and she can't get up."

Kim-Jack got around her and slipped his hands under her armpits. Pulling Cassidy upright, he helped her walk over to a counter and lifted her onto its glass top. Unfortunately, her weight was more than the glass could support and it collapsed with a sickening crash. Cassidy's butt fell into the opening, jamming her tightly in place. As hard as he yanked, Kim-Jack couldn't drag her free.

Marcus finally made his way through the throngs and rushed over to help.

"Grab her left arm, I've got her right." Kim-Jack directed the boy into position. "Then get your other hand under her butt and lock it onto mine."

"Oh, KJ, your hand feels so good right there." Cassidy squirmed, but only succeeded in sliding deeper into the display case.

"Don't move, Cassidy. Your ass is right on top of some huge glass shards." Pushing her up slightly, Kim-Jack did his best to keep the glass from stabbing her in the privates. His hand brushed her crotch and he pulled it back, cutting his thumb as it crossed a broken piece of glass.

"You're bleeding, professor."

Kim-Jack gritted his teeth. "Yeah. I know. Shit, that hurts."

Cassidy managed to get her face close to his and kissed him squarely on the lips. "You're my hero, KJ."

"Oh shit." Marcus clapped his hands. "Your be-atch gonna kick your ass, professor."

"Calm down, Cassidy." Wiping his mouth with the back of his uninjured hand, Kim-Jack looked over at the boy and shook his head several times. "Madeline isn't going to hear a word of this, or you're on the first flight back north. You can sit in jail until I get home. Are we clear?"

Several of the younger members of the crowd had been shooting video and posting photos of the incident. Marcus nodded toward them. "It ain't me you gotta worry about, professor. This shit is going viral right in front of your eyes."

Spinning around, Kim-Jack came face-to-phone with a redheaded girl in a knee-length football jersey and Crocs. She smiled at him and then disappeared into the crowd. Several other bystanders filled her space. All of them were holding cellphones. One was even doing a live play-by-play...in Spanish.

More mall security converged on the scene, breaking up the throngs of people who'd temporarily forgotten they were in a mall and were supposed to be shopping. The three mall cops came over and lifted Cassidy off the broken counter. Noticing the blood dripping on their carpeted floor, an employee of the sporting goods store broke open a first aid kit she'd pulled off a nearby display, and bandaged Kim-Jack's hand.

From somewhere down one of those unlabeled corridors that shopping malls are famous for, a security guard appeared with a wheelchair. With Cassidy loaded onboard, Kim-Jack, Marcus, and the guard set off for the entrance Madeline had designated as a rendezvous point. They were about fifty feet away from the sporting goods store when Kim-Jack turned and ran back.

He grabbed the woman who'd staunched the bleeding and asked her for a furry, winter hat with floppy ears in his size. She told him to wait and jogged to the back of the store, disappearing through a locked door that required her keycard to open. A few minutes later, the woman returned carrying four floppy hats in different sizes. Kim-Jack tried on the first one and was pleased with the fit. He reached into his pocket to retrieve his wallet and credit card, but it was gone.

Feverishly checking every pocket and not finding his wallet, Kim-Jack ran over to the counter that Cassidy had destroyed and searched the floor. The wallet wasn't there, but another piece of glass became imbedded in his thumb, requiring additional first aid from the store employee.

"Are you sure you had your wallet when you came in here?"

He nodded. "Yes, absolutely. My friend, who is shopping with my fiancée, forgot his and I gave him my spare credit card."

"Wait. The woman who kissed you isn't your fiancée?"

"Hell no. She's her stepmother." Kim-Jack laughed. "Christ, she's at least twenty years older than me."

The woman shrugged. "My mom is fifteen years older than my dad. Cougars are cool." She winked. "I'll be a cougar when I grow older. I want to be seventy and have a twenty-one-year-old stud for a boyfriend."

"It's good to have a goal in life." Shaking his head, Kim-Jack snatched a couple of gauze pads from the open first aid kit. "For later. Just in case I bleed through these bandages."

Marcus jogged into the store and waved at him. "We need to go, professor."

The woman looked at Marcus and then back to Kim-Jack. "Let me guess. That's your adopted son?"

Slapping his forehead, Kim-Jack blew out a quick breath. "Not in this life." He chuckled. "We're not even cousins."

They arrived at the mall entrance much earlier than the agreed upon time, so Kim-Jack rolled Cassidy into an ice cream parlor. Amazingly, Marcus had a full stomach and wandered into a high-end men's shop across the way. Without a dollar to his name or a credit card, Kim-Jack knew the kid would only be window-shopping, but he kept an eye on the store's entrance just in case Marcus exited on the run.

Whatever Cassidy had sampled in the liquor store was fading, and she slowly became more coherent. The slurring ended and was replaced by a voracious appetite. While they waited, Kim-

Jack used Cassidy's credit card to stave off their hunger. In a nod to his childhood, he had a chocolate shake with two scoops and chocolate sprinkles, and she plowed through a banana split as though her life depended on finishing it before Madeline returned.

Watching her devour the ice cream, Kim-Jack sat back in their booth and formulated an explanation.

She'll see the video of Cassidy kissing me first. Everything else will be superfluous after that. I know she's going to be pissed. He shrugged. *Well, not at me, but she's going to go ballistic on Cassidy. Hey, it's not my fault she wandered off and got drunk.*

Marcus shook him out of his pondering.

"I need a loan."

"A loan?" Kim-Jack put the beverage he'd been holding on the table. "For what?"

"Clothes." Marcus pursed his lips. "Look, man. All these other chumps in this wedding thing have nice fancy white people's clothes. I look like–"

"A fifteen-year-old street thug?"

"Now, why you gotta do that shit, professor?"

"Tell the truth?" Kim-Jack smiled. "I'm not prone to lying. You should know that by now."

"Fine. Be that way. That's your thing then do it. But I remember hearin' some shit about clothes making the man. Well, I want to be made and that requires clothes and that means I need a loan." Marcus held out his hand.

"How much?"

"Just give me your card, man. You about to marry into Fort Freakin' Knox. Don't be playing that empty wallet shit with me." Marcus shoved his hand closer.

Kim-Jack pushed the hand away. "Find my wallet and I'll be glad to help you become that inner man."

"You lost your wallet?"

"Five'll get you ten that someone pulled it out of my pocket during the melee in the liquor store."

Marcus shook his head. "Damn. This place is more dangerous than the hood."

Looking over at Cassidy, who appeared to be as sober as she normally was, Kim-Jack held out her credit card.

"Don't go anywhere. I'm going to take Marcus over to that men's shop and buy him some decent clothes. I'll reimburse you when we get to the airport." He leaned over and whispered, "What do you remember?"

She whispered back, "About what?"

"About what happened after you got drunk."

"Why are we whispering?"

Kim-Jack stood up straight. "Forget about it. Don't go anywhere, okay?"

"Buy me another banana split before you go."

"Really?"

"Airplane food sucks."

Marcus had already picked out his new wardrobe. All that was necessary was for it to be packed and paid. Kim-Jack stared in disbelief at the price tags as each item was scanned and carefully wrapped.

"One-hundred-and-eighty dollars for a polo shirt? Are you serious?"

Four pairs of silk socks were next.

"Wait a minute. That's twenty-four dollars and change for each pair?" Kim-Jack shook his head. "I buy my socks online. Six pair for fifteen dollars. Six pair, Marcus."

"Do you want me to fit in with your crowd or not, professor?"

"They're not my crowd. Ninety-nine percent of them are Larry Kloppleman's friends and business associates. My crowd consists of Madeline, Tito, and you. And let me clue you in. None of us owns socks that are twenty-four dollars and change per pair. In fact, I've never put a pair of silk socks on my feet."

Marcus grabbed a pair of silk socks off the nearest rack and handed them to Kim-Jack.

"Take off your shoes and socks, then, and put these on."

Kim-Jack hesitated a moment too long.

"I'm serious, professor. We ain't goin' to Antarctica until you try on a pair of twenty-four-dollar silk socks."

"Fine."

Walking over to a nearby bench, Kim-Jack traded his running shoes and white crew socks for a pair of silk ones. He rubbed them smooth and stood, walking casually across the carpeted floor.

"Wow." Slowly scuffing his feet on the carpet, he walked back to the bench and sat, making fists with his toes. "That's incredible."

"Told you so." Marcus grabbed three more pairs of the largest size, in different colors, and handed them to the store clerk who was packing their order.

"What are you doing?"

"Getting you a wedding present, professor. Compliments of the drunk woman who kisses everyone she can." Marcus smiled. "Oh, you didn't see the shit with the security guard."

Kim-Jack finished tying his laces. "And neither did you. Okay?"

Marcus winked at him. "You ain't got nothin' to worry 'bout, professor. I ain't five-oh."

"Good." Kim-Jack stood and took a few steps. "These socks make a huge difference. I can actually feel the floor through the soles of my sneakers." He glanced around the store. "We've still got time. I want to look around."

"Yeah, I knew you would, professor."

Chapter Fifteen

Madeline had seen the videos, the photos, and especially the kiss. Having run into Kim-Jack's father and stepmother in a shoe store where the senior Donaldson was trying on sandals, she sat down next to him and shared the video. Neither of them was shaken by the kiss after watching it several times. Ossie, Kim-Jack's father, had kissed plenty of strange women in his time. He was more concerned with his son's injuries and insisted that a trip to the Emergency Room was in order. Urged by Trisha to heed her husband's recommendation, the group got into a rideshare van and made tracks for the nearest hospital.

Ten stitches, far more anesthesia than was required, a mound of bandages that turned Kim-Jack's hand into a club, and an hour and half later, the group was on the way to the airport. The ER doctor told Madeline that her husband could remove most of the bandages in forty-eight hours. Madeline informed the doctor that Kim-Jack wasn't her husband yet and that they were on their way to Antarctica to get married.

"Antarctica?" The doctor ran his hands through his gray hair. "What's wrong with the beach here in Miami? Lots of nice places for a wedding. Beautiful sunrises from the beach."

Madeline shook her head. "Lots of places that lots of regular folks have already used for their vows. We want something unique."

"Well, Antarctica is certainly unique, but have you considered some place *really* unique?" The doctor smiled. "I got married the first time in the Galapagos surrounded by iguanas and sea lions. You should see the pictures."

"Interesting, but my best friend was married there two years ago. She said the smell from the animals was so off-putting that she vomited and they ended up holding the ceremony on the ship instead."

The doctor was not going to be outdone. "My second wife was a skydiver."

Madeline held up her hand. "My cousin was married in midair with a group of twelve other couples and a priest, who performed the mass wedding ceremony on the way down."

"Well, enjoy Antarctica." Walking toward the door of the exam room, he turned and scratched his head. "Where are you going to find a priest?"

"We brought one." Madeline grinned. "And a rabbi."

By the time they arrived at the airport, the balance of the wedding guests had arrived. Larry ushered their group into the private lounge in the executive terminal and stood behind a podium. Holding his hands in the air, he called for silence and welcomed everyone.

"From near and far, you have all come to witness the marriage of my daughter to Kim-Jack Donaldson. Our expedition to Antarctica begins in forty-eight hours and I'm as thrilled to be going to the seventh continent as I am to see my daughter finally become a wife."

The applause was loud and enthusiastic. Larry gave the crowd a few moments to cheer, and then silenced them so he could continue.

"At noon on December thirty-first, Rabbi Horowitz and Father Gustafson will perform a joint ceremony on the actual land that makes up Antarctica. Following the ceremony, the crew from our ship will arrange a polar plunge where the newlyweds and the bridal party will jump into the crystal-clear Antarctic Ocean."

Kim-Jack grabbed Madeline with his undamaged hand.

"What the hell is he talking about?"

"We're going to jump in the Antarctic Ocean." Madeline laughed. "I'm going to total the wedding dress, but just think about the photos!"

"You're insane." Kim-Jack stood up from his front-row seat. "We'll freeze to death. This is going to be the shortest marriage in history. Good thing all these people will be there for our funeral."

She pulled him back down.

"Relax. You'll be in the water less than five seconds. They tie a rope around your waist and haul you out before you have a chance to freeze." Shaking her head, Madeline pointed at his father and stepmother. "Ossie and Trisha are going to take the plunge in the nude."

A buffet dinner was served shortly after Larry's remarks. Tito parked himself in front of a platter of meatballs and consumed most of them while the other guests stepped around him. Dressed in khakis, a silk shirt, and Italian loafers, Marcus was exploring foods that he couldn't pronounce.

Kim-Jack had corralled his future father-in-law before the man had a chance to grab a plate and was holding him hostage in a corner of the room.

"I can't swim and I'm scared to death of cold water."

Larry put his hands on Kim-Jack's shoulders. "You don't have to swim and you'll be out of the water before your testicles freeze." He smiled. "I'm not going to take a chance damaging your ability to provide me with grandchildren."

Glancing over at Tito, Kim-Jack tried a different approach. "There's no way that Tito is going in the water. He isn't going to trust a rope to save his fat ass from freezing. And my father has a heart problem. The shock of the cold water could kill him." He shrugged. "Do you want to be responsible for two deaths on your daughter's wedding night?"

"I spoke to Tito earlier."

"Oh?"

The wealthy real estate mogul smiled. "You'd be amazed how quickly a thousand dollars can change a person's outlook on life. And if you want to throw heart problems on the table, remember what I just went through." Larry reached for his wineglass. "If I can do it, anyone can."

Neither of them had seen Marcus wander over.

"Yo, professor, cold water ain't no big thing. The last time I had a hot shower I was still in diapers and hadn't left the hospital." He grinned. "You ain't gonna stay hard like in a hot shower, if that's what you're thinkin'. That much I can guarantee, but you ain't gonna die neither."

Kim-Jack frowned. "Thanks for your vote of confidence."

With a wink to Marcus, Larry Kloppleman slipped away, waving at a group of people at the opposite end of the buffet.

"If I'm going in the water, then so are you, Marcus." Kim-Jack sneered. "Consider it a pass fail situation that will affect your final grade."

"Bullshit." Dropping his half-empty plate of food on a nearby table, Marcus jammed his hands into his hips. "You can't do that, professor. This ain't school. Plus, it's still vacation until January fifth."

"Education isn't limited to the four walls of a classroom." Kim-Jack held his arms outstretched. "The whole world is a classroom, Marcus. From the day you're born until your last breath, you will learn about life every time you step outside your house."

Marcus stood in front of Kim-Jack in silence for a few uncomfortable moments before turning to walk away. He stopped after a few paces and spun on his heel.

"If I do this thing, I want an A for the year."

Kim-Jack closed his eyes for a moment. "How about I guarantee that you won't fail my class?"

"How about a B then?"

"I'm not going to bargain with you, Marcus. You started this expedition with a passing grade. Where you go from there is up to you."

"You drive a hard bargain, professor."

Kim-Jack raised his eyebrows. "So, you're accepting the challenge?"

Marcus walked back over to him. "You do it first."

"Deal." Holding out his hand, Kim-Jack shook his head slowly. "What could possibly be next?"

What came next was a flight that Kim-Jack would always refer to as "his first taste of excessive luxury." Larry Kloppleman always traveled in style. First-class was the low end of the spectrum where he was concerned. As someone who traveled over a million miles a year, Larry insisted on the best and nothing less. Bestowing that luxury on his daughter and her future husband was a requirement that he accepted with pride.

Boeing's 787 Dreamliner was designed to have forty-four fully reclining first-class seats that they called "pods." The actual seat slid down to become a bed, making a long flight much more enjoyable and less stressful for the frequent flyer. Larry was able to convince the company to configure a Dreamliner with one-hundred and twenty of the luxurious pods to accommodate his entire wedding party and their guests. The nine-hour-flight Kim-Jack had been dreading had been transformed into a good night's rest with a gourmet breakfast when he awoke.

Madeline had other plans.

Five hours into the flight, when everyone else was snoring, she came around to Kim-Jack's pod and pressed the button to raise him into a sitting position. Coming out of a dream, with an erection, Madeline's hand covered his mouth as he realized what she wanted.

"Shush. Not a word."

Kim-Jack had changed into sweats for the flight with nothing underneath. Madeline had removed her panties hours ago. Climbing onto him, the thought of joining the Mile High Club had prepared her for effortless penetration. She took him deep inside and began rocking back and forth while holding onto his shoulders.

Even though it was not the best sex they'd ever had, Kim-Jack was turned on by the sheer danger of discovery at thirty-five-thousand feet. For the briefest moment, he wondered why they didn't go into the bathroom for sex, and then realized it was probably too small.

Now, fully awake, they synchronized their motion. Reaching under her t-shirt, Kim-Jack smiled. Madeline was braless. She loved when he played with her nipples, it was the last element she needed for an orgasm.

Well, not exactly the final one.

Within a few seconds of his fingers squeezing her nipples, Madeline began to hum "*My Way*." Kim-Jack tried to stop her, but his mind was locked onto *his* approaching orgasm, and the rest of the world had become background noise.

Madeline's voice became a soft whisper, and then loud enough to draw his attention. But it was too late to stop. She was only a few moments away from the peak of pleasure, singing loud enough to bring two flight attendants running down the aisle.

They were too late. However, Kim-Jack and Madeline were on time. He howled. She screamed out the song. Around them, dozens of passengers awakened and turned on their overhead reading lights to see what had happened.

Larry Kloppleman ran down the aisle on the wrong side of the plane and climbed over from Madeline's pod, landing on top of Kim-Jack, who was doing his best to pull his sweatpants over his glistening erection. He missed his future son-in-law's face but brought his knees down, squarely on Kim-Jack's abdomen.

By this time, Madeline had scrambled down the aisle and back to her pod. She also yanked on her sweatpants and grabbed her bra from the floor, running for the bathroom as the rest of the nearby passengers awoke and turned on their reading lamps. Coming out of the bathroom, still in the afterglow of sex, she didn't realize that the t-shirt was inside out and backwards.

Doing her best to maintain an air of dignity, Madeline walked back to her seat, smiling at each of the people she passed, and ducked under the covers in her pod. Moments later, her father pulled back the thin blanket and looked down at his daughter.

"You couldn't wait until we got to the hotel in Ushuaia?"

Madeline shrugged. "It's so rare that KJ and I fly together. I didn't want to miss an opportunity."

"You're impossible."

Another shrug.

Just then, Trisha walked over to them and offered Madeline a high-five. "Welcome to the club."

Madeline looked at her father for a moment with a grin on her face before she accepted the gesture.

Leaning close to Larry, Trisha whispered, "You and Cassidy are in the first two pods. You should do it. Nobody cares."

"I care." Larry shook his head. "The Governor is six rows back. Two senators are behind him."

Trisha laughed. "The Governor is a closet nudist. He goes to Jamaica, but not the same resort as us. I've seen the pictures on Facebook. You can't see his face, but the man has a distinctive scar on his ass. We've seen it. And those two senators have probably screwed their office staff in parts of the Capitol that are off-limits to the public for just that reason." She smiled. "Face it, Larry, sex is everywhere. Even in a fancy jet on its way to Antarctica."

A faithful advocate of the natural life and creative lovemaking, Trisha was talking loud enough that everyone heard her admonish Larry Kloppleman. Several of the passengers cheered. Almost all of them applauded. From her seat, Madeline raised her clasped hands over her head in victory.

On the other side of the plane, Kim-Jack slid under the pair of blankets he'd requested before takeoff and pulled them over his head. His erection was gone, probably never to return. Marcus, in the pod across from him had been videotaping the entire tryst.

Just as the reading lamps were extinguished, his student leaned over and winked. "Do we need to discuss my final grade again, professor?"

They landed in Ushuaia four hours later. Kim-Jack was unable to get back to his dream even though he always fell into a deep sleep after sex. Madeline spent the time talking with Trisha about nude beaches and who had a better voice: Sinatra or Nat King Cole. The rest of the passengers also slept until the lights came on for breakfast. No one mentioned the incident they'd witnessed out loud, but while they were in line for Customs and

Immigration at the airport, it was the topic of whispered conversation.

With their passports stamped and their luggage stuffed into the cargo holds of three large tour busses, the group left the airport, heading to the newest hotel in the city at the bottom of the Earth for an overnight. In the morning, they would take those same busses down to the port and board their ship to begin the Antarctic expedition. However, before that, Larry had arranged a massive feast at the city's most popular restaurant.

King crab was a New England delicacy that most of the group rarely enjoyed. The supply each season was more limited than the year before. Overfishing and climate change had reduced the northern hemisphere's haul to a trickle. Crossing the equator, the southern part of the planet had few places that the tasty crustaceans called home. However, the tip of South America was one of their favorite breeding grounds, and every restaurant in the tiny city featured them during crab season.

El Viejo Marino, the Old Marine, was the most famous of the king crab restaurants in Ushuaia. Travelers who passed through the city on their way to Antarctica made reservations months in advance for a table during the king crab season. Locals couldn't afford to eat there and without a reservation, neither could anyone else.

Larry had booked the place less than a month ago by offering the manager twice the price shown on the menu for everything his group would order. He made certain that the manager knew they were coming for king crab and that he would give the man a hefty tip if everyone left there stuffed with crabmeat.

What Larry hadn't foreseen was someone with Tito's appetite. Of course, Tito aside, he also didn't figure Marcus into his plans. Having lived on the bare minimum of food to sustain life for most of his fifteen years, the boy was making up for lost meals with a vengeance. He'd managed to sweet talk a flight attendant into bringing him three breakfasts. While most of the passengers slept, prior to the sex show, Marcus was making the rounds of the four galleys onboard the giant aircraft, sampling the snacks. By the time they landed, the khakis he'd purchased in Miami were tight and he no longer needed a belt to keep them snuggly wrapped around his waist.

Seated in the restaurant, a team of servers brought out a platter of king crab legs for each table along with a gravy boat filled with melted butter. Never having tasted crab legs before, Marcus was leery about the strange-looking shellfish until his first bite. Looking over at Tito, seated opposite him in the El Viejo Marino, Marcus cocked his head to the side.

"You like this shit?"

Tito nodded with a mouth full of crab. "Mmmm."

"They's okay, not as good as shrimp." He took another bite.

"Dip it in the butter." Tito pushed the gravy boat closer to him.

Marcus did as instructed. "Now, all I taste is the butter." He swallowed and pointed at Tito. "I'll bet I can eat more of them than you." Standing, Marcus repeated the challenge to the entire group. "I'll bet there's no one in this restaurant who can eat more than three of these bad boys."

Kim-Jack frowned. "Three whole crabs? That's eighteen legs. Nobody can eat that much crab."

Tito swallowed. "I can eat three, maybe four."

"Yeah?" Marcus leaned over and rested his knuckles on the table. "I tell you what, Professor Czerwinski, I bet you a hundred dollars that I can eat four. Shit, two dozen of those skinny little legs? I can do that shit with one hand tied behind my back."

Kim-Jack shook his head. "Where are you going to get a hundred dollars, Marcus?"

Cassidy stood and opened her purse. "I'll cover that bet."

Looking over at Kim-Jack, Tito held out his hands. "I don't have a hundred dollars. Just a credit card."

Trisha pulled her wallet from her back pocket and gave him a Franklin. "Now you do."

With that, wedding guests strolled over and placed hundreds and twenties in front of Kim-Jack, assuming him to be the dealer in this challenge. Before long, nearly five-thousand dollars had been wagered on the outcome of the contest. Even the senior Kloppleman was in for a hundred. However, he was the only bettor to put his money on Marcus Tigue.

Madeline, who spoke more Spanish than most of the group, explained the contest to the restaurant's manager. There was some back and forth about not having enough king crab for the coming weekend, but when Larry Kloppleman opened his wallet that concern vanished.

Everyone else had finished their meals and were now crowded in a semi-circle around a table that had Marcus on one side and Tito on the other. A couple of servers came out of the kitchen, each with a king crab dinner on a sterling silver platter. They laid the enormous plates in front of the contestants and hurried back to the kitchen for more crab.

"You don't have to eat the fries or corn on the cob." Kim-Jack held up an ear and took a bite out of it. "Same goes for the body of the crab, but you must eat all the meat out of each of the six legs for that crab to count." He looked at Tito and then at Marcus. "You both understand the rules?"

Marcus nodded. "Got it, professor."

Tito shook his head. "Enough bullshit, let's eat."

The big man had a distinct advantage. Not so much because of his size, but he'd eaten crab legs for years and knew exactly how to break them open so that every tender morsel of meat could be accessed. Trisha asked the group if it was okay for her to show the boy how to crack a crab leg. The consensus was yes.

Tito finished his six crab legs first, but eating quickly was not part of the challenge. Sucking the last tiny chunks of crabmeat from his sixth leg a minute later, Marcus held it up and received a round of applause. The next crab dinners came out moments later and both eaters dug in, emptying the legs mere seconds apart.

They plowed through their next crab in record time. A dozen legs each so far. Kim-Jack figured it was at least eight pounds of meat and wondered if some professional eater had already set the bar. Madeline searched the web on her phone and was unable to find a world record. Several of the guests had been shooting video. She told them they were witnessing history.

The manager came over and explained to Larry in broken English that he'd never seen crab legs eaten so quickly and wanted some photos for the restaurant's social media pages. One of the servers produced a camera and instructed the two eaters to pose with crab legs in their hands and then chunks of meat going into their mouths. Tito filled his mouth with food and then held it open, making a roaring sound from deep in his throat.

As fast as the servers could bring their food from the kitchen, Tito and Marcus ripped it apart. The chef shouted that he needed more time. His pots had to be refilled and the water brought to a boil. Brazenly, Tito ate the ear of corn. Marcus shoved a handful of fries into his mouth while they waited.

The fourth crab dinner for each contestant came out and they attacked them, albeit somewhat slower and with less gusto than their earlier pace. They both finished. Marcus first and with a happier expression than his opponent.

"We both ate four crabs." He shrugged. "Now what?"

"We need a tie breaker." Dropping the last empty leg shell onto the platter, Tito looked up at the manager. "One more dinner each."

The man shook his head. "We only have one crab left. I'll get more in the morning when the fishermen return from the sea, but you've eaten all that we had except for the old big one in the tank."

Kim-Jack turned around and stared in awe at the largest king crab he'd seen them eat so far. "Oh, my god. That thing's a monster. It's easily as big as two of the crabs you've been eating."

Marcus burped. "No problem, professor. We'll split the last one in half. Unless the big man's bowin' out."

"Not a chance, junior." Taking a long, deep breath, Tito nodded once and asked for a glass of ginger ale to settle his heaving stomach.

Coming out of the kitchen, the chef walked over to the tank and lifted the massive crustacean out of the tank with tongs and a steel mesh glove. He showed the beast to the crowd, nodded once, and disappeared into the kitchen.

Seven minutes later, two servers carried the cooked monster from the kitchen and placed it between the two combatants. The chef had split the crab evenly down the middle and garnished it with parsley. Tito grabbed what appeared to be the smaller of the two pieces and dropped it on his plate. Marcus took the larger one and immediately ripped off a leg and cracked it open. He finished the first leg and repeated the process with the second one while Tito was still struggling with his first leg.

"You turnin' green, Professor Czerwinski." Marcus laughed. "All that fat and you can't find room for a tiny, little crab leg?"

"Kiss my ass, Marcus." Cracking another leg, Tito pulled out the meat and ate half of it before he passed out.

He was only out for a few minutes, but when Tito came to, he was on the floor of the restaurant with the other diners crowded around him. Marcus was kneeling alongside with his hand on Tito's forehead.

"Somebody was takin' bets that you were dead, Professor Czerwinski."

Tito grabbed a chair and pulled himself into a sitting position.

"Did you eat the third leg?"

Marcus shook his head. "I was waiting to see what you were gonna do." He shrugged. "I guess we know."

Rolling over on his side, Tito moaned. "I think I'm gonna be sick."

Kim-Jack grabbed one of his friend's arms and told the man standing across from him to get the other.

"Let's get him into the bathroom."

With their help, Tito got to his feet. He was unsteady for a moment and grabbed the table.

"I'm okay."

"Are you sure?" Holding him by the elbow, Kim-Jack guided Tito into a chair. "I'm sure if it was pizza, you would have won."

Marcus came around the other side and held out his hand. "Too bad you ain't my teacher. I've already got an A for the year from Professor Donaldson. This could have been a double A or maybe even a triple."

Tito belched and looked up at him, frowning. "This isn't over, son. In fact, it's just getting started."

Chapter Sixteen

According to the printed schedule that Larry handed out as the weary travelers clomped into the hotel after dinner, everyone was to attend an expedition briefing in the hotel's Orca lounge at eight o'clock Sunday morning. A mixture of grumblings and sighs tumbled from their mouths, however, of the one-hundred-and-twenty guests all but two were either on time or half an hour early for the mandatory lecture the following day.

Marcus strolled in, holding his stomach, at five minutes past the hour. Tito stumbled through the door, taking the last available seat ten minutes later. Fortunately for both of them, the expedition's team leader was having trouble with her slide projector, and the actual briefing started at twenty after eight.

Wearing thick, black utility shoes that gave her an additional inch, the woman hit five feet. While she had considerable girth, it was easy to see that she could punch a hole in a sheet of plywood or carry any one of them to safety if the need arose. She introduced herself as Gwendolyn McMartin in an accent that was a hybrid between Irish and Dutch.

"Good morningk, good morningk. Let me welcome you to the bottom of the world."

Kim-Jack whispered in Madeline's ear, "Where did your father say she was from?"

"Brooklyn, New York, but she's been living here for most of the last seventeen years."

"That's an Argentinean accent?"

Madeline shushed him and sat forward in her chair.

Gwen, as she preferred to be called, spoke for thirty minutes about the ship, Antarctica, and the wildlife they expected to see. She went into detail with regard to the Drake Passage, saying that there were two possibilities: the Drake Shake or the Drake Lake.

"Twenty and thirty-foot swells are possible, or it will be no worse than a windy day on a lake. From the weather forecast I received ten minutes ago, it looks like we're going to be in for some rough seas, but we're quite well prepared for it." She smiled. "For those of you who favor rollercoasters, this will be a treat."

With mumbles of fear and concern from the group, Gwen shifted gears and showed the group dozens of slides that elicited oos and ahs. Brilliant blue icebergs, smiling seals, and wobbly penguins tamped down concern over the crossing. She brought up a map of their journey and then showed slides of each base they would visit with waving scientists and happy sled dogs that appeared to be eagerly waiting for visitors.

For her closing act, she introduced the ship's doctor, a Philippine native who was able to smile with all his teeth showing and speak at the same time. Of course, no one understood a word he said, but his nurse took over and explained that seasickness pills would be available after the meeting and around the clock once they set sail.

"Don't be a hero. Everyone gets seasick. The pills are free, they don't have any long-term side effects, and they will keep you from turning green." Her last comment brought a few laughs, but the vibe in the room was less enthusiastic than it was an hour ago.

The ship's first officer, a stalwart blond well over six feet tall with a dimpled chin and blue eyes that seemed to glow, was the next speaker. He also welcomed everyone and then proceeded with a fresh set of slides and a safety briefing. The photos ranged from calm to crisis, detailing every possible scenario for calamity at sea. When he finished, to the silence of a stunned audience, he asked if there were any questions.

Getting up from his seat in the back, Marcus raised his hand.

"I just want to make sure this boat–"

"Ship." The officer smiled. "You can put a boat on a ship, but you can't put a ship on a boat."

Some scattered laughter came from the crowd, but Marcus squinted at the man and shook his head.

"Whatever that means. Anyhow, boss, with all those icebergs floatin' around, I just want to be sure this ship ain't been built by the same folks that built the Titanic."

The rolling guffaws, slapping thighs, followed by hacking coughs from the smokers was finally brought under control by the first officer, who had to wipe away his laughter tears.

"No, sir. The Queen of the Wind was designed and built in Japan. She's been afloat for six years and in service for Antarctic expeditions for five of those six."

"Made in Japan?" Marcus rubbed his stomach and covered his mouth while he burped. "What do the Japanese know about icebergs?"

More laughter from the audience and a smile from the officer.

"We'll be visiting a Japanese base as part of your expedition. I'm certain they'll be glad to discuss shipbuilding with you." He folded the pad with his notes and looked over at Gwen. "That concludes our briefing. The busses will be here at ten. Please finish packing and we'll meet in the lobby at nine-forty-five."

Marcus walked over to Kim-Jack as everyone was filing out. He waited while his teacher discussed the Citizen Scientist program Gwen had introduced with the ship's science officer. Shaking hands with the officer, Kim-Jack turned around and bumped into his student.

"Yo, professor."

"Marcus, how's your gut this morning?"

"Anybody put a crab leg in front of me gonna get that thing stuck in their eye."

Kim-Jack nodded. "I'll keep that in mind. What's up?"

"Up until a few minutes ago, I thought this whole thing was bogus. I didn't really think we was going to get on a ship and float around some big ass icebergs. And that Drake Passage shit? Are these people nuts? How many ships sunk? Man, I don't know if I'm up for this shit, professor."

"So, you're scared?"

"Whoa, Captain Obvious has arrived." Marcus blew out a sharp breath. "Man, I'm shittin' bricks and it got nothin' to do with all them crab legs."

Kim-Jack put his arm around the boy's shoulders and led him over to the floor-to-ceiling windows that overlooked the harbor.

"Do you see that gleaming blue and white ship down there?"

"That's the Queen?"

"Look at the size of that ship compared to every other ship near it." Kim-Jack spread his arms apart. "This is the Queen." He brought them together. "And this is the next largest ship."

Marcus nodded. "It's bigger."

"Now who's Captain Obvious?"

By one o'clock in the afternoon, everyone was onboard. The luggage had made its way to the correct staterooms. Four passengers had locked themselves out of their rooms and needed help finding their keycards. And both Tito and Marcus had already run out of toilet paper.

It was time for the mandatory lifeboat drill.

One of the perks the wedding guests received was a waterproof red parka with a hood and silver stripe running down the back. The lifeboat drill required all passengers to attend wearing the parka, a life vest, and boots. As part of the boarding process, each passenger selected a pair of heavy rubber boots to be worn while transiting from the ship to the shore. Gwen explained that the crew took sanitation seriously and that the boots would be washed with disinfectant every time they left and returned to the ship.

Nearly half the guests had to exchange their boots for a proper fit after walking from their cabins to the appropriate lifeboat station. By the time they had been properly outfitted, not only would the ship have sunk, but it would have taken all twenty-four empty lifeboats to the bottom of the Antarctic Ocean as well.

Kim-Jack wondered if there was any real purpose to the drill, but kept his musings to himself. To him, one-hundred-and-twenty people, all dressed in identical red coats with red hoods, resembled a collection of fire hydrants. Standing at the rear of his group at the lifeboat station, he dug into his pocket and pulled out his cellphone. This was certainly a Kodak moment.

Several of the passengers had yachting experience and knew how to properly don the life vest. Most of the others either had it on backwards or upside down. One woman had simply tied the straps around her waist. As they would be wearing a life vest every time they left the ship, the crew took extra care to see that their charges would survive.

Walking back to their stateroom, after the drill had ended, Madeline stopped in the middle of the corridor and turned to face her future husband. Seconds after the all clear was sounded, she'd stripped off the life vest, unzipped the heavy parka, and yanked her feet out of the boots.

"If this ship sinks, we're never going to make it on to those lifeboats with all this clothing. They're going to have to give us twenty minutes notice to get dressed if they want to have an emergency." She dropped one of the boots and bent over to pick it up. "And why do we have to wear these stupid boots? What's wrong with the ones we brought with us? Do they think we've never walked around in snow?"

Kim-Jack leaned against the wall and opened his zipper a few more inches. He'd watched the Kloppleman's accountant, a veteran yachtsman, put on the life vest and was still wearing it.

"Did you listen to the safety briefing this morning? You were sitting right next to me."

"That woman's accent was so irritating that I put in my earbuds." Madeline sighed. "I'm falling in love with Frankie Valli's voice."

"Who is Frankie Valli, and should I be concerned?"

Madeline dropped the boots and punched him in the shoulder. "Lead singer of an amazing vocal group from the sixties.

He perfected the falsetto. Sang like a bird. I'll play you some of his music when we get in bed tonight."

"Instead of Sinatra?"

She kissed him and retrieved the boots. "I already have a tune in mind."

The ship sailed at four o'clock Sunday afternoon, blowing its horns several times as a phalanx of tugs guided it out of the harbor. A few clouds spotted the sky, but the sun was in charge. Most of the guests were on deck, waving at locals who lived close enough to the seventh continent but would never have the cash to make the journey. Few of them waved back. The tourists were leaving and the economic bell curve was headed south along with their credit cards.

Kim-Jack found his father and stepmother on the forward deck, sipping champagne. Grabbing a flute of the cold beverage for himself and one for Madeline, who was still unpacking, he leaned next to his father on the rail.

"It's a good thing we have one of the owner's suites."

"The king size bed is a real treat on ship." His father took a gulp of bubbly and sighed. "Trisha and I took an au natural cruise to a bunch of ports in the Caribbean last summer. Most of the passengers were having too much fun to get off the ship. But our cabin was one of the smallest and we couldn't wait to go ashore." He looked around for a moment. "Where's Maddy?"

"Please, dad, she can't stand that nickname."

"Pardon me." Ossie tilted his head back and held the tip of his nose. "Where's Princess Madeline?"

Kim-Jack shook his head. "Still putting clothes away."

"How much crap did she bring?"

"Four suitcases." Jamming his tongue into his cheek, Kim-Jack shrugged. "Nine days means a lot of clothing changes if you're style minded like her."

"There isn't gonna be a whole lot of style once the weather changes."

"That's what I told her."

Sipping the champagne so that he would have enough for a toast once Madeline arrived, Kim-Jack turned his attention to the pilot ship that was cruising alongside. Just after the lifeboat drill, he'd watched a man jump from the tiny ship to the Queen. Not having had much cruising experience, he asked one of the officers if it was a late passenger. A member of the crew laughed and explained that the pilot was required to get the ship out of the harbor and safely into deep water.

"The Captain can't find his way?"

The crewman shook his head. "The pilot can do it blindfolded. The Captain rarely takes the chance."

Trisha walked over with a refill for Ossie and a plate of crackers covered with an orange paste. "Where have you been?"

Kim-Jack shrugged. "Unpacking. How'd you guys get up here so fast?"

"One suitcase between us." She smiled. "Don't worry, we'll be naked in our stateroom, but dressed on deck."

"What's on the crackers?" Ossie took one off the plate and ate it before Trisha could answer. "Yuck. Salmon goop." He spit the cracker into a napkin and washed the taste away with champagne.

Trisha ate the two remaining crackers and swallowed them with the flute of champagne she'd brought over for her husband. A server with a platter of food spiked with toothpicks walked past and she grabbed several of the treats without asking what they contained. "This also tastes like fish." She offered one to Kim-Jack. "Try it."

He bit off a small piece and immediately spit it out. "Sardines. Ewww."

Searching for something more edible, Kim-Jack spotted Marcus on the opposite side of the deck with a serving platter balanced on the rail. Walking over, he smiled. The boy had taken a full tray of little hot dogs and mustard from one of the servers and was consuming them at a pace that could earn him a spot at Nathan's on the Fourth of July.

"I thought you weren't hungry."

"Man, if I'm breathin', I'm hungry."

"You gonna share those?"

Marcus nodded. "Only with family." He stabbed a hot dog with a toothpick and handed it to Kim-Jack. "We cousins now, professor."

A musical fanfare suddenly blasted from speakers set up on the deck. From a door behind them, came a procession of officers and crew. They formed a semicircle at the bow of the ship as the servers and food disappeared. With the crew assembled, Gwen walked to the middle of the group and introduced the ship's captain, who marched out to a crescendo in the music. Madeline was holding his arm, dressed in a formal gown and heels.

"Fellow explorers raise your glasses in toast and welcome Captain Benjamin Columbus."

Kim-Jack laughed so hard that he nearly passed the champagne through his nose. Leaning over toward his father, he whispered, "Looks like a chip off the old block."

Trisha whistled. "I'd love to see what's under that uniform."

The Captain signaled for quiet. "Ladies and gentlemen, welcome aboard the Queen of the Wind and to the start of the wedding between Madeline Kloppleman and Kim-Jack Donaldson." He motioned to Kim-Jack to join them. "Four days from now, on December thirty-first, we will gather for the ceremony that will unite these two lovers. It will also be the day you will step onto the continent of Antarctica for the first time."

A cheer went up from the crowd.

"However, today is the beginning of the most amazing journey you will ever take, and we honor those who came before us and opened the way. We are most fortunate to have Rabbi Horowitz, who has known Madeline since her birth, here today to lead us in prayer as we begin the expedition of a lifetime."

Stepping forward, the rabbi took the microphone from Captain Columbus and sang the benediction. Not having prepared for the impromptu blessing, he adlibbed with chunks of the prayer for the deceased. Those familiar with the prayer, chuckled and sang along with him. Next, he blessed the champagne and took a drink, handing the glass first to Madeline and then to Kim-Jack.

"This is truly a wonderful night. The seas are calm. Birds are escorting us with their songs and in a few days, we will have a party that you will remember forever. We are traveling to one of God's last unspoiled landscapes to celebrate the most sacred of vows. Raise your glasses and toast with me." He took another drink and then said, "L'chaim!"

Father Gustafson stood from his front-row seat and added, "Amen."

The cocktail party wrapped up soon after, and the guests made their way to the Gentoo dining room, named after one of the penguin species they were soon to encounter. For their first dinner onboard, Larry had insisted on place cards with each guest's name. They would sit in the same configuration for the wedding reception and it had been Cassidy's recommendation that they try out the table assignments for dinner rather than do it for the first time after the ceremony.

"There will always be people who don't want to sit next to someone else. Let's get those conflicts resolved before the actual reception."

The head table was reserved for the immediate families. An extra chair had been added for Marcus, who unwrapped a fresh suit for the occasion. Seated between the two fathers, he did his best to join the conversations, but none of it concerned him, and most of it was beyond his comprehension.

Until they started talking about the schedule.

"Can I ask a question?" He looked at Larry with raised eyebrows.

"Of course."

"New Year's Eve is at midnight. Wouldn't it be more special to get married on New Years Eve than during the day?"

Larry nodded. "Yes it would be, but then you have to consider the tax implications."

"Taxes? There's a wedding tax?"

Laughing, the wealthy realtor shook his head. "As far as the IRS is concerned, if you get married on the last second of the last day of the year, you're considered to be married for the entire year in terms of tax benefits."

"I don't pay taxes."

"Not yet, but you will some day."

"Nah, I don't think so. Why would I give away my money?"

Ossie leaned in. "If you don't pay your taxes, the government will come in and take them anyhow."

Larry added, "And hit you with penalties and interest."

"What I get back for givin' them my money?"

"A safe place to live." Ossie sighed. "And a few bucks leftover for food."

Marcus shook his head. "That's bullshit, man. I got a nice place where to live and I pay rent. Government didn't give me that shit, I earned it."

Larry cocked his head. "You're fifteen-years-old, how did you earn enough money to pay rent and buy food?"

Stepping in before the boy could open a can of worms, Kim-Jack cut him off. "Perhaps this is a discussion for another time and place."

"Yeah." Marcus looked over at Kim-Jack and nodded. "What he said."

Lifting his wineglass, Ossie shifted gears. "A toast to the future Madeline Donaldson and her husband-to-be, my one and only child, Kim-Jack."

A round of cheers came from the nearby tables as their first course was served. It would be the last food most of them would eat for the next thirty-six hours.

Chapter Seventeen

The sea grew angry several hours after everyone except the bridge crew, Gwen, and the night staff had gone to bed. Kim-Jack got up to pee and the floor came up to meet him before he was able to stand. Making his way into the bathroom, he held onto the doorknob. A sudden drop caused the door to slam on his damaged thumb and he screamed loud enough to wake Madeline from a deep sleep.

She rolled out of bed and crashed into the floor as the ship tossed in the heavy sea. Crawling over to him, Madeline was able to reach up and turn on the bathroom light.

"What the hell is going on? Are we sinking?"

"I think this is the Drake Shake." Kim-Jack pulled himself over to the sink and turned on the cold water, shoving his thumb underneath to squelch the pain.

Madeline was able to get into a sitting position outside the bathroom and stared out the balcony windows, trying to see the waves.

"I can't see shit from here." She crawled along the floor until she reached the balcony door. "I think I can see–"

She bit her tongue as the ship jumped out of a twenty-foot swell.

"Ow! God dammit."

Kim-Jack was within a few seconds of peeing on himself, but managed to get close enough to the toilet to drop onto the seat. Holding onto the toilet with one hand and the sink with another, he was able to empty his bladder without making a mess on the floor, but the toilet paper popped out of the roll before he could tear off a sheet.

The only way to get back into bed was to crawl the way Madeline did, but a lull in the waves gave him false hope that the crisis had ended. He was only a few steps away from reaching his goal when a huge swell rocked the ship to one side and he fell, face first, onto the carpeted floor. Creeping along the floor in the dark,

Kim-Jack touched the blanket and pulled himself onto the bed. No sooner did he get horizontal when the ship pitched violently to the right and he rolled over to Madeline's side and onto the floor.

Madeline had finally crept back to the bed. She was about to drag herself onto it when Kim-Jack collided with her. They held each other for several minutes, hoping that the bouncing would either soften or stop, but it only got worse.

"My stomach is sending me evil signals."

Kim-Jack nodded and took a deep breath. "When did you take a seasickness pill?"

"Hours ago, but I don't think it's working." Madeline burped. "I'm gonna puke."

"Can you get to the bathroom?"

"No. But there's a small trashcan by the desk."

Rolling onto his back, Kim-Jack crab-walked over to the desk and kicked the empty can in her direction. From there, he crossed the cabin to the bathroom and pulled a towel off the rod in front of the sink. Crawling from the bathroom to the bed, he tossed the towel over to the other side before turning on the desk lamp closest to the bed.

The room was a shambles. Everything that wasn't tied down was on the floor. The extra pillows they'd thrown off the bed and onto a nearby chair were scattered in front of it. Thanks to a chain holding the chair in place, it was still upright, but the luggage that Kim-Jack had stored in the closet had rolled out and toppled over.

"What happened to the wineglasses that were on the desk?"

Madeline held up one of them. "I've got the empty glass, but yours still had some wine in it. I think it spilled and the glass is wedged between the desk and wall."

The ship listed to the right and dropped several feet. Kim-Jack jumped onto the bed as it came back up and reached across for his fiancée's hand. They touched fingers, but Madeline pulled her hand away and grabbed the trashcan to catch what her digestive system was rejecting.

"You should take another pill."

"And immediately puke it back up?" Madeline shook her head. "Got any other stupid ideas?"

"Yeah. I'll crush it and mix the pill with water."

"Oh, that'll work." She held up the trashcan. "Most of what I'm puking is water at this point."

There was a knock at the door and Kim-Jack slid off the bed and grabbed the wall of the open closet for support. Working his way around the corner, he switched his grip for the bathroom door, and finally made it to the door to their stateroom.

Dragging the heavy door open against the rocking and rolling of the ship, he reached out and grabbed the hand that was about to knock again. Tito fell into the room, taking Kim-Jack to the floor with his massive bulk. The two men struggled to unwind themselves. Tito managed to grab the closet wall and pulled himself inside, bracing his legs on either side of the doorframe.

"I couldn't sleep and I was walking the hallways. I heard you two shouting and knew that you were awake."

"We could have been having sex." Madeline slid the trashcan under the desk, but kept it within arm's reach.

Tito pointed at the waves that were cresting over their balcony. "With that shit going on? You'd have to be acrobats."

"Are you feeling okay?" Hoisting himself onto the bed, Kim-Jack braced his legs against the nearest wall and held onto the mattress. "Madeline's puking her guts out."

Reaching into his pocket, Tito pulled out a joint and a lighter. "You can trust big pharma if you want, but I'm going to put my faith in the natural herb."

Kim-Jack pointed at the smoke detector in the ceiling. "What about that?"

Yanking a plastic bag from another pocket, he wrapped it around the smoke detector and tied the bag in place with a shoestring that he'd removed from his sneakers.

"Ziploc bags. Never leave home without them."

Making his way to the bathroom on his hands and knees, Tito stood up just long enough to turn on the powerful exhaust fan. Satisfied that the smoke from his prerolled was not going to be a problem, he lit it, took a hit, and handed the joint across the bed to Madeline.

Kim-Jack had never seen his fiancée smoke pot. Even when he barbecued, she stayed upwind rather than inhale smoke that would foul her singing ability. However, Madeline claimed to have a past that she was waiting to reveal...after they were married. Taking a long, deep toke off the joint, she held it for nearly a minute before coughing out the smoke.

"Wow. That brings back memories."

Tito smiled. "Take another hit."

The effect was immediate. Madeline lay on the floor and stared at the ceiling. Even when the ship jumped twenty feet from a swell, she barely moved. Kim-Jack asked if she was still nauseous and Madeline mumbled something that he couldn't decipher. Making his way around to her side of the bed, Tito took the still lit joint from her fingers and smoked half of it in one toke.

He offered it to Kim-Jack, even though he knew that his friend and fellow teacher would refuse.

"This works better than those stupid pills."

"I'll take your word for it."

"Sure?"

Kim-Jack nodded. "Yeah. I've been clean for over ten years. No way will I start again. It's just not worth the risk. We'll get home and before they let us through the metal detectors, we'll have to piss in a Dixie cup."

Stubbing out the joint, Tito shrugged. "Suit yourself. But sooner or later, those pills are going to fail and you'll be begging me for relief."

With that, the big man crawled to the door and let himself out. Kim-Jack waited until there was silence in the hallway and the ship was momentarily steady to reach up and remove the Ziploc bag from the smoke detector.

Madeline managed to grab the corner of her pillow and pulled it down to the floor. "I'm staying here until this shit is over."

"Do you want company?"

"There's room."

"Catch my pillow." He threw it over the bed. It landed on Madeline's face. "Sorry."

Dragging the blanket behind him, Kim-Jack crawled to the other side of the bed and lay down next to her. He did his best to cover them both with the blanket, but he was over a foot taller than Madeline and ended up with his feet sticking out the bottom.

As Sunday night faded into Monday morning, the swells worsened. Madeline slept, thanks to the pot. Kim-Jack rolled back and forth, doing his best not to wake her while at the same time, trying to force himself to sleep. He may have dozed off, but at six o'clock in the morning, the speaker in the ceiling crackled to life with a "bing-bong" alert that he thought was a fire alarm.

Gwen's voice was loud enough to wake the dead. "Good morningk, good morningk. Well, we are in the worst part of the Drake Passage. Checking the weather, there is no good news, so my advice is to stay in bed if you're not feeling well, but do join us in the Chinstrap lounge at seven for a lecture by our science officer. Breakfast is being served in the Gentoo dining room and the buffet will be open until nine this morning."

Kim-Jack crawled up the foot of the bed and then over to his side. He didn't know how many muscles were in his back, but every one of them was screaming in agony. Swinging his legs from left to right, he tried to loosen the kinks and relieve the pain, but it was useless. The cabin floor was carpet, but there was no padding underneath. It was worse than falling asleep on a pebbled beach.

Their stateroom was equipped with a fifty-inch television. Reaching up to the desk, Kim-Jack found the remote and turned it on, muting the volume before it could awaken his fiancée. Channel one was a live feed from the bow camera. It was the default channel when the set was powered on, and he sat with his back against the wall, watching the bow go up and down with the swells for several minutes.

On the left side of the screen, a scale followed the swells, indicating their height in meters. Kim-Jack did the conversion in his head.

Twenty-two feet. Seventeen. Twelve. He sighed. They were decreasing. The next one measured thirteen feet and the one after that was eleven. Taking advantage of the relative calm, he jumped onto the bed just as a twenty-foot peak rocked the ship.

Desperately, he grabbed at the mattress, but the sheet slipped out from underneath and Kim-Jack rolled out of control toward Madeline, still on the floor and sleeping soundly.

Until he landed on top of her.

"What the hell?" She shoved him off. "I was sleeping. What's our rule about sex when one of us is asleep?"

"Trust me, Madeline, sex was the last thing on my mind."

Another twenty-foot swell tilted the ship, causing Kim-Jack to slide into her.

"This shit has got to stop eventually." Getting up on his hands and knees, he snatched the last pillow off the bed and collapsed alongside her. "I'd pull the mattress off the bed frame, but they've strapped it in place."

Madeline wiped the sleep from her eyes and lips and glanced at the television. "Is that real-time video?"

"And a scale to let you know just how bad it is outside. Can you do meters to feet in your head?"

"Three-something times the number, plus a few inches." She pointed at the screen. "That's nineteen. That's fifteen. Holy shit, that's twenty-one."

They held each other as the scale topped thirty, twice, before settling into the teens for a few minutes. Madeline was able to grab a bottle of water that had taken cover under the bed and swallowed a seasickness pill.

"How much pot did Tito bring with him?"

"I really don't want to know."

"I should ask him for another joint."

Kim-Jack frowned.

"For an emergency." She forced a smile. "And a Ziploc bag."

"I'm not taking the laces out of my sneakers."

Channel one was mesmerizing. Several times over the next hour, they discussed surfing the limited selection and checking out the free movies, but then a twenty-five-foot swell would have them hanging on to each other as the ship rocked from side-to-side. Madeline's bladder broke the spell and she made a mad dash for the toilet as the waves calmed to the low teens for a few minutes. She returned with a bottle of mouthwash and a glass.

"Your breath could kill a moose at fifty feet." She handed him the bottle. "Spit into the glass."

"Why don't I just use the trashcan?"

"Trust me, you don't want to use the trashcan. I sprayed it with deodorant and it still smells like puke. Play the part of the hero and dump it in the toilet."

With the sea still at a mild pace, Kim-Jack had enough balance to handle the task. He took advantage of the situation to relieve himself and brush his teeth. Several sturdy aluminum handholds were strategically mounted around the bathroom and he found them perfect to deal with even a large swell. He was going to shave, but his Norelco had bounced off the counter and into the main part of their stateroom at some point.

Coming out of the bathroom, Kim-Jack was surprised to see Madeline, the comforter, and all the pillows back on the bed. She had removed the soiled t-shirt, replacing it with a knee-length gray football jersey. Her favorite crooner was smiling on the front in a larger-than-life image, and the words "I Did It My Way" were in blue letters above his fedora.

"Are you hungry?"

Kim-Jack fell onto the bed as another deep swell tossed the ship. "I'm horny. Does that count?"

"Might I suggest self-service?"

"What if I get you one of Tito's joints?"

Madeline raised an eyebrow. "You'd go out in the hall, down a flight of stairs, get a joint, and bring it back? All with the good ship Lollipop bouncing like a horny kangaroo just to get laid?"

"Now that you put it that way, I'm not so sure."

Sliding closer, Madeline reached into his sweatpants and caressed him. Softly, she whispered in his ear, "Go get the joint before you change your mind."

Reluctantly working himself free of her grasp, Kim-Jack changed into a clean shirt and made his way to the door.

"As long as I'm risking my life, I'm going to check on Marcus."

"Whatever. Just don't return empty-handed."

Following the instructions of the safety officer, Kim-Jack navigated the hallways and stairs with one hand always holding onto the ship. He passed a handful of passengers on the way, most of whom were strangers to him, but they all wished him good luck or congratulations. Working his way downstairs, Kim-Jack decided to check on Marcus first and then collect a prerolled for Madeline on the way back.

He reached Marcus' stateroom, three decks down, and knocked several times. A steward cleaning a nearby room leaned out and pointed at the stairway to the crew quarters.

"Your cousin is down one deck. Go. You'll hear him."

"He's not my cousin." Kim-Jack was about to explain their relationship, but the man ducked back into the room to continue cleaning.

From halfway down the stairs, he could hear Marcus talking to a pair of dice. Gambling in the high school was forbidden. However, it was also the most popular use of the restrooms. Every teacher knew the sound of the dice and chants that went with them.

Marcus and five stewards were in a corner of the crew's mess. A young Filipino girl was braiding his afro into cornrows.

"What the hell are you doing?"

Marcus looked up with the dice held high. "Yo, professor, you want in?"

"Where did you get the money to gamble?" Kim-Jack glanced up and down the corridor. "If someone catches these kids gambling, they're going to lose their jobs."

"Money?" Marcus laughed. "These guys ain't got enough coin to make change on a dollar." Reaching behind, he lifted a plastic bag with Tootsie Rolls. "We're betting on candy, professor. They're crazy for chocolate. I bought a five-pound bag at the candy store in the mall while you were screwing around with the drunken be-atch in the sporting good store."

Kim-Jack shook his head just as a swell shook the entire ship. "Are you feeling okay? Taking the pills?"

"For what? My cousin drives worse than this. Anybody gonna get seasick better not get in a car with him."

He tossed the dice and rolled a seven. The Filipinos cheered and grabbed candy from the pile on the floor.

Kim-Jack left him and headed upstairs to Tito's cabin, but not before snatching a couple of Tootsie Rolls from the pot.

He knocked several times then banged loud enough to bring a steward running down the hall.

"Have you seen my friend?"

"Big guy?"

"Yes, big guy."

The steward grinned. "He got good smoke, you know?"

Oh, shit. Tito's gonna get the entire crew wasted. "Yes, I know. Have you seen him?"

"He went to breakfast."

Kim-Jack glanced at the clock on the wall next to a painting of seagulls. "Breakfast ended an hour ago."

"Oh. He come back."

"Is he in the room?"

The steward pointed at the little green light above the door. "Yes. He inside."

"He's not answering the door. Can you let me in? I want to make sure my friend is okay."

A heavy swell hit the ship and Kim-Jack lurched across the corridor and into the steward, taking him to the floor as he fell.

"Always hold onto the ship." The steward pushed himself off Kim-Jack and pointed at the wooden rail that ran the length of the corridor. "One hand on ship at all times."

Using the keycard that hung on a lanyard around his neck, the steward opened the door to Tito's stateroom and backed out of the way. A cloud of sweet smoke poured out of the room and Kim-Jack rushed in, shoving the door closed with his hip.

Tito had transformed the cabin into a fort. With a steak knife he borrowed from the Gentoo dining room, he'd slashed the bindings that held the mattress to the bed frame and leaned it against one wall. Both ends of the fort were covered in blankets, but his friend's feet jutted out from the end closest to the balcony doors. Everything else in the room that wasn't tied down had been tossed to the floor and then shoveled into one corner.

Kim-Jack knelt at the entrance to the fort, opposite where Tito's feet were visible. Peeling back the blanket, Tito covered his eyes against the light and pulled out his earbuds.

"What's up?"

"Just how stoned are you?"

Tito smiled. "As stoned as I need to be, KJ."

"I like your fort."

"I'd invite you in, but there isn't much room."

Kim-Jack sat down, Indian-style, against the wall. "I want to thank you for doing this."

"Your best man?" Tito shrugged. "I'm your only friend. Who else were you going to ask?"

"Marcus?"

"Yeah, Madeline would have gone along with that plan in a heartbeat."

Kim-Jack nodded. "This is some really crazy shit. We should be home working on pizza boxes."

"Maybe they'll have pizza on the buffet."

A large swell rocked Kim-Jack off the wall, and he grabbed the edge of the mattress for support.

"Hey, don't ruin my fort."

"Sorry." He let go and reached for the nightstand. "Madeline sent me down here for a joint."

Tito grinned. "Yeah, they work much better than those stupid pills." He lifted a small, jeweled case from a corner of the fort and took out a prerolled. "Here. No charge."

"I wish you wouldn't get all the crew wasted."

"Heaven forbid." Tito shoved his stash back into the corner. "So far, I'm just helping my friend Jaco."

"The guy who let me in here?"

"He's a prince." Tito smiled. "A real, honest-to-god prince. Or so he says."

"I don't think they have a royal family in the Philippines."

"Not the Philippines. He says he's from Burundi."

Chapter Eighteen

Over the next few hours, the seas gradually calmed. The swells dropped to single digits, and for a few minutes, the sun came out from behind the clouds. Gwen announced that the most recent weather forecast was promising and that another lecture from the science officer would be held late in the afternoon.

The wedding couple made an appearance at the nearly empty lunch buffet, a few minutes before it was supposed to close. Madeline had the munchies and settled for the last piece of chicken breast that she sliced and ate on a croissant with arugula and ketchup. A chef brought out a tray of cookies and small pastries that she collected on a salad plate for later, and she ended the meal with a glass of white wine.

A plate of cold hamburgers together with the last dregs of pasta salad covered Kim-Jack's need for food and the two grabbed a table in the corner, where they could watch the waves and eat in private.

He found that if they faced either the bow or stern of the ship, the rocking was less offensive. Kim-Jack went into a detailed description of the human inner ear that she ended with an obviously fake yawn. Finished eating, they began a slow circuit of the room, greeting guests, and attempting to act married just for practice.

Halfway around the room and at the limit of his patience, Cassidy and several of her friends corralled Madeline, insisting they escape from the men, and headed off to the Chinstrap lounge at the other end of the ship.

Relieved that being a husband was still a few days off, he borrowed a parka from a man that Kim-Jack recognized from Larry's staff, who was the same size, and shoved open the heavy door to the main deck.

There were more people roaming outside than Kim-Jack figured he would see. Most were strangers that he would meet at the reception, but he smiled at everyone who greeted him and offered congratulations or told a corny joke.

Among the sightseers, he spotted his father leaning against the rail and shooting video of the waves and passing icebergs. Ossie's expedition parka was hanging loosely on his shoulders and the outline of his private parts was exactingly distinct on his waterproof pants. Kim-Jack mentioned his father's wardrobe, wondering if he had the wrong size clothes.

"I'm not wearing anything underneath." His father continued videoing. "It's chilly, but I didn't feel like getting dressed."

Kim-Jack slapped his forehead. "Dad, this is not Jamaica."

"No kidding?" Ossie punched his son's shoulder. "You're pretty smart for an inner city science teacher. Maybe you should also teach geography. They'll give you a raise."

Trisha came up from behind and wrapped her arms around her stepson. Turning slowly, Kim-Jack asked what she was wearing underneath her parka and sweatpants. Lowering the zipper a few inches, her all-over tan answered his question.

"You two are impossible." Kim-Jack walked to the opposite side of the ship, trying his best to erase the image from his mind.

A pair of back-to-back violent swells made everyone grab a rail, and darkening clouds sent most of them back into the safety of the dining room. Larry came up to Kim-Jack and put his arm around his future son-in-law's shoulder.

"Are you ready for this?"

"Getting married?"

He laughed. "No. Antarctica. Penguins, seals, giant humpback whales." Larry waved his arms. "Icebergs. The challenge to mankind to survive in such a hostile environment. Did you know that more than twenty-thousand people have died making this crossing?"

Kim-Jack blew out a breath. "And we have to come back this way, too."

"You'll be a better person for accepting this challenge."

"Again, I'm wondering if you're referring to Madeline or the icebergs."

Larry thought about it for a few moments. "Probably a little of both."

Returning to the dining room, he gave back the parka and drank two cups of hot cocoa from a station by the door. The swells were increasing, and passengers were scrambling for the safety of their cabins. He followed a line of guests up the stairs single-file as they held onto the wooden rails for support.

Larry and Cassidy were just going into their stateroom, and Kim-Jack shouted at them to wait.

"Where's Madeline?"

Cassidy shook her head. "We were drinking in the Chinstrap lounge and I left when the swells got worse. Madeline didn't seem to be bothered by them." She leaned toward him and whispered, "I think she was stoned."

Shoving his wife into the stateroom, Larry turned to Kim-Jack before closing the door. "She's drunk. Madeline wouldn't smoke pot. She knows it will screw up her throat."

Kim-Jack nodded. "I'm sure you're correct." He pointed down the corridor. "The Chinstrap lounge is that way?"

"Down two decks and head toward the stern."

"The stern?"

"The back of the ship." Larry pinched the bridge of his nose. "Wait until I get you out on my yacht. Then you'll learn all about sailing and which end of the ship is which."

On the stairs, Kim-Jack felt as though he was swimming against the tide. Everyone was going up while he was fighting his way down. Both sides of the stairs were being used for the same direction and he had to step around people, which meant letting go of the safety rail. Timing his moves so that he was holding the rail as the boat rocked up, he managed a few steps at a time as it was settling.

The forward staircase that he was descending was at the opposite end of the ship from the Chinstrap lounge. However, as he approached midship, Kim-Jack could hear singing in the distance.

That's Madeline's voice. He stopped and strained to make out the melody. *What is that she's singing? I've never heard her reach notes that high before.*

Walking into the lounge, Madeline noticed him immediately and motioned him toward the small stage. A karaoke machine was lit in the far corner and she was seated on a stool, holding the microphone.

"What song is that? And what's with the falsetto?"

"Oh, my god. That's Frankie Valli and the Four Seasons. Can you believe his vocal range?"

Kim-Jack shrugged. "Sounds weird to hear a guy sing that high. On you, the notes fit perfectly."

Several guests got up from their seats and walked over to shake Kim-Jack's hand. Even as they introduced themselves, he forgot their names. One elderly woman asked if they would sing a duet.

"Not this afternoon." Madeline smiled at the woman. "KJ's a bit under the weather and I don't want to strain his voice."

Another woman claimed that Rabbi Horowitz told her that the couple was going to sing their wedding vows. Kim-Jack turned to Madeline and asked if that was true.

"I may have mentioned it in passing."

"How do you sing 'I do'?"

Madeline reached into her back pocket and pulled out several folded sheets of paper. "Here. You need to study this."

"What is it?"

"Our wedding vows."

Kim-Jack took the vows from her and read through them slowly. The top of the first page was the standard set of declarations he'd heard his father and stepmother take when he was a young boy. Reading further down, he became concerned and by the time he flipped to the second page, Kim-Jack was fuming.

"I promise to keep the house tidy and clean? You're not going to help? I thought we discussed maid service months ago and agreed that the townhouse wasn't big enough to justify the expense."

"I am trying to head off the problem of housekeeping when I sign my record contract."

"Do you even have someone offering you a contract?"

She shrugged. "Not yet, but I can feel my luck changing."

"And what's this shit about pleasing you even when I'm not in the mood?"

"Just because you can't enjoy sex sometimes doesn't mean that I should suffer." She looked at the group of women sitting in the first row. "Am I right?"

They nodded in unison with one woman wagging a finger at Kim-Jack to admonish him for even thinking this was wrong.

Most of the second page followed a similar trail. Kim-Jack came close to ripping the document to shreds, but stifled the urge, figuring they could discuss this in private and come to a compromise. The last page appeared to be taken from a standard contract. It had both their names with a signature and date line as well as blank lines for witnesses.

"Will I need to place my hand on a bible before signing this?"

"That page was my father's idea."

"So we don't need it?"

She scratched an itch on the back of her neck. "I don't know. Daddy was insistent that the vows be signed."

"In blood?"

"Now you're being stupid."

Kim-Jack handed the vows back to her. "I have no problem with the first page, but everything else is bullshit. I'm not buying a car or signing an employment contract. The purpose of our vows to declare our eternal love for each other, not bind us to chores."

"Well, you're going to have to discuss this with my father."

"I'm not marrying your father."

Madeline sighed. "I knew this wasn't going to be easy."

"Easy?" Kim-Jack slapped his forehead. "If you wanted easy, we should have stayed home. I can't imagine what your father went through to put this expedition together for a hundred-and-twenty people, but I'm sure that his favorite synagogue would have been much less expensive."

She started to retort, but he held up his hand.

"Don't tell me about how much money he has and that it doesn't matter to him how much this wedding costs. Your father's a businessman and not prone to frivolous spending, even on his daughter's wedding."

"And if I told you that you're wrong?"

Kim-Jack shook his head. "I'd have a hard time believing you."

Walking over to the karaoke machine, Madeline switched it off and laid the microphone on a stool. She got her wineglass refilled at the bar and crossed the room to where Kim-Jack was standing. Taking his hand, they started for the door, but the ship heaved and the wine spilled. Gulping what was left, Madeline placed the glass on the floor and grabbed the rail with her free hand.

"Let's go."

"Where?" Kim-Jack hesitated. "To talk to your father?"

"No. To yours."

"Do you really think my father is going to side with you?"

Madeline paused to let a couple of guests pass. "You obviously don't trust my father's opinion, so let's see how you react to his."

Kim-Jack shook his head. "I have a better idea. Let's ask Marcus."

"Your criminal cross-dresser?"

"I told you he claimed the purse was for a cousin and the boots were a spur-of-the-moment lark."

"You want me to discuss our marriage vows with a fifteen-year-old?"

"His knowledge of the streets is unsurpassed."

Madeline stepped back and covered her eyes with a hand. "I can't believe I'm hearing this."

"What?"

"What the hell does street sense have to do with marriage?"

With the ship bouncing harder and higher, Kim-Jack was having trouble maintaining his balance. He took her by the hand and led his fiancée over to a booth.

"After three years in that hell hole of a school, I've learned more about the realities of life than I could from a library full of books. These kids are survivors, and to survive the streets of any major city, you have to know how to live with the barest of essentials."

Madeline was unconvinced. "What does that have to do with marriage?"

"Well, first off, none of them even think about marriage. Their day-to-day existence precludes long-term planning."

"Yeah, most of them don't live long enough to get married."

"But even those who do avoid the subject because of their focus on themselves."

Nodding, Madeline smiled. "A bunch of self-centered miscreants."

Self-centered? Madeline, really? Kim-Jack shoved the comment to the back of his mind. "In the extreme, yes. But that's not what I meant."

"Okay." She pursed her lips. "Let's go get some streetwise suggestions on our wedding vows from a self-centered cross-dresser."

The craps game had ended and they found Marcus in his cabin, counting Tootsie Rolls. Only, he wasn't alone. Father Gustafson was sitting at the desk helping the boy tally his winnings. The priest looked up from the sheet of paper he was using to keep score and smiled sheepishly at Madeline.

"With the economy tightening, the church needs to find new ways to cover our expenses." He held up a Tootsie Roll. "If these were cash, young Marcus over there would have won nearly five-hundred dollars."

Kim-Jack shook his head. "Gambling is illegal in our state."

"Except for church functions." The priest winked. "How do you think we got away with bingo for all these years?"

Father Gustafson was at the tail end of young. While most of his hair was black, spots of gray had formed and the top was thinning. Kim-Jack was hard-pressed to believe the priest had never heard of craps.

"I grew up in the Midwest. If you want to talk corn, I'm an expert. However, inner city mores and the culture of crime are subjects I've just begun to investigate."

Marcus finished the count and offered everyone a free Tootsie Roll. He insisted that he'd played fairly with the Filipinos and that the dice weren't loaded.

"I'll take your word for it." Kim-Jack shrugged. "I don't know why I should trust you, but the more this ship bounces my brain around my skull, the more reason I have to believe I've got a concussion."

Madeline had been standing in the open doorway all this time, with a look of annoyance on her face. Kim-Jack asked her to come inside and sit, so they could talk.

"I want the criminal to apologize first."

"For what?" In the process of unwrapping another Tootsie Roll, Marcus paused and pointed the candy at her. "What I do to you to deserve bein' humble?"

"What you called me in the limo."

Marcus looked over at Kim-Jack. "What she talkin' on, professor?"

"You called her a bitch."

"No. I called her your fine-lookin' be-atch." Marcus shook his head. "College degree and all that shit and you can't understand how we talk in the hood. That shit is a compliment, professor." He turned his attention to Madeline. "If I apologize, I'd be takin' that shit back. You want me to take back a compliment?"

Madeline pursed her lips. "I don't believe you."

Shaking his head, Marcus nodded at Kim-Jack. "White girls don't know shit."

"This is stupid. I'm going upstairs." She turned to leave.

"Hey. Don't leave angry." Getting up from the bed, Marcus walked over to her. "Any time someone leave angry, I gotta worry they gonna come back mad. Mad people do crazy things and I don't need no more crazy in my head than I already got." He took her hand. "So, if you want an apology, I'll give you one."

"I'm listening."

Marcus grinned. "Marcus Tigue hereby apologizes for callin' the professor's girlfriend a be-atch." He bent down and grabbed a Tootsie Roll off the bed. "Here. We cool?"

Madeline unwrapped the candy, took a bite, and smiled. "Yeah. We're cool."

"What you come down here for, professor? I didn't expect to see you and your fine lady out of the cabin with all this shakin' goin' on. I had a woman, I'd swing the bed around part way and take advantage of all this up and down." Marcus air-humped an invisible mate.

Kim-Jack's jaw dropped. "Why didn't we think of that?"

Glancing up at the ceiling, Madeline was silent, but he could see a smile on her face.

Father Gustafson cleared his throat.

"Do you think you might get married some day, Marcus?" Walking over to Madeline, Kim-Jack put his arm around her shoulder.

"No." Marcus laughed. "Why would I do that? They's more women in the world than men. Why would I only want one of them?"

Madeline was unconvinced. "First of all, how do you know there are more women than men?"

"Men fight the wars. Men go to prison. Men be dying all day long. Just makes sense that there's more women left than men when the bell ring."

"Interesting observation." Kim-Jack winked at his student. "Extra credit as well."

"I knew this was a waste of time." Madeline shrugged off his arm. "I think you should discuss the vows with Father Gustafson."

The priest raised his eyebrows. "How can I help?"

Kim-Jack was running out of options. "You're married."

"Yes, but my wife has a fear of boats, so she stayed home."

"Who wrote your wedding vows?"

The priest smiled. "God."

Madeline snickered.

"Seriously. God came to me in a dream and told me what to say."

"Did God say anything about cleaning house?" Kim-Jack did his best not to laugh. "And if your wife wants sex and you're feeling under the weather, does God want you to perform anyhow?"

Father Gustafson closed his eyes and lowered his head. "I'm going to pray for you, Kim-Jack. I'm going to ask the Lord to give you strength because you are looking for kernels of corn rather than harvesting the entire field. You are a farmer without focus and your crops are going to suffer. Life is your farm and to be successful, you have to be able to see the whole picture and not just a single ear of corn."

Kim-Jack considered the image for a few seconds and did his best not to lose his composure. He failed. Doubling over, he slapped his knees and roared with laughter.

"Father, I'm not sure I followed half of what you just said, but that is the corniest thing I've ever heard from a priest."

Madeline moaned.

Marcus spit half a Tootsie Roll across the room.

A twenty-four-foot swell hit the ship and the lights went out.

Chapter Nineteen

In the sudden, unexpected darkness, Kim-Jack ran into a wall, trying to reach Madeline who was screaming at maximum volume. Marcus illuminated a small corner of the room with his disposable lighter, but the fuel was nearly spent and the tiny torch only lasted a few seconds. In that short time, Father Gustafson pocketed the dice and a handful of Tootsie Rolls. When the lights came back on, a couple of seconds later, he blessed everyone in the room and left.

The bing-bong of the public address system was followed by Gwen, who apologized for the incident and then Captain Columbus who assured the passengers that it was just a single circuit breaker that was being replaced as he spoke. Gwen came back on after he was finished and reminded everyone that dinner would be served at six followed by a science lecture in the Chinstrap lounge and a kayaking discussion in the Albatross room.

Madeline, now calm, asked what if they wanted to go to both?

"You're going to kayak?" Kim-Jack was skeptical. "Have you ever tried one before?"

"No, but I want to learn. It looks like fun."

"I'm sure you'll love it. Especially the part where you do a barrel roll and get dunked underwater."

Madeline shoved her tongue into her cheek. "That's bullshit."

"Don't believe me. Go to the discussion and see for yourself." He smiled. "If I'm lying, then I'll go with you."

Marcus got up from the bed and began collecting his remaining Tootsie Rolls. "I got company coming in half an hour. You guys done here?"

"Company?" Turning to Madeline, Kim-Jack nodded once. "Marcus has company coming. Who's the company?"

"Ain't none of your business, professor, but her name is Ulla and she promised to teach me how to speak her language."

"Are you considering a move to the Philippines?" Madeline smiled. "Permanently?"

Kim-Jack grabbed her wrist. "Let's get out of here and give the boy his privacy."

They made their way up two decks and stopped to check on Tito, but the Do Not Disturb sign was hanging from his door, so they continued up to the owner's suite.

"What if we skip the vows?"

Madeline shook her head. "Are you crazy?"

"Sometimes." He grinned. "But not right now. We have the rings, the priest *and* a rabbi, let them do their thing."

"You can't get married unless you recite the vows."

"Okay, then let's just use the standard stuff and be done with it."

Taking his hand, Madeline pulled Kim-Jack down to sit next to her on the bed. She said nothing for a few seconds and then turned to face him.

"What about this wedding do you think is standard?" He started to reply, but she held up her hand. "Is coming to Antarctica standard for a wedding? What about bringing a fifteen-year-old criminal along or your four-hundred-pound best man?"

"I don't–"

"No, you don't and you shouldn't. A wedding is all about the woman. It's her moment to shine, to show the world that she's no longer a little girl."

Kim-Jack shrugged. "I thought that happened when you lost your virginity."

Madeline punched his shoulder. "You are such an asshole sometimes."

He winked. "At least it's not 'round the clock."

A knock on the door interrupted their discussion. Kim-Jack got up from the bed and yanked it open without checking through the peephole. The man standing there in cowboy boots and leopard print jacket had a red moustache, snow-white eyebrows, and mostly blue hair. His roots were gray and it was obvious to Kim-Jack that the man needed a touchup if he intended to maintain the patriotic appearance.

He introduced himself as Dr. Zametsky, going so far as to show Kim-Jack his Kloppleman Industries identification card. "I'm the inventor of the foil you need for your pizza box. Larry said you'd probably want to talk to me about it." He leaned into the room. "This is a much bigger stateroom than mine. Mind if I come in and sit down? My back isn't much for standing with this ship tossing around."

Kim-Jack stared at the laminated card until he could form actual words. "You're the guy? You. I mean the foil." He slapped his forehead. "Madeline, this is the guy. The foil thing I told you about. The pizza box. Holy shit. What are you doing here? I mean, yeah the wedding and all. But, wow. I can't believe it's you."

"Larry also said that you would have that reaction." He smiled. "Yes. It's me and I'm here because your future father-in-law wanted us talk about your pizza box. He's very interested in its potential application to other food groups. He used the term profit center. Not a pair of words that Larry Kloppleman uses together on a regular basis."

"Wow. This is amazing." Kim-Jack pointed at the desk chair with his parka draped over the back. "Have a seat. Please." He turned to Madeline. "I should call Tito."

"You saw the sign on his door, right?"

He nodded. "Yeah, but I think this warrants waking him up."

Madeline shrugged and nodded toward the doctor. "What if he's you-know-what?"

"Stoned? When he hears why I woke him, he'll get his shit together and actually run up the stairs."

"A one-man herd of elephants." She smiled at the doctor and then turned toward Kim-Jack. "Call him."

Kim-Jack shook his head. "No. He probably put the phone on silent." Looking over at Dr. Zametsky, who was unwrapping a Tootsie Roll, he smiled. "I'm going downstairs to get my partner."

"The communist from Canada?" Zametsky chuckled. "That's what Larry calls him."

"He's not a communist."

The doctor shrugged. "That's okay. I am." Pulling his wallet from a back pocket, he retrieved an official American Communist Party membership card and showed it to them.

"So, you're a real commie?" Madeline took a step back. "How did you get a job with my father?"

"When you say, 'a real commie' I have to assume you're thinking along the lines of the Russians and how they are the sworn enemy of the United States."

She nodded. "Good guess."

"The ACP has nothing to do with a dictatorial environment. We are communists in the true sense of the word. For us, it's all about economics and equal distribution of wealth. Everyone does their fair share of the work. Everyone benefits. Everyone is equal."

"Ah, the utopian version of communism." Madeline nodded at Kim-Jack. "I wrote a paper on that shit to get an A in sociology, first year. The professor tried to get it published, but the college stopped him."

"Let me guess. The dean got a visit from the guys in blue windbreakers." Kim-Jack shook his head. "A guy in my physics class disproved some theory that the top brains in the world swore was true. He also got his paper three feet away from the press before every copy of it disappeared and his computer was stolen."

Dr. Zametsky sighed. "I hear these stories all the time and more. It's part of the reason I don't vote or drive a car and I never eat red meat unless it's well done, almost to a crisp."

Kim-Jack scratched an imaginary itch on his neck. "Okay, then. I'm going downstairs to get Tito. Madeline, are you okay entertaining our guest for a few minutes?"

"A few minutes." She shuddered. "A very few minutes."

Pulling himself down the corridor with both hands on the rail, Kim-Jack fell into rhythm with the ship. He took the steps two at time and reached Tito's cabin at a lull in the swells. Yanking the

Do Not Disturb placard off the doorknob, he pushed the bell several times in rapid succession and then started knocking.

Cabin doors across and next to Tito's opened with curious faces popping out. Kim-Jack waved to each one, explaining that his friend had been meditating for too long and he need to return to reality in time for dinner. He was about to ring the doorbell again when Tito pulled the door open to the length of the security chain.

"Oh. It's you." He closed the door and Kim-Jack could hear the chain clatter against the metal frame. From inside, Tito shouted, "It's open!"

The fort was still standing, but everything near the balcony door was covered with wet towels. A puddle at the foot of the door, almost two feet in diameter, was swaying back and forth with the ship. Tito was wearing the expedition boots, a bathing suit, and his parka.

"There was a lull and I wanted to see how cold it was outside."

"So, you opened the balcony door." Kim-Jack blew out a long breath. "Okay. There's a steward cleaning a cabin at the end of the hall. Get dressed and we'll get him to clean this place up."

"Get dressed?"

"You'll never believe who's upstairs in our stateroom."

"Chelbe Udulu and she wants my body."

"Yeah. She flew in by helicopter and rappelled onto the deck."

Tito came around to the dry side of the room and sat down on the bed. "This better be worth it. Give me a hand with these stupid boots."

The bing-bong first call for dinner sounded while Dr. Zametsky was wrapping up his presentation. Too stunned for words, Kim-Jack and Tito had no questions, and watched him leave in silence.

Madeline whistled. "Do you understand what my father's offer means?"

"I could get a bigger apartment."

"Tito, you could get a friggin' penthouse with a view of the lake and never set foot in Bohi again." Kim-Jack jumped off the bed. "Did you know about this?"

"Uh, uh. I've never seen the guy before. Very patriotic with the red, white, and blue thing going on, though."

The second call for dinner slid reality into the mix.

"Let's go eat." Tito got up slowly from the bed. "I'm hungry enough to eat a whale."

The Klopplemans and Kim-Jack's parents were holding court at a table for ten in the dining room. Kim-Jack heard his father's voice from the corridor leading into the buffet and could tell that he was drunk. Thinking it awkward to insert themselves into the discussion at their table, he steered Madeline and Tito to a table as far away from them as possible.

"You should go over by yourself and thank daddy."

"I can hear my father telling baby stories about me from where I'm sitting."

"Does he have pictures in his wallet?"

Kim-Jack laughed. "No, but I'll bet he's got some on his phone."

"Let's eat and then go over together." Madeline leaned around Kim-Jack to get a better view. "Maybe some of them will be gone by then."

Forty-five minutes later, after eating as slowly as they could, the group surrounding Larry Kloppleman's table had grown, nearly tripling in size. As nearby diners finished their meals, they slid their chairs into an ever-expanding circle. From where Kim-Jack sat, it was easy to hear the drunken voices of his father and Larry telling jokes.

Waves of laughter roared across the dining room as tables emptied and the guests either joined the throng or tottered off to bed. Servers and busboys cleared the vacant tables and in short order, Kim-Jack, Madeline, and Tito were isolated in their corner of the room. Of course, this made them easy to spot, and Cassidy stumbled over to retrieve the missing pieces of the wedding party.

Tito used the restroom excuse and vanished before anyone could protest. The bride and groom were left defenseless and marched over hand-in-hand.

Someone retrieved the karaoke machine from the Chinstrap lounge and was projecting the lyrics on the large white wall next to the entrance. Sinatra was singing and Larry wanted her to sing along. He got the guests at all the tables, now some thirty people, to chant "Madeline, Madeline" while pounding their fists in unison.

However, Madeline wasn't interested in Sinatra. She walked over to the karaoke machine and selected the tune she'd been practicing all day. Horns opened the piece and several of the older guests sat up, instantly recognizing one of the songs from their youth, and started to hum. The vocals began and Madeline joined Frankie Valli in perfect harmony, hitting the high notes and belting out the lyrics.

Holding out her hand to Kim-Jack, she motioned him over with the music.

"Can't take my eyes off of you." She threw him a kiss. "You're just too good to be true."

The guests at the table joined in and even those who'd never heard the song before sang the chorus. Three more of the Four Season's greatest hits were stored in the machine. Madeline had spent most of the day singing their number one hit, but she had a tight grip on the other two, and managed a successful performance.

A distant cousin from San Francisco who knew Madeline's mother came up to her as they were powering down the karaoke machine. They'd been introduced at the soiree in Miami, but she didn't remember the woman's name.

"I can't believe how much you resemble your mother. That little crook in your nose reminds me of when she fell and broke her nose. You were still in diapers."

"I broke my nose when I was ten." Madeline sighed. "Daddy was trying to teach me how to ride a bike and I crashed into a garbage can."

"You've got Frankie's falsetto down cold. You should reach out to him and see if he'd be interested in a duet."

Madeline held her breath. "He's still alive?"

"Yes. And occasionally performing." The woman pulled a pen and a small leather-bound pad from her purse. "He lives in my building. I cook for him occasionally." She scribbled his phone number. "Call him and say, Scoochie gave you his number."

"Scoochie?" Madeline laughed. "Is that your real name?"

The woman winked. "That's what he calls me, dear."

Kim-Jack waited until they were upstairs behind closed doors to ask the question. "Do you think she's for real?"

Madeline kicked off her sneakers and sat down on the bed. "I've been trying to Google his name, but the internet is still down."

"Why would he live in San Francisco of all places?"

"He got tired of the East Coast? Maybe he's a stoner and wanted to live in a legal state."

"Every state is a legal state now."

"Maybe he likes earthquakes." Madeline slipped off her shorts and got up to brush her teeth. "I love his music and if there's a chance to meet him, we should take it."

Kim-Jack laughed. "Fly out to San Francisco on a wild goose chase for a singer from the sixties. I love adventure, but I think after this expedition we should stay grounded for a while."

"What if Dr. Zametsky asked you to fly out to the West Coast?"

"That's different."

"Ah. So my voice isn't as important as a pizza box."

Kim-Jack wondered how she'd managed to smuggle the trap through airport security. However, he was now an expert when it came to avoiding its jaws.

"You're right. The potential of a recording contract certainly outweighs the millions of dollars that your father wishes to lavish on us for a silly pizza box." He grinned and then ducked when she tossed a sneaker at his head.

"One of these days, you're going to eat those words with a mountain of cold pepperoni pizza."

Kim-Jack balanced the sneaker on top of his head. "Mmmm. Cold pizza for breakfast."

Chapter Twenty

The Tuesday morning bing-bong followed by Gwen's "Good morningk, good morningk" was a half-hour late. Sounding as cheerful as an executioner, the expedition's team leader welcomed the passengers to calm waters for their third day at sea.

"We'll be cruising through one of the most beautiful channels and into the Gerlache Straits shortly, and we expect to see whales. After that, we'll have our first shore excursion to a small island in Fournier Bay where you'll be able to visit a Japanese research station."

Kim-Jack nudged his fiancée. "Or we can just go down one deck and look at Tito."

"Or we can stay in bed and watch the real whales on television."

Gwen paused to listen to someone on the bridge. She continued, a bit more excited. "I've just been told that a large pod of orcas is about a hundred yards off the bow on the starboard side."

"That's the left, right?"

Kim-Jack nodded. "Correct. Left side of the ship if you're facing forward."

"We should get dressed and take some pictures."

"What happened to staying bed?"

"How often do you get to see whales?"

"I took my class to the zoo. They have whales there, so the answer to your question is just about any time I want to, I can see a whale." Kim-Jack grinned. "Now, can we discuss staying in bed?"

Madeline rolled away from him and got up. "I need a break. Get dressed and find the camera."

All one-hundred-and-twenty guests were on deck. Everyone had on their red expedition parka with the silver stripes. And every guest had a camera. Gwen directed the action over the public address system, calling out distance and direction. The passengers stared through the lensfinder of their cameras and tried to capture the perfect "tail shot" as the massive animals dove under the ship.

Kim-Jack shot stills and then video and then back to stills, but every picture was blurry. Around him, the other passengers were having similar luck, and moaned about it to each other.

"This is like watching a NASCAR race." He ran to the starboard side as the whales surfaced again. "You stare at the track for hours, watching the cars make left-hand turns. The minute you look down for your beer or to take a bite of a hot dog, there's a crash and you missed it."

Madeline pointed at a small black object in the water. "Is that a whale?"

Squinting, Kim-Jack zoomed the lens to its maximum setting. "No. Just a chunk of ice."

Someone behind him yelled, "Over here!" but by the time he and everyone else rushed over, the whales had gone deep.

The sun was dipping in and out of the clouds, but the wind was constant. It wasn't long before the chill worked its way through their parkas and the guests began disappearing from the deck. Marcus had been viewing the confusion from the observation deck above the main and made his way down.

"You get any good pictures, professor?"

"If I was trying to get blurry images, I succeeded." Kim-Jack showed Marcus his attempts to capture the whale as it was diving. "Everyone's talking about a good tail shot." He shook his head. "I should take some photos of Madeline's butt. There's a good tail shot for you."

Marcus laughed. "Yeah, but you ain't gonna put them pictures on Instagram."

Losing its battle with the clouds, the sun disappeared and rain began to fall. Kim-Jack tucked the camera into one of the large outer pockets of the parka and slipped on the hood.

"It's cold, but the fresh air is a welcome change." He wrinkled his nose. "Our stateroom is starting to smell like the boy's locker room back at school."

Marcus moaned, "Now why you gotta bring up school when we're a million miles away, dealin' with whales and shit?"

"Did you think it would be gone when we got home?"

He shrugged. "It could be for some of us."

"What's that supposed to mean?"

Holding his hands out, palms up, the boy looked around the deck. "Look at this, professor. It's pure and clean. Ain't no poleese. Ain't no sirens from ambulances. Nobody shootin' nobody. This place is what heaven must look like."

"I don't think heaven is this cold."

"And hell ain't as hot as the city on Saturday night."

Kim-Jack nodded. "There's plenty of truth in those observations, Marcus. But you need to finish school. That's a cold, hard fact. Regardless of what you do after high school, without a diploma, you'll always be walking down a dead-end street."

"None of the Filipinos got any real schoolin' and look where they are, professor? Down here in Antarctica with a bunch of rich folk, seein' the same sights and gettin' paid for it. Ain't that some shit?"

"Do you see how hard they're working?"

"They's gettin' paid big coin. The lead sled dog told me he's makin' eight large per trip and he's signed for seven trips this season." Marcus shook his head. "That's gotta be a whole busload of coin compared to what the city pays you, professor."

Kim-Jack found it difficult to disagree with the inner city youth's view of the world. Fifty-six-thousand dollars was a tidy sum of money, especially when he compared it to his annual compensation for teaching at Bohi. However, the decision was out of their hands.

"I hate to cast cold seawater on your plans, but as your legal guardian, I can't let you walk away from high school."

Marcus rubbed his chin. "What happens if you do?"

"I'm not a lawyer, but there are several of them on the guest list. I can pretty much guarantee that if I simply let you disappear, and the state can prove it, I'll go to jail." Kim-Jack shook his head. "And that's not going to happen."

"What if I run away?"

"Well, you've still got charges hanging over your head, so I guess they'd send someone after you?"

Marcus smiled. "A bounty hunter?"

"I don't think that's what they call them anymore, but yes, they would look for you."

"Look, professor, I don't want to get your ass in a sling, but they's a whole lot more future for me on the deck of this ship than in your classroom."

Madeline had been silent throughout this exchange. But the thought of Kim-Jack going to prison for the kid was enough to make her explode.

"You won't have to worry about a bounty hunter, Marcus. If anything happens to my husband–"

"Future husband." Kim-Jack grinned.

"My *future* husband, I will hunt you down myself and bring you back to the city dead or alive." Madeline stood and walked over to stand between them. "And either way, I will cut your balls off and use them as whale bait."

Marcus took a step back and laughed. "Chill, Mrs. *future* professor. I ain't gonna cause no grief for you or my favorite teacher. We just talking hy-po-thetically. We cool?"

She nodded. "Yeah, hypothetically."

"Okay, confrontation over. This is supposed to a fun adventure, let's put reality back into Pandora's shoebox and live for the moment." Kim-Jack waved his arms at the black mountains with snow icing drizzled in the cracks. The sun had conquered the sky and the continent's frozen beauty held center stage. Rocking softly with the light swells, the ship cut through the dark water with a steady thrum of its engines. "How can you even think about anything else in the world with all this magnificent scenery?"

Marcus rubbed his stomach. "I can think about breakfast."

"Well, at least we agree on that." Madeline nodded. "Come on. Table for three."

The sluggish rail-hanging and apprehension of the first two days onboard was replaced by colorful blurs of activity. The expedition team, in yellow chest-waders and orange life vests, scurried down corridors and out through hatches marked CREW ONLY in red letters. A kayak team was headed out to test the waters wearing green waterproof parkas with yellow stripes down the sleeves.

The bing-bongs were frequent with Gwen opening most of her instructions with an extra "good morningk." The dining room staff seemed to have doubled. Shouts in a variety of languages came from the kitchen. Freshly washed cups and saucers appeared from both ends of the buffet line while the servers shouted, "Fresh coffee, fresh decaf." Stewards passing in the hallways with walkie-talkies close to their ears added to the cacophony, as they moved underlings into position. From every corner of the ship, the crew had moved into expedition mode.

Standing in the dining room, passengers froze the buffet line, watching as each orange kayak was gingerly lowered past the floor-to-ceiling windows. Massive cranes swung back-and-forth as they waited their turn to grab a boat. Gwen bing-bonged into the activity and announced that the Captain had made better time than expected. The passengers would have their first chance to step ashore early that afternoon, probably right after lunch. They wouldn't be stepping onto the actual land mass of Antarctica, but instead a small rocky island several miles off the coast with a working research outpost. A cheer went up from the dining room. Not wanting to be late, several full tables of guests stopped eating and marched back to their cabins to prepare.

Kim-Jack grabbed a cup of coffee and some Danish. Madeline loaded up a plate with cheese and cold cuts. Topping it off with a few croissants, she stuffed a bottle of water in each pocket of her expedition parka and followed Kim-Jack out of the dining room.

In short order, the crowded room had been reduced to Marcus at one table and three young women, friends of the bride, at another. They did their best not stare at him, but with no one else in the dining room, it was obvious he had their full attention. He smiled, looked away, looked back, and smiled again. Finally, he got up from his table and sauntered over to the trio.

"I figure you all are friends of Miss Madeline's."

A tanned brunette leaned across the table and smiled at him. "We are. And who are you here with?"

Marcus pursed his lips. "I'm not supposed to say."

"Are you a spy?"

He shook his head. "Not exactly."

"Do you work for Kloppleman?"

He smiled. "Good guess."

The brunette turned to her friends. "I knew it." She nodded and looked back at Marcus. "You're in that new research group that Madeline told us about."

"Research?" He nodded quickly. "Yeah. Research. I'm workin' with the two professors on a secret project."

Squinting at him, the woman shook her head. "I'm in HR and I don't recognize you. What's your name?"

Marcus looked around the room and lowered his voice. "Kirk, James Kirk. I'm the captain of my team."

The brunette frowned at him. "I don't know a Kirk in research. And captain of what team?"

"The secret research team that you don't know about."

A server walked over and told them that the buffet was about to close and did they want anything else to eat?

Marcus looked at the man and shook his head. "I've got experiments to run. No time for food."

Glancing at her friends, the brunette decided for the group that they were finished as well. "I'd love to spend some time and hear about your secret experiments, but our boyfriends are waiting for us."

"Yeah, I'll bet they is." Marcus nodded at the women and marched out the door ahead of them.

Prior to boarding and knowing that it would be necessary to divide the guests into small groups for the shore expeditions, Larry had suggested that the groups would be easily arranged by table number. One-hundred-and-twenty guests, which included the wedding party, made up twelve tables of ten. The Zodiacs, an inflatable short run boat that rode across the waves on two large rubber tubes, could hold ten people and a driver. The plan was simple, and it kept friends together for the short trip to the rocky beach.

As luck would have it, Marcus, the odd man out, ended up on the Zodiac with the three women and their boyfriends. He did his best to ignore them, but the men kept making snide remarks for the ten-minute ride to shore. Upon reaching the rocky landing, Marcus let the others get off the boat first, but blocked the three men until just the four of them were left onboard.

Marcus stood and looked down at the three boyfriends. "That brown-haired be-atch is your girlfriend?"

The man sitting in the middle nodded. "Yeah, what of it...Captain Kirk?" He chuckled. "Where's your spaceship?"

"Don't be worrying about no spaceship, jamf. Your be-atch almost begged me to show her a good time."

"Bullshit."

"Seriously, jamf. She and her two buddies waited until the dining room was empty before they come over to my table and start talking trash. The be-atch was starin' at my johnson and droolin' like it was a big piece of candy." Marcus reached down and grabbed his crotch. "I gots a girlfriend back home, so I ain't gonna toss a hump on no strange chick." He smiled. "Man gots to have values, right?"

The man jumped from the rubber tube and threw a punch at Marcus, but the boy saw it coming and easily ducked under the fist. He fell forward with the momentum, and all Marcus had to do was help him slide over the other tube and into the frigid water. Both of his friends rushed over and pulled him out, but they were too late to grab Marcus, who was already on shore, and walking over to Kim-Jack and his group.

"Somebody fell in the water." Madeline covered her mouth in shock.

"I think he wanted be the first one to take the polar plunge." Laughing, Tito made a snowball and tossed it toward the Zodiac, but it fell short, landing in front of a group of penguins instead.

Up ahead, Ossie and Trisha were organizing the group for a short hike up a path to the peak of a small hill where the research station was located. Gwen was several yards up the trail already, motioning them to follow. Kim-Jack looked at his fiancée and stage-whispered, "Bing-bong."

Weighted down with the parka, boots, and heavy undergarments, the passengers struggled to ascend the smallest hills. With expedition team members leading the way and others bringing up the rear, it didn't take long for the lines of hikers to spread out hundreds of yards. Kim-Jack and Madeline were the first to reach the top of the peak that Gwen had conquered with ease. They stood there, breathing heavily and sweating until she walked over and had them open their coats.

"It's easy to get heat stroke unless you remove layers as you get warm."

Kim-Jack understood the science, but was skeptical. "Even in this cold?"

"Two below zero with full sunshine is a lot warmer than you think." Gwen already had her coat wide open and unbuttoned her sweater halfway down. She grinned. "Wait until you're standing on the beach in your wedding dress."

Madeline sucked in a breath. "Shit. I didn't think about that."

"You're going to need warm undergarments." Gwen shouted to a group of passengers who'd wandered off the path to get back on it. "It's the simple things in life that confuse so many of us."

"I have a long-sleeve white t-shirt you can wear." Kicking a clod of snow, Kim-Jack looked at Madeline. "And I also have white long johns if you want to keep your ankles warm."

"Screw that shit." Madeline slapped her thigh. "I'm wearing the gown and nothing else."

"Not even panties?" He grinned. "You could freeze down there and then what would we do?"

Gwen shook her head. "I don't need to hear this. Enjoy the view and be careful on your way down."

Exhausted from the climb, they took a quick glance inside the research station. A Japanese scientist was typing data into a computer, but he stopped to explain the various instruments and answer questions. Someone wanted to know how long he stayed in Antarctica and the man replied, "Too long" to polite laughter.

No one had come to talk to scientists. Antarctica was all about the scenery and wildlife. As quickly as they had wandered in, the group left the research station, pulling their cameras out to capture the beauty of nature instead of the boredom of numbers.

From where they stood, the view presented the harbor as a semi-circle with two mountains at either end. The mountain to their right had a glacier that seemed to erupt from a deep black crevasse on the side closest to them. It split in two halfway down, ending at the water. Penguins were everywhere. Their light brown poop stained the snow and indicated precisely where the humans should not tread. Several large birds circled overhead and a light breeze blew wisps of snow off nearby peaks.

Kim-Jack shot photos from every angle he thought significant, capturing several interesting candid images of Madeline, his father and Trisha, and Tito, who had finally conquered the hill. Below them, on the beach, Gwen blew her whistle three times, indicating the first Zodiac was ready to return to the ship.

"We should head down. If it took this long to get up here, going down might be worse." He took a tentative step and slipped, catching himself before he could fall. "Watch your footing. The melted snow has been packed into ice."

Tito stepped off the path to get around the others and returned to it just past his friend. "I should go first. If I fall, I could start an avalanche."

"Good plan." Kim-Jack nodded. "Watch yourself."

A few stragglers were just reaching the summit. Tito took a step off the path to give them room, but his foot landed on an ice-encrusted boulder and he lost his balance. Tumbling sideways, his girth, nearly doubled with the thick parka and four layers of sweaters, hoodies, and a t-shirt underneath, was too wide for him to reach out and stop.

He slammed into a couple from behind who had started back down moments earlier. Rolling over them, Tito shouted an apology, and promptly plowed into Kloppleman's director of security and her husband. Between the two of them, they tried to stop Tito's forward progress, but gravity was no longer their friend. The husband fell to the left, the wife to the right. From where Kim-Jack stood, it looked as though a bowling ball had crushed two pins.

Tito left the path where it merged with one of the many penguin highways. Narrow, but hard-packed, he picked up speed and was less than a hundred feet from the water. Moving too quickly to focus, especially since his glasses were still in his cabin, he didn't see the boulder that was between him and the rocky beach.

Two fat Chinstrap penguins, standing on top of the boulder, must have felt the vibration of Tito's gargantuan bulk rolling toward them. They jumped, but in the wrong direction, and ended up cushioning the big man from serious damage. Unharmed but obviously stunned, one of the flightless birds skittered away and jumped in the water. The other, quite perturbed by the human incursion into its domain, waddled over and pooped on Tito's head.

Chapter Twenty-One

Dinner was mostly passengers running from one table to another to share photos. Several of the guests had brought professional camera equipment, laptops, satchels full of lens and filters, and tripods that folded up so small they fit into a pocket. Kim-Jack stared in awe at screen after screen of pictures on one passenger's laptop until he felt dizzy from the rapid-fire display.

Gwen worked the room offering photographic advice: angles to avoid shadows, being aware of the sun, leading the whale with the lens in order to get the best shot. It was only after dinner, on their way back to their cabin, that Kim-Jack and Madeline noticed that every framed photo in the corridors and stairways was signed Gwendolyn McMartin.

They'd gone to a kayak briefing before dinner and Kim-Jack was swayed by the magnificent images the instructor had shown them. Sven, who had arms thick enough to bend a kayak in half, made it seem as though paddling a fiberglass boat in freezing waters with whales that viewed the orange boat as a target was as simple as riding a bike. Something that neither had done in years.

Despite what seemed to be certain death from Sven's description, Kim-Jack signed up for the first group to go out on Wednesday morning. Madeline swore she'd only go with a gun to her head and reminded him that they were supposed to marry the following day.

"He's exaggerating."

Madeline raised an eyebrow. "Oh, really? Did you see how close that orca came to tipping over the kayak in the video?"

"Yeah, but did *you* see how easy it was to right the thing?"

"Ah yes, after suddenly dunking in water that's cold enough to freeze a penguin's penis, you'll have the wherewithal to flip the kayak over and just go on as though nothing happened." She slapped her forehead. "What was I thinking?"

"I don't plan on getting wet."

"The Titanic didn't plan on sinking."

Kim-Jack laughed. "Okay. Fair point, but I'm still going to kayak in the morning." He scratched the top of his head. "Maybe we should have sex a couple of times, just in case I don't come back."

"How about you reverse your decision to tempt fate or we don't have any sex tonight?"

"One of these days, you're going to say that and mean it." Kim-Jack pulled his t-shirt over his head. "You know as well as I do, that you've been thinking about that Frankie Valli song all day long." He grinned. "You can't wait to jump into bed."

Madeline slipped off her wool socks and shook her head. "That's not fair."

Stepping out of his trousers, Kim-Jack nodded. "If life was fair, it wouldn't be fun."

Kim-Jack was brushing his teeth when the morning bing-bong sounded. Excitement tinged Gwen's voice as she announced their first kayaking expedition. Yesterday, the team had spent several hours checking out various routes through the icebergs and reported that everything was perfect. He rinsed, spit, and left the bathroom without flossing.

Rolling over, Madeline shook her head. "I can't believe you're doing this."

"My father is going as well."

"Two widows for the price of one."

He dropped his cellphone on the bed. "You know my password, right?"

"31479, Albert Einstein's birthday."

"Good." Zipping up his waterproof pants, Kim-Jack sat down on the bed. "If I drown or get eaten by a whale, there's a list of all my other passwords in the files."

Madeline clapped her hands. "Oh, for joy. I can clean out your checking account."

"If you need the hundred and ten dollars that badly, go ahead."

She sat up and took his hands. "Don't drown, okay?"

"What about getting eaten by a whale?"

"Take Marcus with you and use him as bait. I doubt a whale would eat both of you at the same time."

"I haven't seen him since we got back onboard yesterday afternoon." Kim-Jack tied his laces. "I'll stop at his cabin on the way downstairs."

Madeline grabbed his arm and pulled him over, kissing him on the lips. She hugged him and then pushed him off the bed. "Go. But you better get back in time for lunch."

Marcus was closing the door to his stateroom when Kim-Jack came down the corridor. With the exception of a black baseball cap emblazoned with an orange and yellow fire-breathing dragon, they were wearing identical clothes.

"Nice hat."

He smiled and flipped it around backwards. "I won it last night playing blackjack with the boys."

"What happened to craps?"

"Can't find my dice."

Kim-Jack pointed at the large group of passengers also dressed for kayaking that had gathered at the end of the hallway. "Wow. I didn't think so many people would do this."

"Where's your be-atch?"

"Probably unlocking my cellphone as we speak."

Marcus started down the hallway and then stopped. "You ever done this shit, professor?"

"Nope. But there's a first time for everything."

"There's only a last time for dyin'."

"Are you scared?"

Marcus pursed his lips, but then grinned. "Nah. This ain't about shit. If you can do this, so can I." He turned and took a couple of steps before pausing. "I watched that video on the TV three times last night. Yeah, I can do this shit."

Kim-Jack raised his eyebrows. "There's a video on TV?"

"Hell, yeah. That lecture that Sven made us sit through didn't show nothin' compared to the video on TV."

It was too late for television. The group ahead of them was already moving to the gangway. Ossie waved to him and then disappeared around the corner. Kim-Jack took several deep breaths, but he was committed to the expedition.

"Let's go, Marcus. But when we get out on the water, I want you to stay where I can keep an eye on you."

"I ain't gonna run away in no kayak, professor."

"Marcus, I'm not worried about you cutting bait and floating away." Kim-Jack lowered his voice. "If I have trouble, I'm going to need your help."

"Whoa." The boy crossed his arms over his chest. "So, now I'm the professor?"

Kim-Jack sighed. "Don't let it go to your head."

***

The kayakers returned to the ship an hour later than planned. Gwen had already radioed in and instructed the dining room staff to plan for an extra long lunch. Kim-Jack was the last one out of the water with Marcus right in front of him...still soaking wet.

Stopping at the dining room, Kim-Jack spotted Madeline sitting with Trisha and several other women he didn't recognize. Bolting across the room, he shouted, "We're getting kayaks as soon as we get home!"

He grabbed an empty chair from a nearby table and spun it around. Collapsing into the seat, Kim-Jack grabbed Madeline's beverage and gulped it down.

"Yuck. What's in there?"

"It's an herbal mix that Trisha brought with her." Madeline took the nearly empty glass and set it out of his reach. "So, how was the kayak experience?"

"Oh, my god. I was crossing a large expanse of open water, and this pod of humpbacks joined us. It was like we were in a parade. Whales, bigger than a school bus, blowing fountains of water twenty feet in the air. And everywhere there are icebergs. Some of the most vibrant blues I've ever seen." Kim-Jack pulled the camera out from a pocket. "I must have taken a thousand pictures."

Marcus ducked in and shuffled over to the coffee station. He stood there drinking several cups before marching out without speaking to anyone.

Kim-Jack watched him and almost raised his hand to wave him over. When the boy was gone, he turned to Madeline and shook his head. "He flipped over three times."

"Oh, my god."

"The last one was intentional."

"What? Why?"

"He got into it with Sven." Kim-Jack unzipped his parka and slipped it off. "I was about twenty yards away, so I didn't hear all of the confrontation, but they were getting loud." Rubbing his hands, he showed the fresh blisters to Madeline. "I tried to paddle over there, but they started jousting with the double-ended paddles, and the next thing I knew, Marcus had rolled over."

"Did Sven push him?"

Kim-Jack shook his head. "No, Marcus just tilted too far to one side in an attempt to smack Sven with the paddle. His momentum carried him the rest of the way."

"And the second time?"

"He went after Sven about ten minutes later. Came up behind him and swung, but his gloves were too wet to hold on to the paddle and it went flying." Waving to a server, Kim-Jack asked for a cup of hot cocoa and whatever pastries were still available from the buffet. "Marcus tried to paddle with his hands and that was when he flipped again."

Madeline rested her elbows on the table and steepled her hands. "I can't wait to hear how he flipped a third time."

Kim-Jack laughed. "He was so pissed off that he rolled the kayak just as we got close to the ship. Apparently, Gwen was on the gangway shooting video and he wanted her to capture something funny."

"Funny?"

"That's what he said. The whole incident was funny."

As it was their last night as singles, Larry and Ossie had arranged a bachelor party for Kim-Jack in the Chinstrap lounge. The women were headed to the Rockhopper room for a similar party, and Cassidy had instructed several stewards to bring the karaoke machine and the screen as well as the champagne fountain into their soiree.

For the men, it was booze and barbecue. A pair of chefs cooked ribeye steaks on charcoal cookers they fired up on the deck. Captain Columbus, while not drinking, ordered a keg of beer to be brought up from the stores. Four of the Filipino stewards fashioned mop top hairpieces and performed Beatles songs with such perfection that one of the guests who had connections in Nashville gave them his business card and suggested an audition.

It was well after midnight when the last partygoers returned to the staterooms. Up on the bridge, Captain Columbus gave orders to get underway. They had twelve hours to get to the designated beach where Kim-Jack and Madeline would recite their vows.

As for the soon-to-be newlyweds, Kim-Jack was snoring. Madeline was writing a song while sitting on the toilet.

With the dawn came the bing-bong and the passengers awoke to a glowing vista as the sun spilled between two mountains that formed the harbor where the Queen of the Wind had anchored. Gwen wished them all several "good morningks" and proceeded with the daily agenda.

"We're anchored in Port Lockery just off Goudier Island, which has the southernmost post office in the world. Granted, it's the British Post, but they're also the only research facility where you can get your passport stamped. The postmaster will be coming onboard shortly to perform a signing ceremony and everyone is invited to attend with their passports in the Chinstrap lounge."

Pausing while the Captain shouted several commands, she continued with details of the day's activities. "We'll work our way around Wiencke Island and drop anchor in Flandres Bay where everyone will go ashore on Zodiacs for the two o'clock wedding ceremony. Following the ceremony, the bride and groom have invited everyone to take the polar plunge with them."

Kim-Jack had been sitting on the edge of bed, trimming his fingernails. Hearing the final sentence, he clipped a nail too deeply and cut into the soft flesh of his fingertip.

"Ow! What the hell? Madeline, I thought we resolved this shit."

She looked up from the notebook where the first chorus of the song was taking shape. "We did. Everyone is going in. Even my father."

"I don't remember agreeing to this part of the ceremony."

"You said you were going to think about it."

"I did." He blew out a sharp breath. "And I decided it wasn't a good idea."

Madeline pursed her lips. "Well, it's too late now. Everyone is expecting you to jump in with me."

"Everyone?"

"My father and Ossie and me."

"That's everyone?"

Madeline shrugged. "Well, everyone who counts."

"You're going to destroy a five-thousand-dollar wedding dress and you want me to trash my rented tux?"

"Look at it like this. You're only going to get married once, why not do something memorable?"

Kim-Jack laughed. "Getting married in Antarctica isn't memorable enough?"

"Did you ever eat a cupcake without icing?"

"No. I usually eat the icing first, though."

"What about a turkey dinner without the gravy?"

He grinned. "Let's not talk about turkey, okay?"

"Fine. What about French fries? Do you ever eat them without ketchup?"

"Not that I can remember." Kim-Jack took her hands. "What's the point you're trying to make? That was the last call for breakfast."

She gripped his hands tighter. "For me, the polar plunge is that icing. It's the gravy. It's the cherry on top of the sundae. We don't have to worry about destroying a five-thousand-dollar wedding gown or a five-hundred-dollar rented tuxedo. But answer this. How many times do you think you'll be back to Antarctica?"

"Never would be my guess."

Madeline smiled. "Then why not make it the most memorable experience possible?"

"By jumping into the frozen Antarctic Ocean?"

"Can you imagine anything more memorable?"

Gwen bing-bonged in to save him from answering. "We have a large pod of humpbacks off the starboard bow."

Kim-Jack grabbed his parka and camera. "If I get a good tail shot, I'll do the plunge."

"If not?"

He shrugged. "I guess I'll still do the damn polar plunge."

Chapter Twenty-Two

The plan for the wedding involved moving everyone from ship to shore, starting at noon with the wedding party going first. As plans go, it fell apart rather quickly. One of the Zodiacs had sprung a leak which was repaired but required six hours of curing time before the boat could once again float. Another Zodiac had a finicky motor that Captain Columbus deemed unsafe, so that boat was unavailable.

    Cassidy started drinking before dawn and was out cold when Larry called their cabin to get her ready for the transit. He called Trisha and convinced her to sit with his wife until she sobered enough to walk, figuring an hour would be enough. It wasn't.

    The decision was made to start early with the guests, moving them onto shore as soon as breakfast ended. A few minutes after dawn, the expedition team went ashore to set up a huge heated tent for the ceremony. It would be warm as soon as the guests arrived and perfect for the ceremony. After the wedding, and the guests were back onboard, they would have to fill in the holes and return the area to its original pristine condition. The Antarctic Treaty was strict when it came to preserving the natural landscape.

    Crossing the harbor, everyone was dressed in the same red parka with silver stripes, heavy waterproof boots and pants. Once they hiked up the tiny hill to where it was flat and the tent awaited them, they were able to strip off the heavy clothes and display their finery underneath with the exception of the boots. Once again, the Antarctic Treaty held all the aces.

    Despite the one requirement, the explorers transformed into partygoers once their parkas were removed. Even though few of the women wore a dress, they were all adorned in lace and silk above the waist. Most of the men had on a tuxedo underneath their waterproof pants and parka. Marcus, in a vibrant purple tuxedo complete with matching cummerbund, cane, and top hat sauntered among the wealthy guests as though he'd just won the lottery.

From the waist up, they were wedding guests. Below that, they were explorers. Madeline instructed the photographer to avoid photos that showed their expedition gear. Kim-Jack thought it would be cool to see the contrast and countermanded her orders.

By one-thirty in the afternoon, more than half the guests were on land with a huge contingent still motoring across the harbor. Cassidy had yet to regain consciousness, but the ship's doctor had stopped by to take her vital signs and pronounced the woman alive. With the help of several large, muscular stewards, Trisha was able to dress her and get the stepmother of the bride off the bed.

They leaned Cassidy against the cabin wall and held one of Larry's unwashed t-shirts close to her nose. Waving her arms to get rid of the foul stench, she reached a level of coherency that made it possible for her to walk. A steward brought in a carafe of hot coffee that they nearly poured down Cassidy's throat.

The last Zodiac, carrying the two stepmothers, the doctor, and a couple of stragglers reached the shore at ten minutes after two.

At Larry's request, all the male members of the actual wedding party wore top hats and carried black canes with silver tips. They were dressed in identical blue tuxedos, several sizes too large so that the pants covered their boots. The bridesmaids had crowns of fresh flowers that he'd purchased in Ushuaia and kept cold in the ship's store. Several of the Filipino cabin attendants had woven their stems into crowns early that morning. Onboard the Queen, all the kitchen workers wore white boots. They were more than happy to have the afternoon off as they handed them over to Gwen for the bridesmaids to wear instead of the black ones the guests used for landings.

The ride across the harbor flushed the last of Cassidy's stupor and she was beaming as though she'd picked the winning horse in the Kentucky Derby. Prancing around the tent, she greeted the same people she'd been traveling with for nearly a week as though meeting them for the first time. Larry, having reached the point in the festivities where he was now a participant and no longer in charge, grabbed his wife by the elbow, steering her to where the rabbi and priest were waiting, and took their seats in the first row.

With the wedding party assembled at the front of the tent, Gwen signaled to the band to start playing. Heads turned toward the back of the tent with the first notes. A pair of ship's officers pulled back the flaps on either side and Madeline stepped inside.

Other than the bride and the seamstress who created the gown, no one else had seen the garment until that moment. For nearly an hour, Madeline had been standing outside in the cold where no one could see her. She had Dr. Zametsky to thank for her survival.

Using his amazing foil, the doctor had designed an inner garment for Madeline to wear that would protect her from the cold by sealing in her body heat. Wrapped around her legs and torso, the foil was skintight. Above the waist, the foil was attached to the inside of the open lace of her gown. With sunlight from the clear panels of the tent hitting the gown as Madeline walked, the effect was a wedding gown covered in diamonds.

Not to be outdone by his employee, Larry Kloppleman commissioned the creation of a jewel-encrusted crown for his daughter to wear, along with a matching four-carat diamond pendant to cover the bare spot on her neck. The two pieces were slated for display in a local museum upon the family's return.

Kim-Jack had fought the blue tuxedo for several weeks before he and Madeline came to a compromise. He didn't have to wear blue, but it had to be a tuxedo. The discussion ended without resolution, but Kim-Jack had solved the problem before they left Miami without telling her how.

Even with all her careful planning, no one had been designated ring boy. It was a minor detail that somehow slipped through the cracks. Madeline checked her wedding spreadsheet several times, even going into the trash folder on her laptop to see an older version. They were an hour outside of Miami when the decision was made.

"What about Marcus?"

She looked up from the laptop. "Are you out of your mind?"

He shrugged. "I ask myself that exact same question every morning."

"The honor of ring boy at our wedding." Madeline raised an eyebrow. "And you want it to go to some criminal tagalong that I still can't believe is here?"

"Why not?"

"Because he called me a bitch."

"No. He called you my bitch. In fact, I believe the word he used was be-atch."

Madeline closed the laptop. "And you think that qualifies him to be ring boy?"

"Uh-huh." Kim-Jack glanced at Marcus, his eyes glued to the airplane window, listening to music through his high-tech earbuds. "There's something about this kid that makes me think he has a chance to survive the inner city. He's from there, but he doesn't belong there. And I don't want him to see me as his keeper. I don't want him to see this chance to be some place he'd never even dreamed of as a prison sentence. I want him to be part of this experience just like every other guest."

"So, you're willing to trust this career criminal, who you have a gut feeling about, with a ninety-five-thousand-dollar diamond ring?"

Kim-Jack smiled. "Even if it came out of a Cracker Jack box."

Standing in front of Father Gustafson in his purple tuxedo, Kim-Jack adjusted the top hat and switched the cane to his left hand. Thinking back to the salesman in the men's store that sold him the matching pair of tuxedos, both in a size too large, he laughed and lifted the top of the cummerbund. Marcus had kept both outfits hidden in his cabin until that morning. On his way back from another failed attempt at the perfect whale shot, Kim-Jack had retrieved his tuxedo. Just outside their cabin, he put on the jacket and top hat, walking in with the cane on his shoulder.

Madeline, in the process of finishing another of Tito's joints, laughed until she had to race for the toilet. She came out of the bathroom with tears still running down her cheeks and promised Kim-Jack that she would bury him in that exact suit some day.

He spotted Marcus in the back row, sitting next to Dr. Zametsky. The boy held up the white box and nodded. Kim-Jack lifted his cane.

By a toss of the coin, Madeline was granted her wish to be married Jewish first. Kim-Jack never saw the coin or the toss, but for the good of their marriage and because he really didn't care, he was fine with Rabbi Horowitz as the opening act.

Not wanting to violate the Antarctic Treaty signed by every expedition operator, the crew had assembled a wooden stage, covered with a waterproof tarp for the celebrants. The rabbi had alerted the crew that a glass would be intentionally broken, although it would be wrapped in a cloth napkin at the time. The head chef provided them with a freshly sterilized cooking sheet to be used as a hard surface.

Cassidy started to cry with the first invocation. The rabbi sang, she wept in perfect harmony. A woman in the front row leaned over and stage-whispered to her husband, "She cries at supermarket openings."

Larry, who was now so deep in the moment that the rabbi had to ask him for Madeline's Hebrew name three times, started to hum along, not knowing any of the words.

Promising eighteen minutes, a lucky number in the Jewish religion, Rabbi Horowitz finished with ten seconds to spare. He looked up at the congregation and smiled. "Who has the rings?"

Marcus stood, twirled the cane under his armpit, and marched regally up the aisle. He stopped in front of Kim-Jack and opened the box.

Time froze colder than the outside air and there was silence in the tent for almost a minute. Kim-Jack stared at the box and shifted his gaze to Marcus.

"What?"

Kim-Jack took a deep breath and whispered, "Madeline's first."

"Oh, shit." Marcus turned toward the bride and shrugged with a sheepish grin on his face.

Taking his ring from the box, she smiled at Marcus and gripped the ring with both hands. Kim-Jack got her ring next and held it up for the congregation to see. A handful of shocked comments murmured through the tent. Apparently, few of them had ever seen a five-carat diamond before today.

Father Gustafson took over next, leading them through a traditional Catholic wedding ceremony. He'd brought wafers and wine and offered communion to any who wished to come forward. No one did. As he reached the point in the service where the bride and groom spoke their vows, exchanged rings, and kissed, Rabbi Horowitz joined him and they finished the service together, pronouncing the couple husband and wife in unison.

Kim-Jack lifted his foot to smash the napkin-wrapped shotglass and slipped on an icy patch that had been exposed as the snow on top of it melted. He missed the glass with his foot, but managed to smash it with his fist on the way down. Looking up at the rabbi as he lay there on the frozen floor of the tent he asked if that counted.

Nodding several times, the rabbi smiled. "It doesn't say you've got to use your foot in the scriptures, so I'll take any extremity...as long as we're in Antarctica." He looked at Madeline. "He's okay."

She helped Kim-Jack to his feet and pulled him close. "Somebody say kiss the bride."

Father Gustafson leaned in front of the rabbi. "You may kiss the bride."

Taking her down on one knee, Kim-Jack gave his wife the deepest soul kiss of his life. He kept her there until Larry finally hissed, "Enough already." Bringing Madeline to her feet, they held up their hands in a triumphant bridge to roaring applause.

Marcus gave Kim-Jack a high five. Tito wrapped his arms around his friend's waist and lifted him off the ground. Hand-in-hand, Larry and Cassidy walked over to the newlyweds.

"Welcome to the family, Kim-Jack." Larry gave his new son-in-law a hug.

Cassidy kissed him on the cheek and whispered, "Now that you're family, I have some great stories to tell you about Trisha and Jamaica."

Kim-Jack whispered back, "I can't wait to hear them."

Next up were Ossie and Trisha, who made the same comment about Cassidy and Jamaica. Kim-Jack smiled. "Now, *those* are some stories worth telling."

While the guests were queuing to offer their congratulations, Captain Columbus radioed that the storm front they had been watching had picked up speed and intensity. They would have to hurry to get the ship battened down and underway toward calmer waters. Putting the crew to task, Gwen sent the passengers down to the waiting Zodiacs as quickly as they got dressed.

Madeline cornered the woman in the middle of the tent. "What about the polar plunge?"

"I don't think we'll have time this afternoon before the weather hits. Let's figure on tomorrow afternoon, okay?"

"It took two hours to get dressed in this thing."

Gwen shrugged. "It'll probably take the same two hours tomorrow."

While they were waiting for the rest of the guests to board a Zodiac and head back to the ship, Madeline worked her way out of the wedding dress and into a parka and waterproof pants. If she wasn't going to do the polar plunge there was no reason to trash the dress. Kim-Jack, still wearing the purple hat, had also switched clothes as the wind was picking up. However, Marcus put his money on style and rode back to the Queen in full purple.

They were halfway back to the ship when Madeline leaned over and shouted in Kim-Jack's ear, "Just think. All around the world people are getting married today. But on this continent, only you and I got married on the last day of the year."

Kim-Jack nodded. "This wedding was one for the record books."

"We're unique, KJ." She leaned over and kissed his cheek.

They boarded the ship just as the first squall rumbled in. Thick bands of rain coupled with piercing wind chased everyone inside. Gwen bing-bonged in to say that the bar was open in the Chinstrap lounge and everyone was invited there for cocktails before the main event began at seven that evening.

Since they'd left Ushuaia, the internet had been shaky at best. Madeline had tried to get email several times, but there was no response from the server. Hoping to at least post a brief message on social media about their nuptials, she powered up her laptop and waited for it to connect. Unraveling the complex hairdo one of the female stewards had created, she let her hair drop and brushed out the curls.

Madeline's home page had a bunch of news articles and blogs. It came up after a couple of attempts by her to refresh the screen. She read the lead story and then screamed for Kim-Jack to come take a look.

"I can't believe it." Madeline stormed into the bathroom and locked the door.

Staring at the screen, Kim-Jack read the short blurb out loud, "The President's daughter was married this afternoon at the McMurdo Research Station in Antarctica to the son of the Egyptian ambassador to the United Nations." He blew out a long breath. "Wow, of all the days."

Madeline called from the bathroom, "What time did they say their vows? Does it say in the article?"

Kim-Jack read further, clicking the link to read the piece in its entirety. He found the exact time in the last paragraph. "The daughter, who is currently the president of NORML, the National Organization for the Reform of Marijuana Laws, insisted on saying "I do" exactly at four-twenty in the afternoon." Kim-Jack shook his head. "What's so special about 4:20?"

Madeline shouted through the door, "How the hell should I know?"

"Well, regardless, we're still unique. McMurdo Station is the complete opposite side of the continent."

"But it's still Antarctica."

"Can't argue with that." Kim-Jack closed her laptop. "Is it that bad to have to share your wedding day with the daughter of the President of the United States?"

"What if it was his son?"

Kim-Jack sighed. "He doesn't have a son."

Madeline came out of the bathroom and threw a wet face towel at him. "You don't care, do you? This isn't important enough for you to get angry. Why? Because there's no science involved? Because you think it doesn't affect your life?"

"Jesus, Madeline, we just got married and you're acting like you came from a funeral." Kim-Jack held out his hand. "Come here and sit down next to me."

"Why? Are you horny? Do you really think sex will make everything better?"

He grinned. "It always has in the past."

She took the chair from the desk and spun it around backwards. Sitting down, facing him, Madeline rested her arms on the back of the chair. "This was supposed to be our special day. Our unique marriage in a place where no one else was going to ever get married. My father spent a fortune to pay off the people who oversee tourism in Antarctica. He had to jump through hoops to get permission to hold the ceremony on that beach. It was supposed to be unique."

Tears rolled down her face and Kim-Jack did what he could to calm her, but his tender touch and soft words only made her cry harder.

And then it occurred to him that because McMurdo was in the American zone, they were also in a different time zone. Reopening her laptop, he found a time zone map for the continent and did the math in his head.

"They got married tomorrow." Kim-Jack slapped his knee. "According to my calculations, the President's daughter was married at 4:20 in the morning on January first."

"Are you sure?"

He did the math again. "Yep. You and I were the only ones to get married on the last day of the year."

"But the article said 4:20 in the afternoon."

"The sun only sets for a few hours. It would have been daylight when the ceremony took place. Obviously, the reporter made a mistake."

"Obviously." She sniffed. "So our wedding really was unique."

He nodded. "Just what you wanted."

Madeline took off her t-shirt and smiled at him. "Well, if that's the case, we should celebrate."

Chapter Twenty-Three

Marching hand-in-hand into the Gentoo dining room at a quarter after eight, the newlyweds waved and smiled as though they'd just won the lottery. Madeline had changed into slacks and a flowered blouse. Kim-Jack had on jeans, a t-shirt that read, "HUSBAND" in bold red letters, and the purple top hat. The band had been playing pop music from twenty years ago. They switched to "*My Way*" by Sinatra as husband and wife danced into the middle of the floor. Having recently heard Madeline sing the song in their stateroom, Kim-Jack chuckled and held her tighter.

    Captain Columbus arrived soon after and led the guests in singing Elvis Presley's hit "*Can't Help Falling in Love*" with a perfect imitation of the legendary crooner's voice. He finished the song, took a bow, and said, "Ah, thank you very much," before heading back to the bridge.

    Gwen was next with the toast. She'd shot video of the entire ceremony, which was playing on the large screen behind her. Everyone applauded when Kim-Jack and Madeline kissed. Holding up her left hand and spreading her fingers, she wished the newlyweds a long and prosperous life together. Several of the guests shouted "bing-bong" until Madeline wrapped her arms around Kim-Jack and kissed him.

    Taking their places at the head table, the newlyweds toasted their parents and sat down for the first course. Tito walked over and shook hands with Larry and Ossie before kneeling next to his friend.

    "Was that our film under her wedding dress this afternoon?"

Kim-Jack nodded. "At least a thousand dollars worth."

"She wasn't cold?"

"Not for a second."

Tito smiled at Madeline. "Congratulations. You've pulled the gold ring."

"You're next Tito." She winked. "I'm going to make sure you catch the bouquet I toss before we cut the cake."

The appetizers were served: freshly made ceviche from fish the crew had caught during the ceremony along with garlic bread baked onboard using a recipe that Madeline got from a Sicilian neighbor. Striking up dance music from the Swing Era, the band drew the guests from their tables and onto the dance floor.

While Kim-Jack was researching music for their reception at Madeline's request, he happened upon a YouTube video of dancers in spats, women in twirling dresses, and a loud, infectious beat that made him forget everything else he had planned for that afternoon. Benny Goodman, Count Basie, The Andrews Sisters, played for hours had turned him into a fan. Seeing the men in spats and suspenders made him envious of the era. When he told Madeline that he would love to dance to those tunes and she agreed, Kim-Jack spent the following weekend in a dance studio with a professional who knew the genre well.

After dancing for nearly half an hour, the bride and groom returned to their table and listened as the various guests came up to the microphone to offer congratulations. Kim-Jack did his best to memorize the names and faces, but after the first dozen, he gave up and sat there smiling. The toasting was continuous and it didn't take long before the booze and the day caught up with him.

His respite came with the pasta course and the hungry husband dug into the plate of extra wide pappardelle noodles and cream sauce with relief. More dancing and congratulating followed the pasta. So much so that Kim-Jack never had a chance to eat his salad. Madeline danced with her father then with Ossie, who was followed by several gentlemen she'd never met. After the last one stepped on her toes, Madeline slipped off the dance floor, grabbing a roll from a nearby table.

After the salad course that Kim-Jack missed, Rabbi Horowitz gave his blessing to a braided loaf of Jewish challah over three feet long and sliced off a chunk that he shared with Kim-Jack and Madeline. "We dip this bread in honey to wish these lovers a sweet and happy life together."

Father Gustafson sidled up to his fellow preacher and offered an "Amen."

While the pastry chef carved up the largest loaf of bread he had ever baked, the newlyweds made the rounds. At each table, the collection of envelopes of all sizes, shapes, and thickness grew in Kim-Jack's pocket. Filled to overflowing, he bent down and picked up the fallen. Marcus walked over and held out his hand.

"Let me carry the coin, professor."

Pleased to have the assistance, Kim-Jack tugged the flock of envelopes from his pocket and was about to hand them to Marcus. Madeline put her hand on his wrist.

"What are you doing?"

"Giving these to Marcus to hold. I can't fit anymore envelopes in these tiny pockets."

"I don't think that's a good idea."

Kim-Jack shook his head. "He walked around with a hundred-grand in jewelry and nothing happened."

"That was different. There's cash in some of those envelopes."

"I know."

"And you trust him with that?"

"They're all sealed. But just to put you at ease, I'm keeping track." Pulling his wrist away from her hand, Kim-Jack sighed. "Marcus, count the number of envelopes and whisper the number in Madeline's ear."

The boy did as he requested, cupping his hand over Madeline's left ear as he whispered the count. Kim-Jack looked up at the ceiling, scratched the back of his head, and finally nodded once.

"Twenty-nine and six of them have cash." He pointed three tables away. "Pick up the next load of envelopes from me as soon as we finish with that table."

They worked halfway around the dining room before the main course of prime rib au jus was served. Ossie, sitting next to his son, leaned over and joked about Trisha turning vegan. The comment earned him an elbow in the ribs.

Moments after they were served, the band started playing Madeline's list of Frankie Valli songs. She was hoping to sing along, but a young Zodiac driver from France who spoke English with such a heavy accent that she still hadn't deciphered his name, took the microphone and sang with a perfect falsetto.

Playing to the younger passengers, the music switched to the current chart toppers. A female steward in a blond wig sang a medley of Taylor Swift tunes. The band jumped into hip-hop and Marcus took center stage on the dance floor as the tables were cleared for dessert.

Father Gustafson took the microphone to lead the group in prayer as the lights were dimmed for the grand entrance of the wedding cake. He thanked the Heavenly Father for providing the wonderful meal. Someone in a far corner of the dining room shouted, "Thank Larry Kloppleman. He's paying the bill." That brought a round of raucous laughter.

At exactly eleven o'clock, the pastry team paraded out of the kitchen. Led by the pastry chef, the sheer weight of the cake required six cooks to push the rolling table. Nine tiers high with the base over two-feet in diameter, the cake was pure white icing over alternating layers of chocolate, vanilla with almond paste, and lemon. One hundred and five icing roses covered the cake with intricate swirls connecting their stems. At the top, a motorized couple danced to the *"Blue Danube"* with their arms intertwined.

The roar of the guests must have frightened whales for miles. The pastry chef was reduced to tears. Letting the applause continue for over five minutes, Kim-Jack and Madeline finally stood and made their way over to the cake.

Empowered by the glory of the day, the excitement of the moment, and the biggest cake she'd ever seen, Madeline gave up fighting the alcohol and pot, and jammed her hand into the cake up to her wrist. Pulling out a fistful of chocolate sponge, she it mashed into Kim-Jack's face. Doubling over with laughter, she grabbed another chunk of cake and shoved it into her mouth.

Kim-Jack was stunned, but only for a moment. Shoving *his* hand into the cake, he loaded up with vanilla sponge, soaked in almond paste, and pasted it all over his wife's face. Then, adding the cake to what his wife had already shoved into his mouth, he laughed and licked his fingers.

Ossie, who considered the late John Belushi worthy of sainthood, jumped up from his seat, yelling, "Food fight! Food fight!" and grabbed a handful of icing roses that he smeared across Kim-Jack's face. He was joined, moments later, by Trisha who covered *his* face with icing, and then slipped on a chunk of cake that had fallen. She landed, face first, in a lemon layer, grabbing Kim-Jack's arm at the last second.

A table of the youngest guests thinking that this was how the older folk partied on New Year's Eve, jumped from their seats and began plastering each other with cake. Not to be left out, a mass of seniors, who had also seen the movie, joined in the melee.

Watching his magnificent creation be destroyed, the pastry chef was frozen in horror. Cake chunks were flying through the air. Icing was stuck to the walls. The dancers lay on the floor, sideways but still moving, although the music had ended. Guests unwilling to participate in the sudden madness cowered in the corners of the dining room, some slipping out the door with napkins over their heads.

A balloon drop, scheduled for midnight, was cut loose, adding to the airborne detritus. Gwen radioed for help to quell the battle and a squad of expedition crew rushed in to restore order. Of course, the crowd, fueled by alcohol and an everyone-is-doing-it-so-why-not-me attitude, attacked the orange vested security force with icing, sponge, and deflated balloons that they used as slingshots.

More help arrived with stewards jumping into the fray while holding pillows and towels for protection. Gwen, seeing that the battle was still out of their hands, made her way to the bank of switches and killed the lights.

The screaming died down quickly. Most of the people in the dining room froze in position. Those with cellphones activated their flashlights, but Gwen didn't need the lights to stay off for very long. Switching them back on, with the microphone in her hand, she checked the time and smiled.

"Happy New Year, everyone. Thanks for coming, but the party's over."

Madeline grabbed a chunk of cake and hurled it across the room. It missed Gwen, but hit her father in the face. She pointed at him, giggled, and passed out cold.

Kim-Jack and Tito carried Madeline upstairs to their stateroom, laying her gingerly on the bed to avoid waking her. After he left, Kim-Jack removed as much of her clothing as he could. The icing and sponge had glued her blouse to her chest, but he was able to pry it off with a damp towel. The jeans were another story. Surprisingly, they were cake free and only had one wet spot where someone had squirted her with a bottle of champagne. However, Madeline favored tight-fitting jeans to accent her figure and getting them off her while she was sleeping would only happen with sharp scissors and plenty of luck.

He covered his wife with a spare blanket and was heading into the bathroom when someone slid an envelope under their cabin door. Thinking it was another gift, Kim-Jack picked it up and was about to put the envelope on the desk with the others when the ship's logo in the corner of the envelope caught his eye. The flap had been tucked inside rather than sealed and he opened it with his finger.

The document it held was a radio transmission from some place called AF1. It was addressed to Jack and Madeline Kloppleman and it had been received less than an hour ago, while the food fight was still underway. Reading further, he held his breath and covered his mouth in disbelief.

Holy shit. Oh, my god. He put the letter on the bathroom counter and stepped back from it. *She's not going to believe this.*

Coming out of the bathroom, Kim-Jack turned on every light in their cabin. He sat down on the bed and shook Madeline awake.

"Who? What? Oh, my head." She grabbed the blanket and slid underneath.

"Get up and look at this." Kim-Jack pulled back the blanket. "You're not going to believe who sent us congratulations."

Facedown, she mumbled, "Unless it's from the Pope, I'm not interested."

"The Pope doesn't know your father, but the President does."

Madeline rolled over. "The president of what?"

Kim-Jack held the letter where she could see it. "The President who flies on Air Force One. The President whose only daughter was married in Antarctica today."

Shaking her head, Madeline grabbed the paper and read it, her lips moving silently with each word. Finished, she handed the message to Kim-Jack and blew out a quick breath.

"My father sent an invitation to the White House, but I thought it was a joke."

"It probably inspired his spoiled brat daughter to want a polar wedding."

Madeline chuckled. "The little twit couldn't come up with an original idea if it hit her in the head."

"You know her?"

"Yeah. She was there when the Governor was running for re-election two years ago. We shared the stage on either side of him."

Kim-Jack pointed at their names. "It would have been nice if he got my name correct. And I thought we agreed on Donaldson and not Kloppleman."

"We did." She shrugged. "I guess you can't expect the President of the United States to get the details correct. He has people for that."

He folded the radiogram and laid it on the desk. "Should we reply?"

"Let's send him some cake." She smiled. "But not the layer with the almond paste. I liked that one the best." Madeline sat up on the edge of the bed. "Do you think there's any left?"

"Tito was heading back down to the dining room after we carried you up here." Shaking his head, Kim-Jack sighed. "He loves almond paste."

"I don't think your friend ever met a food group that he didn't fall in love with at first bite."

"Well, if he had to marry one of them, my bet would be pizza."

***

The sun had been up for several hours before one of Gwen's bing-bongs woke Kim-Jack. He rolled over, onto a pile of torn envelopes, and then rolled back to the comfort of the Egyptian linen top sheet. Madeline was kneeling on the floor and tapping away at her laptop. On one side of the computer, she had a stack of cash. The other side was checks. She looked up from the keyboard when he yawned.

"We missed breakfast."

He burped. "I doubt that I'm ready for food."

"I was going to call for room service, but I didn't know how long you were going to sleep."

"My bladder said it was time to wake up." Sliding out of the bed, Kim-Jack walked quickly to the bathroom. Staring at his reflection in the mirror, he shook his head. "I should grow a beard."

"Not with my sensitive thighs."

He nodded. "Then there's that."

"Do you have any more envelopes?"

"Did you get the ones from my pants pocket?"

"Uh-huh." Tapping a few keys, she looked up and whistled. "Nine-thousand dollars in cash and fifteen-thousand and some change in checks."

"Wow." Kim-Jack sat down on the bed. "We should plan an exotic vacation."

"Somewhere warm."

"How about Hawaii?"

She punched his shoulder. "You just want to go to the nude beach."

"And watch you sing Sinatra without any clothes."

"Pervert."

"Showoff."

Reaching over, he pulled his wife down on the bed and caressed her thighs. Madeline slipped out of her sweatpants and rolled on top of him. She was about to take him inside when Gwen bing-bonged them out of the moment.

"Good morningk, good morningk. We're getting set up for the polar plunge. We should be ready for the bride and groom in about twenty minutes. See you all on the Zodiac deck."

Kim-Jack looked up at Madeline. "Think we can be ready in twenty minutes?"

She leaned over and kissed him. "Only if we hurry."

"What happened to never rush a good thing?"

Madeline pulled off her t-shirt. "It's waiting for us on a beach in Hawaii."

Chapter Twenty-Four

Without the foil, Madeline's wedding gown was see-through. Nothing from her neck to her ankles was left to the imagination. She'd slipped into it after sex and stared at herself in the full-length mirror for several seconds before shaking her head and taking it off.

"They're not going to let you jump naked."

"Well, they're not going to be taking pictures of my nipples, either."

She put on a black bathing suit that she'd purchased at the mall in Miami and slid the wedding dress over it. Checking her exposure in the mirror, she nodded once. "Much better."

"Now I know why they had a bathing suit on the packing list."

"I think it was supposed to be for the hotel in Ushuaia. Did you see their indoor pool?"

Kim-Jack shook his head. "All I remember from Ushuaia was the bed and too many king crab legs."

Gwen sent another bing-bong. "We're waiting for our honored guests. Someone go knock on their cabin door and tell them it's time to get out of bed. Come on you sleepyheads, everyone is waiting."

The knock on the door that came seconds later was followed by Tito's voice. "Come out, come out wherever you are."

Opening the door, Kim-Jack nearly slammed it closed, seeing what his friend was wearing. Tito jammed his foot against the door and smiled at the newlyweds as though he'd heard the funniest joke of his life.

"What the hell are you wearing?"

Tito spun around as gracefully as his three-hundred-and-ten pounds would allow. "After you told me about the dance lessons, I went online and searched for a period costume to match. This one-piece bathing costume with stripes was in every picture I found, so I ordered a suit in my size."

Madeline laughed. "They had one in your size?"

"And bigger." Tito bowed. "I'm ready to take the plunge if you are."

They made their way downstairs to the Zodiac loading deck. Tito spread the crowd with, "Make way for the newlyweds. No one gets wet until they do."

Kim-Jack and Madeline squeezed through to the head of the line. Tito took his place directly behind them.

Gwen was standing in a Zodiac several yards away from the ship. She had a megaphone in one hand and a trident wrapped in gold foil in the other. Seeing husband and wife on the small platform, she raised the trident and lifted the megaphone to her lips.

"As the authorized representative of King Neptune and one who has kissed the holy fish, I welcome you all to your baptism in the Antarctic Ocean." She pointed at the two crewmen with ropes in their hands. "Minions, tie the jumpers securely and prepare them to meet their fate."

The ship's doctor walked over to the pair and made a big fuss about checking their hearts and listening to them breathe. Waving his hand that they were fit to plunge, he took a step back and grinned.

Sven double-checked their bindings and turned to the waiting crowd. "We count backwards from ten and then they jump, okay?"

A roar of "Okays" and "Let's go" came from the other passengers. Kim-Jack took Madeline's hand and they walked to the edge of the platform. Sven reassured them that the crewmembers would pull them out after only a few seconds, and that the doctor was quite proficient at reviving the dead.

Kim-Jack stepped back, but Madeline pulled him forward. "You can't chicken out now, buddy."

Lifting his hand, Sven started the count, his voice getting louder as they approached zero. Neither of the jumpers noticed him getting closer with each number. On one, he pushed Kim-Jack who was holding Madeline's hand. Together they dropped ten feet into the icy blue water, screaming obscenities as they fell.

Kim-Jack felt his entire body go rigid the instant his toes hit the water. By the time he opened his eyes, the rope around his chest and under his armpits had tightened and he was being lifted out of the ocean faster than he went in. He and Madeline plopped onto the deck at the same time and were immediately wrapped in warm towels.

Wiping the water out of his eyes, Kim-Jack turned to Sven and asked him what happened to zero?

"Oh? Nobody told you? Zero is unlucky number in Antarctica. We always stop at one."

Tito was next, but Marcus stepped in front of him. "You gonna jump in an splash all the water out of the ocean, man. You gotta go last, otherwise everybody else gonna be jumpin' into cold, wet mud."

Waiting until Marcus was secured, Tito took the rope from Sven and smiled at the boy. "Go ahead and jump, whale bait."

"That ain't funny, Professor Czerwinski."

"I ain't laughing, Mr. Tigue."

Sven took the rope from Tito's hands and nodded to Marcus. "Go ahead."

"I can't swim."

"You won't have to." Sven let the rope go slack. "Trust me."

"I've heard that shit before." Marcus turned to Tito. "Take the rope, professor. I know you. I don't know him."

Tito obliged the boy, wrapping the rope so tightly around his hands that they started to go numb. "Go ahead. I've got you."

Marcus pinched his nostrils and jumped.

Sven counted to five out loud and tapped Tito on the shoulder. "Pull him out."

Flexing his arms and bending his knees, Tito put every ounce of strength in his body to the task. Marcus flew out of the water and over Tito's head, coughing and spitting. He would have crashed into the side of the ship had Sven not jumped and caught him.

Marcus dragged himself out of the rope and laughed. "Shit, I got dunked and a airplane ride all for the same price."

Ossie and Trisha were next up, stepping onto the platform in bathrobes. Kim-Jack, standing inside next to the space heater, covered his eyes.

Oh god, they're naked.

Madeline wrapped her arms around his waist. "Don't worry, Gwen's the only one with a camera."

Turning around, the couple waved at the crowd and let their bathrobes fall to the deck. Laughter and squealing made Kim-Jack drop his hands and stare at his father and stepmother.

They wore skintight, full body bathing suits. His had the image of a naked white woman, hers a black man in the buff. They were anatomically correct, although a bit exaggerated. The mismatch of skin color made the image even funnier. Kim-Jack shook his head and shouted, "Go Ossie!"

Several other couples took the plunge before Larry and Cassidy reached the platform. Madeline insisted that doctor check her father's heart, "For real this time" before letting Sven tie the rope. She turned away, listening for the splash, and holding her breath until Larry called out, "I'm okay."

Last to go was Tito. For the hour and a half the passengers had been getting dunked in the icy ocean, he'd been giving up his place in line and moving backward. Twice, he ran to the bathroom, as the pace of the jumping seemed to increase. However, the line eventually dwindled to just him and he stepped onto the platform one foot at a time.

"Tie two ropes around him." Sven ordered the crewmen to change places with two more muscular men that had been assisting the plungers.

Tito snugged the lines as tight as they would go and asked for a third.

"Two is plenty." Sven smiled. "We can lift a Zodiac with two lines. Do you weigh more than a Zodiac? I don't think so."

"You drop me and I'll come back from the dead just to strangle you, Sven." Triple checking the ropes, Tito took a deep breath. "Okay. I'm not ready and don't think I'll ever be, but what the hell." He took a step forward and fell into the water.

Once again, lunch was served an hour later than usual. The polar plunge had taken much longer than Gwen had calculated. They would be cruising for the rest of the afternoon. Whales were abundant in this part of the channel and everyone was still trying to get the perfect tail shot. She encouraged those who had taken photos and videos of the plunge to share them, and set up a laptop next to the bar for uploading.

Just as the first group of diners was hitting the dessert station, Gwen lowered the screen and projected some of the stills and videos for everyone to see. She'd done some rapid editing of the raw footage and assembled a collage of the photos. Opening with the newlyweds, she'd caught them at the moment they entered the water and produced a slow motion video of them going in and then being yanked out.

Someone above the Zodiac deck had captured Marcus in midair. The expression of fear that was plastered onto his face brought tears of laughter. Everyone cheered when Larry and Cassidy jumped. The moment was in sharp contrast to the sounds of amazement when Tito went into the drink.

Kim-Jack wondered why his father and Trisha had been eliminated from the presentation. Gwen answered without being asked.

"I have been watching explorers such as you take the polar plunge for eleven years. I have thousands of images and videos, but none will ever compare with Ossie and Trisha Donaldson. Please put your hands together and give them a round of applause. I give you the naked plungers."

Cheering nonstop, the guests roared as they watched the faux naked duo from every angle possible. Gwen had assembled a five-minute video of Ossie and Trisha going into the water at full speed, then slow motion, then in reverse. Kim-Jack couldn't believe how many passengers must have been filming the event. Madeline counted twenty-one different angles.

Captain Columbus walked into the dining room, holding a stuffed fish in both hands. He motioned to a server to bring the Donaldson's forward and leaned closer to the microphone Gwen was holding.

"Only the most daring Antarctic explorers are invited to kiss King Neptune's sacred fish. The kiss will join you in spirit with those who've come before and those yet to experience the wonder and power of Antarctica." He lifted the fish and turned it to face Ossie. "Ossie Donaldson, King Neptune orders you to kiss the sacred fish. Will you obey?"

Ossie was laughing too hard to answer until Trisha kicked his shin. "Yes. I will obey." He wiped away the river of tears and stepped forward, kissing the fish on its lips. With thunderous applause covering his words, he walked back to Trisha and whispered, "It's not plastic."

The Captain turned to Trisha and gave her the same order. "Will you obey?"

"Sure." She looked at Ossie. "If he can do it, so can I." Stepping over to the stuffed fish, she whispered, "You're kidding. It must be plastic." Trisha touched her lips to the fish's upper one and immediately wiped her mouth with back of her hand. Walking back to her husband, to cheers from the guests, she shook her head. "I don't think I'm ever gonna eat sushi again."

To great fanfare, piped in over the public address system, Captain Columbus, Gwen, and a group of stewards marched out of the dining room. Rabbi Horowitz walked over to where the newlyweds were seated and nodded several times.

"You are truly blessed to have such interesting parents."

Kim-Jack chuckled. "Rabbi, you don't know the half of it."

Even though he'd eaten a hamburger, a hot dog, and a piece of chicken, Kim-Jack was still hungry and the cooks had just refilled the shrimp container. Having a loaded a bowl with his favorite seafood, he had just slathered them with cocktail sauce when Gwen bing-bonged in with a whale alert.

"We have humpbacks on our starboard side and a pod of young orcas passing to our port."

Fortunately, Kim-Jack and dozens of his fellow travelers had gotten used to keeping both their camera and parka nearby. He bit off two of the shrimp without bothering to dunk them in cocktail sauce and dropped the bowl on a server's tray. Madeline saw him coming and ran to meet him at the exit door to the deck.

"Good luck." She kissed him. "Shoot straight and remember what Gwen said, lead the whale with your lens, anticipate when it will blow and when it will dive."

"Yeah, and don't stop to drink your beer or bite your hot dog. You'll miss the crash."

The bow was packed, but Kim-Jack found an open section of railing on the port side. A large utility box blocked the wind, and it wasn't long before several other amateur photographers were standing alongside him.

One of them pointed at a black spot to their right that seemed to be moving. Lifting his camera, Kim-Jack zoomed in tight. It was moving, but it was only a seal and he already had dozens of seal photos. Someone up ahead shouted that a whale had just blasted a fountain from its spout and was heading toward them. Two of the passengers standing next to Kim-Jack ran forward.

He lifted the camera and tried to scan the water, but the rocking of the ship made focusing impossible. Several penguins swam past and he shot a few seconds of video just to make sure the camera was working.

Stepping back into the windbreak, Kim-Jack thought he saw a light green shadow move under the ship. He was tempted to cross to the starboard side, with the hatchway just steps away, when a humpback blew and surfaced right in front of him.

Rushing up to the rail, Kim-Jack was about to start snapping pictures when he made the snap decision to switch to video instead. The whale was less than two car lengths away and passengers were running toward him with their cameras held out in front of their faces.

No one spoke, although there was quite a bit of heavy breathing and lots of soft oos and ahs. The whale paced the ship for almost a minute before diving into the clear blue water. It flipped its tail right in front of Kim-Jack and disappeared. Turning to the stranger next to him, Kim-Jack took his first breath in nearly two minutes.

"I got it. I got the whale shot."

"Me, too." The man gave Kim-Jack a high-five. "I've been shooting so much video I ran out of SD cards. This is my last one."

"Damn. Erase some of the other ones."

"Nah. I'm about burnt out from taking pictures. I think I'll spend the last few days of the expedition just looking at the sights with my eyes."

Kim-Jack laughed. "Yeah, that sounds noble right now, but wait until the next whale bubbles past." He reached into his camera bag and pulled out a sealed SD card. "I've got ten spares. Take one. Consider it a gift from the groom for coming to our wedding."

The man took the card and held out his hand. "We haven't been formally introduced. I'm Dr. O'Malley. I'm Dr. Zametsky's nephew and his senior research assistant. You and I will be working very closely together in the coming months to develop products for his foil."

"I wasn't aware that I'd agreed to any of this yet."

Dr. O'Malley laughed. "Larry Kloppleman doesn't believe in wasting time. I think he already ordered business cards for you and your partner."

"Wait, Tito? Tito only knows the bare bones about the offer Larry made me and I haven't accepted it yet either."

The doctor nodded. "But you will. You both will. Larry Kloppleman doesn't negotiate. He gives instructions and then moves on to the next project." Holding out his hand, Dr. O'Malley smiled. "Welcome to the Kloppleman family."

Chapter Twenty-Five

For most of the afternoon, the whales seemed to be following the Queen of the Wind. As the ship paralleled the coastline of Antarctica, they continued blowing fountains of seawater into the air and diving under the ship just as a group of passengers readied their cameras for a whale shot. Penguins stood at attention as the ship passed their iceberg perch. Smiling seals basked in the sun.

Pleased with his photos so far, Kim-Jack took a seat at the stern of the ship under a heat lamp and ordered a beer from a waiting server. Unzipping his parka, Larry Kloppleman sat down facing him moments later.

"Hell of a party last night."

Kim-Jack blew out a hard breath. "I can't believe they cleaned up the dining room in time for breakfast."

"I'm sure they've done it before. Have you ever been to a New Year's Eve party that *didn't* get out of hand?"

"I slept through one in college and missed it." Kim-Jack shrugged. "I woke up with green hair, wearing nothing but a pillowcase for a diaper."

Larry slapped his knee. "I hope there's a photo."

"The internet never forgets."

A group of passengers came over and greeted them. Kim-Jack tried to capture as many names as he could, tying them to faces, accents, hand gestures, anything that made the person unique. It was easy to do with students. They sat in the same place every day at the same time and with the same disinterested expression. Adults were different. They could sense when someone was trying to catalog them and often put on a façade.

Kim-Jack loved to give them nicknames. The heavyset man with the jowls was Churchill. His wife with curly red hair that was completely out of control he tagged Bozo, even though the original clown was male. From there it was easy for Kim-Jack to remember that Churchill was actually Theodore Hilly, one of Larry's childhood friends and a fellow real estate investor. Bozo's real name was Beth, and she was a retired hairstylist.

The server finally returned with Kim-Jack's beer. Larry asked the girl to bring him a ginger ale and slid his chair closer to his new son-in-law.

"So, how does it feel to be married? Stupid question, I know, but it had to be asked."

"I've called her my wife several times in conversation and it doesn't feel weird or anything." Kim-Jack took a drink and put the bottle on a table between them. "It's almost like a switch was thrown in my brain and the proper nouns just fell into place. Two days ago, she was my fiancée, my girlfriend. Now, she's my wife. But the nice thing is that she's still Madeline."

"Once a Kloppleman, always a Kloppleman."

Kim-Jack was tempted to ask how that worked with his ex-wife, Madeline's actual mother, but thought the better of it and changed the subject.

"So, what am I supposed to call you?"

"Whatever makes you feel comfortable."

Kim-Jack analyzed the situation, holding the beer in his hand for support. "Well, I'm not going to call you Dad. I only have one father."

"Who you quite often call by his first name."

"At his request." Kim-Jack smiled. Ossie had let the first time pass without comment when his son was twelve. After that, Kim-Jack assumed it was normal. "Do you have a problem if I call you Larry?"

"As long as you don't call me late for dinner, I really don't care." Larry grinned. "Even the woman who cleans my office five days a week calls me Larry."

"So, if I come to work for you, Larry is okay? Even in a meeting with world bankers or heads of state?"

Shaking his head, Larry laughed, which led to a coughing fit that he quenched with Kim-Jack's beer. He held up his hand and caught his breath a moment later.

"First off, under what set of bizarre circumstances do you imagine yourself in a meeting with world bankers or government officials?"

"Well, the pizza box–"

"I have two-hundred-and-four people in the marketing department. After each one of them meets with the bankers and there are still questions to be asked, I'll bring you in."

"Oh."

Grabbing his ginger ale off the server's tray before she had a chance to actually serve it, Larry drank half the glass and set it on the table.

"KJ." He paused. "Madeline calls you KJ. Is it okay if I do the same?"

Kim-Jack nodded.

"Good." Larry started to reach for his beverage, but dropped his hand in his lap instead. "You are a scientist and the most important thing I've learned about scientists is that you must keep them away from anything that isn't science. Economics has no basis in science. It's closer to a game of craps than anything else. Marketing is science, but it's weird science. Marketing seems to be affected by the moon and stars, which takes it out of the realm of science and back into our game of craps."

"So, you see my role as more mad scientist than used car salesman?"

Larry laughed, grabbing his soda before the coughing could kick in. "Dr. Frankenstein and his pizza box."

Kim-Jack failed to see the humor. "And what about Tito?"

"Your friend, the communist?" He shrugged. "Dr. Zametsky likes him."

"We're a matched set. You can't have one of us without the other."

"What about your ring boy?" Larry gulped the rest of his ginger ale. "Is he part of the team now?"

"Nah. Marcus has his sights set higher than the laboratory. He wants to see the world." Kim-Jack sighed. "Take a kid out of the inner city for a little southern vacation, and they'll never want to go back."

Getting up from his seat, Larry walked over to the rail. Without the artificial sun to provide warmth, he zipped up his parka and pulled his hat down over his ears. Kim-Jack finished his beer and joined his father-in-law just as a humpback dove no more than ten yards off the stern. The two men watched in silence as it surfaced further back, pointing out the possible track of the massive animal to a trio of passengers still trying for that perfect tail shot.

The ship reached the end of the long channel and slipped into the open ocean. They were beginning the trip home. In two days, they would be in the heart of the Drake Passage, after that, twenty hours in the sky. Any hope of getting a photo they could brag about was slowly slipping away.

Icebergs in the coolest blue floated past on the port side as they traveled north. Arches so tall that birds flying over them were only pinpoints in the sky. Ragged pillars with sides sanded to a reflective smoothness by the wind. Seals basking in the sun on floating rafts of white snow-packed ice.

Kim-Jack sighed. "Why can't the whole world be this calm and serene?"

"Because nothing would ever get done, and people would spend their lives trying for a level of perfection they'll never achieve." Larry shook his head. "Reality sucks, but fantasy doesn't pay the bills."

"It does if you write comic books."

"Do you want to write comic books, KJ?"

Kim-Jack shook his head. "I can't draw for shit, but as a last resort, I guess I could learn."

"Once your pizza box has been perfected, you'll be able to do anything your heart desires."

"What if I want to go back to teaching?"

"You'll be able to buy a school or start your own."

Rubbing some warmth into his hands, Kim-Jack turned to face Larry. "It must be very empowering to know that you can buy whatever you want."

Larry nodded. "It takes the worry out of shopping for a gift."

"I would think it diminishes the joy."

"You'll think differently in a few months."

Taking a step from the rail, Kim-Jack shook his head. "I don't think so. Money has never been my motivation."

Larry held out his hand. "Congratulations, you're the first person I've met who had the balls to say that. I was worried that you saw my daughter as a way out of your life and into a better one."

"A teacher's life may not be the best one, but every successful person knows they never would have reached that pinnacle without a good education." Kim-Jack shook Larry's hand. "Your daughter was never worried about changing me. I think she realized from day one that I was carved from a block of granite and that all the chisels in the world weren't going to turn me into a work of art."

They hadn't noticed Madeline walk through the hatchway with a glass of white wine in her hand. She walked over to the heated section of the deck and called the two most important men in her life to come over and keep her company.

"My father and my husband. No two humans on the face of the Earth mean more to me."

Kim-Jack kissed his wife and pulled a third chair over so they could all sit in warmth. "I think after the bang-up job that Marcus did with the rings and the gifts, he's cemented himself into third place."

"A position he shares with Tito, who gets my vote for bringing pot to Antarctica." She took a sip of the wine. "I don't know if I would have been able to go through with the ceremony if I wasn't stoned."

Larry doubled over with laughter. "Keeping the great Kloppleman family tradition alive. Your mother was so wasted for our wedding that when the rabbi asked her the question, she replied, 'Do I what?' She stumbled into your grandparents on our way out of the synagogue and got into the wrong car for the ride to the reception."

"Whose car did she get into?" Madeline turned to Kim-Jack. "I never heard this story before."

Larry slapped his thigh, laughing so hard that almost fell out of the chair. "There was a funeral in the small church across the street at the same time. Your mother got into the hearse."

Ossie and Trisha came around from the starboard side of the deck and pulled chairs over to the group. Larry, who was now coughing so hard that he started to turn blue, covered his mouth with a napkin and held up his hand.

"He either wants to go to the bathroom or ask a question." Kim-Jack pointed at his father-in-law. "Mr. Kloppleman, you have the floor."

Larry took a deep breath and wiped his lips. "Madeline tells me that the video of you two in your bathing suits has gone viral."

Trisha nodded. "We hit two-hundred-thousand views an hour ago."

"Our private parts were pixelated by Instagram." Ossie shook his head. "Goddamn puritans."

"Did you see Gwen's video of Marcus?" Digging his cellphone out of an inner pocket, Kim-Jack scrolled through his social media feed until found the video. "If he had only put his arms out in front, he could have been Superman."

Madeline scrolled the images on her phone and held it up to her father's face. "This one of the Senator is classic."

Larry nodded. "Good thing he had on a jockstrap. I guess that bathing suit was a couple of sizes too large."

Several members of the expedition team, including Sven, rounded the corner and set up three pairs of binoculars that were so big that they had been mounted on metal stands with wheels. One of the women adjusting the equipment pointed at a mass of white birds, perched on the side of a mountain.

"Come, take a look at this albatross colony. It's one of the largest in the world. Over a hundred birds in one place. Almost unheard of for this species." She checked the stability of the stand and moved on to the next one.

The scientist in Kim-Jack had him first up as he jogged over to take a look. Focusing the gigantic field glasses, he locked onto the birds and whistled. "Holy shit. Most of them have at least a seven-foot wingspan."

"Eight to ten feet is not unusual." Sven focused the second set of binoculars and got out of the way, as Madeline jumped from her chair.

"I'll bet they taste like chicken." She squinted. "Look at the little chicks. They're so cute."

"You thought the penguins would taste like chickens." Scanning left and right, Kim-Jack found nothing of interest and returned to the albatross colony. "Just because a bird can't fly, doesn't mean it's a close relative of chickens."

Madeline stood up and looked at him. "Chickens can't fly?"

"Not really. They can get airborne for a few feet at a time, but they're not going to nest in a tall tree." Kim-Jack leaned over and kissed his wife. "No extra charge for the science lesson."

"So that really wasn't penguin we ate for lunch?"

Gwen bing-bonged before Kim-Jack could answer and invited everyone to a science lecture in the Chinstrap lounge. She reminded one and all that tonight was barbecue night. The cooks would be roasting several small pigs on cookers set up on the aft deck and the chef had prepared kosher brisket, "Jewish style for those who don't eat pork."

Kim-Jack took his wife's hand. "I know it's probably too late to ask this question, but I've never seen you eat bacon or a ham sandwich. You're not thinking about going kosher, are you?"

"And give up BLTs? Are you out of your mind?"

"Speaking about Jewish food, we have a surprise for you." Ossie opened his parka and took out a small, gift-wrapped box. "A buddy of mine who we often see in Jamaica is from Brooklyn. He owned a soda fountain and stationery store that was recently sold to a developer. He said to make egg creams and drink one to celebrate your marriage and his retirement."

Madeline opened the box and took out a bottle of U-Bet chocolate syrup. "Oh, my god. Egg creams. It's been years."

"Your mother used to give you one in a bottle instead of breastfeeding. Eventually, you would only drink her milk if she mixed in a little U-Bet." Larry took the bottle and checked the expiration date. "He must have just bought this."

"Probably just took it off the shelves when he sold the store." Ossie laughed. "I'll bet he's got a garage full of notebooks, copy paper, and chocolate syrup."

Marcus, who had just stepped through the hatchway, heard the magic word and ran over. "Is that chocolate syrup? Real chocolate syrup, not that one-hundred-percent no-taste shit they have at the bar?"

Madeline handed him the bottle as though it was the king's crown on a velvet pillow. "Marcus, there is no finer chocolate syrup in the known galaxy and we're about to mix a drink with it that will change your life."

Leading the way into the dining room, Madeline held the magical elixir close to her heart. Kim-Jack, already baptized in the beverage, secured a half-gallon of whole milk and a bottle of seltzer from the bar. Joined by several servers who were prepping the tables for dinner, the group surrounded the largest hi-top and watched as she twisted off the cap. Removing the inner safety seal with a flourish, Madeline replaced the top of the squeeze bottle and dabbed a tiny drop of chocolate heaven on her ring finger.

Standing next to her, Marcus held out his thumb. "Yo. Pass the dutchy."

Madeline looked first at Ossie and then at her father, who nodded. "Go ahead. There's plenty to spare." Popping the lid open to expose the small hole that held the powerful condiment in check, she repeated the process and quickly snapped the lid closed.

Marcus stuck his finger in his mouth, holding it there while he licked it clean. Pulling it out, he checked to make sure that every molecule of chocolate was gone. "Damn. White people got the best chocolate. Ain't that some shit?"

"I'll get glasses and spoons." Kim-Jack nodded at Marcus. "Come, give me a hand carrying this stuff."

They walked over to the bar and were waiting for the bartender to load up a tray when Marcus asked about the eggs.

"Not in an egg cream."

"So, why you call it egg?"

Kim-Jack shrugged. "I have no idea and it won't matter to you either once you drink one."

"This a Jewish drink? Brother, you ain't Jewish, you just married to one."

"I eat pastrami rye and bagels with cream cheese and lox. And believe it or not, I know how to make chicken soup. Food has nothing to do with religion. Food comes from culture."

"Can you barbecue? Can you cook collards? You from black culture, professor. Can you cook your culture?"

Kim-Jack counted out seven spoons and placed them on the tray. "No. I can't cook my culture, I'm sad to say. I can't even cook a turkey, and that's about as basic as cooking gets. But my wife is a great cook and I'm willing to learn."

Marcus gave him a high-five. "You one wise man, professor. No shit."

Chapter Twenty-Six

Their last dinner before the Drake Passage was both a gala and a solemn affair. Knowing that they were about to be shaken apart again, many of the passengers ate light. The salad bar was a big hit as were the desserts. Tito, in his glory with a chance to consume suckling pig, insured that there would be no waste or leftovers. Happy that he'd found four stowaway joints in the bottom of his suitcase that he didn't realize were there, the munchies drove his hunger to the brink.

Kim-Jack did the math and figured if he stopped eating by eight, the food would be sufficiently digested before the bad swells hit. As much as he loved barbecue, wasting it with bouts of nausea held his eating in check.

After dinner, the crew put on a talent show that brought more groans than applause. The music was dated and the performers true amateurs, but the more everyone drank, the louder they clapped. Captain Columbus made an appearance, playing Buddy Holly tunes on an accordion while Gwen sang along. They received the loudest applause.

The Captain announced that the bar would remain open until two instead of closing at eleven. Someone joked that they had too much booze leftover from the aborted New Year's Eve party. Another guest stood and toasted Larry Kloppleman to cheers and table thumping.

Realizing that it was New Year's Day and that all the party goods that were staged for last night were still sitting in the back of the kitchen, the servers rushed to distribute party hats, noisemakers, and feather boas to the guests. The band took the stage and dove into their prepared set list for what would have been a New Year's gala. It would be a few minutes before two in the morning when they would play "*Auld Lang Syne*," closing the bar and putting the wraps on an extended New Year's party.

A few hours later, Kim-Jack, unable to sleep, bundled himself in his parka and waterproof pants, and, grabbing a spare blanket, went up to the aft deck. The heaters were off, so he pulled a chair against the bulkhead and draped the blanket over his legs.

What a trip. I still can't believe I came. He shook his head. *I can't believe I'm married. Madeline's my wife.* He spoke the word out loud several times. *It sounds weird to say it, but so does husband. Like I belong to a band of some kind. A hus band. What kind of music does a hus band play? Can you sing karaoke to it?*

Pulling another chair over, Kim-Jack put his legs up, still covered with the blanket, and used his gloves for a pillow. The sun was coming up over the distant mountains and a light breeze was blowing from port to starboard. He was sleepy, but not tired enough to close his eyes.

I drank too much the other night. Shit, I hope Larry didn't notice. Madeline can easily drink me under the table, but I doubt anyone was watching her.

Dragging the chair closer with his heels, he bent his knees and found a much more comfortable position.

Do I really want to work for Larry? He's pretty intense. And what about Tito? I get the feeling he's not wanted in the Kloppleman family business. That's bullshit. I'm not cutting him out after all the work we've done on the box.

A swell bounced the ship and his foot chair toppled over. Getting up, Kim-Jack wrapped the small blanket around his shoulders and righted the fallen chair. He was going to reposition it and sit back down, but another swell, stronger than the first one, hit the ship and he almost lost his balance.

When he returned to their cabin, Madeline was awake and watching the swell meter on channel one. A lit joint sat in a saucer she'd taken from the dining room and the Ziploc bag was back in place on the smoke detector.

She smiled as he walked into the room and stripped off his clothes. "We're almost into double digits. Are you sure you don't want a hit?"

"Thanks, but no. I took a pill right after dinner and I'm going to take another one before I get into bed."

"I'm glad that you'll be getting out of that school and into a real job."

"You don't think that teaching is a real job." He frowned. "It's one of the most important jobs on Earth. If you were never taught to read, how would you acquire the skill? How would you even know how to write a song?"

Madeline exhaled a cloud of smoke and watched it zip into the bathroom and out the vent. "You're twisting my words. I don't mean that you don't have a real job with a paycheck and everything, it's just that there's so much risk involved that I can't understand why you would put yourself in harm's way for a bunch of kids who don't give a damn about their education."

Waving the next gust of smoke out of his face, Kim-Jack sat on the edge of the bed as far away from Madeline as possible. "When you met Marcus for the first time, did you think he was one of those kids?"

She nodded. "I could tell he wasn't an honor student."

"But now that you've spent a week with him, do you feel the same way?"

"Well, I trust him more than I did in the beginning."

Kim-Jack smiled. "That's a huge jump from seeing him as someone who doesn't care about learning. He's one of the few passengers that's been to every one of the science lectures."

"I think he's got the hots for the science officer."

"She's twice his age and taller than me."

Madeline shrugged. "Maybe she likes young boys."

Three loud knocks pounded through their stateroom door, followed by a thud and an "Ow!" as the ship hit the bottom of a ten-foot swell. Kim-Jack grabbed his sweatpants and slipped into them.

"You better hope that's not security." Walking over, he peered through the peephole before yanking open the door.

Tito stumbled in, grabbing the edge of the desk as the ship tossed again. "I hit my head."

Kim-Jack checked the door. "No dents." He shoved it closed with his hip. "Why are you up at five o'clock in the morning?"

Collapsing onto the chair where they'd hung their parkas, Tito folded his hands in his lap. "I'm not going back to Bohi next week. In fact, I'm done teaching."

"What?" Kim-Jack shook his head. "You're stoned."

"Yes, but hear me out." Leaning forward, Tito took a deep breath. "All my life, I've wanted to be a chef. Not a restaurant chef, but one who does mass production of high quality food."

"Like banquets." Madeline took a hit and offered the joint to Tito, who declined.

"Banquets, huge family dinners." He paused and grinned. "Maybe even the White House."

Kim-Jack grinned. "Chef Czerwinski, the President's personal cook. Might as well go for the summit if you're going to climb."

"The internet came back on about an hour ago. I've been reading a book by Anthony Bourdain online and was able to finish it." Tito sat up straight in the chair. "He understood more about feeding people than I could ever hope to learn, but I'm willing to try. The Culinary Institute is accepting candidates on January fifteenth. I put in an application. Now I just have to figure out how to pay for the tuition."

"Will the monthly check from your stepfather cover it?" Tightening the knot on his sweatpants, Kim-Jack pulled two bottles of water from the minibar and handed one to Tito.

"Part of it, but we're not on the best of terms, and I can't ask him for more."

Madeline reached under her pillow and pulled out the envelope with their wedding loot. "Here's nine thousand dollars with the proviso that you'll cater our first anniversary dinner." She grinned. "I promise it will be someplace warm."

Jumping from the chair so quickly that it toppled sideways, Tito bent over and gave her a hug. "I'll pay this back ten times over some day. That's my promise to you."

Kim-Jack twisted open the bottle of water and took a long drink. He shook Tito's hand and told him he was thrilled that his friend had the guts to make such a major life change. But the moment the door closed, he dumped the rest of the water down the drain in the shower and tossed the bottle in the trash.

"What the hell just happened?"

"Were you asleep?"

"My best friend just dumped me for a saucepan and a pound of butter." Dropping onto the bed, Kim-Jack shook his head. "I can't believe it. We've been working for three years on that pizza box. Now, your father is about to throw millions of dollars at us to actually produce it, to make our dream a reality, and he's jumping ship."

Madeline pursed her lips. "Not in the literal sense, I hope."

"He might as well."

She smacked his shoulder. "Don't talk like that. You don't really mean it."

"And to think I was worried about your father not wanting him onboard."

"All these nautical references are making me seasick." She burped. "And hungry as hell. Are there any more of those whale crackers in the fridge?"

Kim-Jack untied the knot in his sweatpants and pulled them off. "Thank you for helping his dreams come true."

"Are you being sarcastic?"

"Ah, Captain Obvious is in the house."

Madeline sat up and stuffed a pillow behind her back. "If the money is the problem, get over it. I can spend nine grand in one store in less than five minutes and not even make a dent in my checking account."

"No." He sighed. "It's not the money. It's the ease at which he's able to walk away."

"You can do it, too."

Kim-Jack lay down next to her. "Some day, maybe. But there are kids like Marcus that need me to stand in front of that classroom and teach them that life is more than a fat bank account or a sharp blade."

She stretched up and kissed him. "You are such a romantic, KJ."

"And you are so wasted."

"Mmmm. And so horny. Turn out the light, husband, and satisfy your wife before the ship turns upside down."

***

Neptune was pleased with the Queen of the Wind and gave her the Drake Lake instead of the Shake for its two-day northern passage. Several swells topped twenty feet, but most were less than ten and the sun lit the way without a cloud for shade. Arriving in the port of Ushuaia at dawn, she was the only ship to unload and everyone was on dry land by seven-thirty.

Three large tour busses took the passengers and their luggage from the dock to the airport where the group began to disassemble. A large contingent was flying directly to London from Ushuaia to begin a European ski vacation. Kim-Jack joked that some people just couldn't get enough cold weather. Another group, from the West Coast, had booked direct flights to either Houston or Denver, but those departures weren't until later that afternoon and they took taxis back into town after checking their luggage.

The bulk of the now seasoned explorers were headed back to Miami, but the route came with a hitch. From Ushuaia, they had to fly to Buenos Aires and land in the domestic airport. Larry had chartered two busses to take them across the busy metropolis to the international airport, a one-hour drive in bumper-to-bumper traffic.

He put Madeline and Kim-Jack in charge of Cassidy, who vehemently denied she was drunk each time she stumbled into something on her way through the first airport. Marcus and Tito managed to load up on local snacks with wrappers in Spanish that neither of them could read.

Arriving at the international airport the group entered a world of chaos. Yesterday's monsoon had resulted in major cancellations, and the terminal was overloaded with weary travelers and short tempers. The bus drivers moved their luggage from the bowels of the bus to the nearest sidewalk and left. What few baggage handlers weren't already engaged wanted tips before they touched the bags, and only in Argentinean pesos.

In the commotion, Marcus disappeared.

Anxiously, Kim-Jack waited outside the security checkpoint until they announced last call to board for his flight to Miami. Sitting next to Madeline on the plane, he stared at the empty window seat and shook his head.

"What do I tell the police?"

"You tell them that he ran away." Madeline squeezed his hand. "You tell the truth. Daddy's lawyers will handle the rest."

"What if he got hurt? What if he was kidnapped?"

"I don't think they kidnap fifteen-year-old inner city gangsters who don't have rich families to cover the ransom."

Kim-Jack slapped his forehead. "If something happens to him, it's going to haunt me forever."

First in Spanish and then in English, a flight attendant instructed the passengers to prepare for departure. Kim-Jack was about to switch his cellphone into airplane mode when it binged, indicating a text had been received.

He opened the message, read it, and laughed until tears rolled down his cheeks. It was from Marcus and it read, "Thanks for everything, professor, but I'm hittin' the trail. I traded my ticket for a one-way flight to Burundi. I'll tell the King you said hello."

Epilogue

Kim-Jack slipped off the headphones and handed them to the recording engineer. They'd been in the Nashville studio for almost four hours. He thought the first take was the best, but Madeline didn't like the way the backup singers handled the chorus. The band had left after the fifth take. She was fine with the music, but the vocals were giving her the fits. The coffee pot in the recording booth was running low again.

They were due to leave for Honolulu in the morning. Both sets of parents were already there along with Tito and two other chefs from the Culinary Institute who were using the anniversary dinner as their final exam. Chelbe Udulu and her most recent husband were flying in this afternoon along with several of Madeline's friends in the music business.

Marcus' latest email was from a small town in the Swiss Alps. For his sixteenth birthday, his girlfriend had bought him skiing lessons. The brown-haired girl from the Antarctica trip, who had dissed him by not believing his story about Captain Kirk, had followed Marcus to Burundi after her other two friends dared her to get on the same plane. They were heading to Marseilles in a few weeks, where her family had a summer home and would send a gift, but had no plans to fly to the other side of the world.

With the pizza box licensed to the largest box manufacturer on the East Coast, Kim-Jack's experimentation had come to an end. The box, branded with "Hot4Ever," was being produced for seventy-six cents.

Despite constant lobbying by his father-in-law, Kim-Jack signed a two-year extension on his contract with the Board of Education, and planned to extend it again before it expired.

Madeline strolled into the sound booth and dropped into a chair next to the engineer. She yawned and stretched her legs before asking for the playback.

"I think that's the best version. You and the backup singers are in perfect harmony." Kim-Jack looked at his watch. "It's getting late and I'm starved."

"We still have another thirty minutes." She coughed. "One more time?"

"Your voice is getting raw." He handed her a cup of water. "Do you really think you can do better?"

Madeline shrugged. "I can always sing better..." She smiled. "Tomorrow."

The engineer took off his headphones. "So we're done?"

She nodded.

"Great." He started shutting down the thirty-two track mixing board. "How about we go for pizza?"

Kim-Jack and Madeline looked at each other and groaned. They turned to the engineer and answered him in unison, "Anything but pizza."

From the author

Thank you for reading this novel. I hope that it sparks a desire in you to see Antarctica for yourself. Having made the journey, and survived the Drake Shake (in both directions), I highly recommend the trip to anyone in good health. An Antarctic expedition is a rigorous undertaking that only gets more difficult as you age. Our trip was stalled for five years due to the pandemic and a variety of other factors. I felt those five years with every heavy footstep in the Antarctic snow. Go now, while you're young, but don't let age keep you away. I was seventy when I set foot on the seventh continent and there were plenty of folks older than me on our ship.

Antarctica is so different from every other place in the world that words can only whet your appetite, photos are mere glimpses, and even videos fail to capture the beauty you should witness firsthand. The Earth's climate is changing faster every second of every minute of every day. With those changes, the seventh continent is being transformed, and what we see today will be radically different next year. An Antarctic expedition will make you aware of these destructive changes, and hopefully make you understand how important it is for all of us to save our home.

For your enjoyment and to further persuade you to take the polar plunge, please visit my website at: www.fawnridge.com/trip_antarctica/antarctica.htm or scan the QR code below.

Made in the USA
Middletown, DE
10 April 2025